D1228234

'Twas a Famous Victory

Deception and Propaganda
in the War Against Germany

'Twas a Famous

Famous

BENJAMIN COLBY

ARLINGTON HOUSE·PUBLISHERS
NEW ROCHELLE, N. Y.

Manufactured in the United States of America

Library of Congress Cataloging in Publication Data

Colby, Benjamin, 1901-
  'Twas a famous victory.

    1. World War, 1939-1945--Propaganda.
2. World War, 1939-1945--United States. 3. World
War, 1939-1945--Germany. 4. World War, 1939-1945--
Influence and results. I. Title.
D810.P7U34   940.53'2   74-19165
ISBN 0-87000-254-6

'And every body praised the Duke
    Who this great fight did win.'
'But what good came of it at last?'
    Quoth little Peterkin:
'Why that I cannot tell,' said he,
    'But 'twas a famous victory.'

—Southey, *After Blenheim*

Contents

'Twas a Famous Victory

Introduction

The United States fought World War II in Europe for the stated objective of bringing peace and freedom to peoples everywhere. As set forth in the Atlantic Charter and held before the American people, the aim was "to see established a peace which will afford to all nations the means of dwelling in safety within their own boundaries, and which will afford assurance that all the men in all the lands may live out their lives in freedom from fear and want."

The war against Germany in particular was portrayed as a holy war. General Eisenhower entitled his experiences *Crusade in Europe*, and not with tongue in cheek, for that is the way it was presented to the American people and the way most of them came to accept it. The forces of good were ranged on one side and the forces of evil on the other, and unconditional victory over evil became necessary at all cost to establish a just and durable peace. It was a war to the death for virtue.

The miliary aim was achieved. The Nazi regime was destroyed and all Germany was prostrated. But the victory, instead of bringing peace and freedom for all, set up a vastly expanded Communist Russia as an oppressive colossus of Europe. Lithuania, Estonia, Latvia and eastern Poland became part of the Soviet state. German territory was handed to the Poland that remained, and all was turned over to communism. The remainder of eastern Germany became a Communist Soviet satellite. Communist regimes were installed in the "liberated" countries of central and eastern Europe, and far more people were placed under Stalin's despotism than had ever been subjected to the dictatorship of Hitler.

As Winston Churchill wrote in the preface to *The Second World War:* ". . . after all the exertions and sacrifices of hundreds of millions of people, and of the victories of the Righteous Cause, we still have not found peace or security, and . . . we lie in the grip of even worse perils than those we have surmounted."

A cold war soon developed between the United States and its

Soviet ally. American forces engaged in a bitter conflict in Korea against armies organized and supplied by the Soviet. Only a sharp confrontation brought the removal of Russian-installed missiles from Cuba, and the Soviet-buttressed regime of that country, just off American shores, has sought to promote Communism wherever it could in the Western Hemisphere. At every possible point, the Soviet Union has aided the spread of political philosophy and governmental systems totally alien to democracy, while continuing political repression at home. The United States has disengaged at last from a disastrous war in Vietnam which it entered to try to halt the Communist march in Asia. In the Middle East, Russia and the United States arm rival nations engaged in a continuing struggle.

The cold war has thawed and there has been marked improvement in the relations of the United States with the Soviet Union, where the most murderous aspects of Russian communism have been at least suspended. But there is still no political or personal freedom in the Soviet, and the iron heel of communism is still on the European states over which it acquired control with unconditional victory in the war. And despite expanding commercial relations between the world's two strongest nations, they confront each other with terrifying arsenals of nuclear weapons which could be unleashed in an instant. Basically, the former allies maintain a truce, armed to the teeth.

Germany, subjugated and carved up by the victors, was to be held powerless for the long future. But soon after the war it became the West's chief European bastion against Russia. United States forces are maintained there to discourage any warlike Soviet moves. The United States and Germany jointly develop weapons of war and German army flyers train above the deserts of Arizona. The nation which the West proposed to reduce to little more than a bare existence is an industrial giant and the chief proponent of economic union of the European democracies.

The continuing military confrontation with Russia and the defensive rapprochement with Germany are not simple perversities of history. They came about inevitably as the United States belatedly faced the consequences of a wartime alliance with a nation which was fighting for entirely different aims, and balked at accepting the inevitable results of unconditional military victory with Russia as a partner. The Kremlin, however, had not hidden its aims from the governments of the West. They had been made quite plain from the start. The Soviet Union's principal territorial designs, quite contrary to the Atlantic Charter, were affirmed to the United States government long before this country entered declared hostilities. Soon after the war with Germany began, Stalin laid his demands flatly on the line, and he never retracted them.

Throughout the war, the governments of the United States and Great Britain—but not their peoples—fully understood the Russian territorial and political intentions and their implacable nature. Long before the war ended, the Russian intention of communizing much of Europe was evident, and, indeed, the substance of the Russian plans for actual territorial seizures were secretly but specifically approved by President Roosevelt when the war was but half over.

Maintaining popular support throughout a war which would inevitably secure these Russian aims posed two necessities. The first was trust in Russia. The Soviet territorial objectives and political intentions had to be concealed. This was the central and all-pervading deception during the period of actual war. It was accompanied by an unremitting effort to whitewash the Soviet record and create a new Soviet image. The 1939 deal, permitting Stalin to seize the Baltic states and eastern Poland while Hitler crushed the remainder, was fresh in the public mind. Just before that Stalin had liquidated potential political opposition in vast, murderous purges. Religious freedom and other liberties did not exist. All this had to be gilded over, denied if possible, pushed into the background if not.

The President himself moved behind the scenes in an effort to evoke a picture of religious freedom under Stalin's rule. When the Soviet subscribed outwardly to the Atlantic Charter, with secret territorial reservations which rendered its allegiance meaningless, the act was portrayed as wholehearted support of the charter's aims. The Communist barbaric mass massacre of thousands of captured Polish leaders in the Katyn forest was laid to the Germans. Every effort was made to erase the Communist past and to set before the American people the fiction of a new and benign Russia, moving toward democracy and desiring only peace and freedom for all.

The second necessity was hatred of Germany, and this was achieved more easily. Even before 1939, Adolph Hitler's Nazi dictatorship had become odious to most Americans. The persecution of the Jews and the brutal suppression of political opposition and civil liberties had cumulatively provoked abhorrence of the Nazi regime. After the war broke out in Europe, President Roosevelt continuously promoted fear of a hypothetical world domination by Hitler, accompanying this by increasingly belligerent policies and actions. Hatred

13

swelled as American *de facto* war on the Atlantic in 1941 resulted in naval encounters. When the German declaration of war followed the Japanese attack on Pearl Harbor, hatred of Nazi Germany (and of course Japan) mounted spontaneously.

Americans did not know that less than two weeks before Pearl Harbor President Roosevelt had discussed with his advisers the problem of maneuvering Japan "into the position of firing the first shot." Nor did they know that Roosevelt had told Churchill the United States would probably go to war against Japan even if not attacked. As to Germany, they did not know that the President had issued orders from the Atlantic Conference in August for American naval vessels to seek incidents on the Atlantic which would justify war; that Roosevelt—as the British cabinet papers have now documented—was "determined" to go to war against Germany. The German declaration, which was in fact a long-delayed recognition of the fact that the United States was already conducting war, was accepted as showing Germany wanted war; it buttressed the interventionist argument that Germany was out to conquer the world.

Hatred of Germany, which had been directed mostly at the Nazi regime, widened with actual conflict. Hating the enemy is natural. When unconditional surrender was adopted as a minimum war demand, barring any other peace even if Nazi rulers were overthrown, the war logically had to be fueled by the most intense all-encompassing hatred of the entire German people. Otherwise, a war to such an extremity made no sense. It was necessary to believe that virtually all Germans were iniquitous and war-loving; that the German nation—Hitler or no Hitler—was permanently dangerous to the United States; and that only by crushing Germany utterly at all costs could great and permanent peril be removed. The effort to create and maintain such a belief was largely successful, and by the end of the war the people of the United States had been whipped to a frenzy of hatred and vengeance, not merely against the Nazi dictatorship but against Germans generally.

This book describes some of the deception, secrecy, propaganda and falsehood employed to promote trust in Russia and hatred of Germany in a war which brought unconditional military victory and disastrous political defeat. It is concerned primarily with the period beginning with aid to Russia and ending with the policy change which sought to make friends with vanquished Germany and build it up as an ally against Russia. The first two chapters briefly describe the course of events preceding that period.

Part I

Getting Into the War

1

Prelude to War

Any of a number of dates could be named for the effective beginning of the second war between the United States and Germany. Whatever the date chosen, the United States was at war *de facto* long before the German declaration which followed the Japanese attack on Pearl Harbor, December 7, 1941. From the start of hostilities in Europe in September 1939, the course was progressively away from neutrality and toward belligerency. The transfer of 50 destroyers to Great Britain in 1940 was a belligerent act. There is now general agreement that the Lend-Lease Act of March 1941 was, as the *Encyclopaedia Britannica* put it, "a virtual declaration of war."[1] In the spring of 1941, the navy began preparations to convoy ships carrying war goods for Britain across the Atlantic, and within a few months it was actively protecting convoys, and seeking out and engaging German submarines far from United States territorial waters.

Our story starts with convoying because with that began the actual shooting war. We are not primarily concerned with previous deception and efforts to influence public opinion toward participation in the war, which have been recounted in many books. Nevertheless, a brief chronicle of the progression from 1939 neutrality to the effective belligerency of the Lend-Lease Act is an essential prelude to a description of the propaganda and deception that followed.

Hitler's invasion of Poland, September 1, 1939, was followed by Stalin's occupation of eastern Poland and the Baltic states of Latvia, Estonia and Lithuania, according to a previously negotiated German-Soviet pact. Great Britain, which had given a guarantee to Poland, declared war on Germany and was followed by France. The American people were sympathetic to Britain and France, but nevertheless convinced that they wanted to stay out of the conflict, no matter who won or lost. A public opinion poll of October 29, corroborated by other polls, showed that only 3.3 percent wanted to enter the war, and that only 13.5 percent more would be willing to enter it even to keep England from losing.

By the fall of 1941, a large segment of the public, still opposed to actual participation in the war, had come around to a reluctant acquiescence in assistance to England of a kind which almost certainly would bring on war sooner or later. In August 1941, a poll showed that only 12.4 percent of the people were for getting into the war immediately; another 41.3 percent agreed it then appeared that they should back England until Hitler was beaten, although it had not looked like their war at first. By September 52 percent were in favor of convoying goods to England with American navy vessels, although most still said they were strongly opposed to a "shooting war."

This erosion of a national determination to remain neutral was brought about by a powerful and unremitting campaign under the leadership of President Franklin D. Roosevelt. As the public was encouraged to accept one step leading to war (portrayed as a peaceful move), preparations were made for another.

According to the Washington correspondent of the *New York Times,* concealment of what policies would mean until the public was unexpectedly confronted with stern reality "was fixed executive practice in the critical prewar period of 1937-41."[2]

Space should be taken here to ask *why* Roosevelt led the nation to war. Like most Americans, he detested Hitler's repressive and murderous regime, but it was no worse than that of Stalin's Russia. Indeed, when the United States entered the war, the number of persons murdered by Hitler had been but a handful compared with the millions whose lives had been extinguished by Stalin. As shown in the final chapter, Hitler had no designs on the United States or on anything across the Atlantic. The sympathies of Roosevelt and of Americans generally lay with Britain, but this did not justify linking the safety of the country with military victory by a nation whose power was even then declining.

The answer must lie primarily in the psychic needs of Roosevelt's own character. He could be content only as a big mover on a big scene. His magnified opinion of his own sagacity, depth of perception and general abilities was matched only by his conviction that he had to put them to use for the benefit of the entire world. His refusal to be conquered by a crippling physical affliction that would have broken the spirit of many men fortified his estimate of himself. In the view of Arthur Krock, long-time Washington correspondent of *The New York Times*, who knew Roosevelt well, he believed his own talents to be "protean and absolutely indispensable to mankind."[3]

Roosevelt had put these talents to use in a series of dramatic New

Deal schemes which had been struck down by the Supreme Court. Congress had decisively rejected his bitter effort to enlarge the court with sympathetic appointees and had refused his bid for more presidential powers by means of a governmental reorganization. His attempt in the 1938 election to purge Congress of dissidents within his own party had failed signally, while the Republicans had made some gains in Congress and among the governorships. On top of this, with unemployment from the 1932 depression still huge, a new economic decline brought a stock market collapse. Increased spending to relieve unemployment had had little effect.

In this situation, Roosevelt was insensibly impelled by his belief in his own great abilities to turn further toward world affairs, with which he had been toying since 1936. In that year he had conceived a grandiose scheme to dissipate growing war clouds by calling a conference of the King of England, the Emperor of Japan, the President of France and the Chancellor of Germany—and Stalin if he would come. This idea he dropped, but in 1937 he had sent "feelers" for a conference with Hitler and Mussolini on the high seas and was rebuffed.[4] In October 1937 he suggested that aggressor nations be "quarantined" by others. With the home situation deteriorating, Roosevelt, always restless for dramatic action, turned to warlike threats. By April 1938 he had moved to the point of assuring Canada—which was in no danger of attack from anybody—that the United States would come to its assistance if the Dominion was invaded. Though he talked peace, his course thenceforward was toward war.

Although Roosevelt brought the nation to war by deception, he was true to his conception of himself. He felt he could and must be the saviour of the world. America was led to war because of Roosevelt's belief that it was necessary for him to participate in settling the conflict—by his vision of his own indispensability.

In a radio broadcast to the nation on September 3, 1939, President Roosevelt said he hoped and believed the United States would keep out of the war, and he gave his hearers "assurance and reassurance" that every effort of the government would be directed toward that end. "This nation will remain a neutral nation," he pledged. But at the same time he took pains to discourage a neutral attitude: "I cannot ask that every American remain neutral in thought as well . . . . Even a neutral cannot be asked to close his mind or his conscience."

The President's own actions were far from neutral. Even before the actual outbreak of war, the German ship *Bremen*, in New York harbor, had been ostensibly searched for contraband munitions exports so thoroughly that it was delayed two days in sailing, giving a British cruiser at Bar Harbor, Maine, time to trail it across the Atlantic for a quick attack if war was declared enroute. When war broke out, the President immediately accepted the resignation of the American ambassador to Germany, who had already been recalled to Washington.

From the start of the war, presidential actions and statements were calculated to generate belief that the nation was in great danger from Germany. On September 8, Roosevelt proclaimed the existence of a national emergency, called up navy and army reserves, and ordered that recruiting be augmented. Laid-up destroyers were recommissioned for a "neutrality patrol" to keep war from American shores.

The President had issued a proclamation on September 5, as required under the 1937 Neutrality Act, prohibiting the export of arms and munitions to belligerents. A few days later, however, he called an extraordinary session of the Congress to repeal the arms embargo provisions. When the Congress convened September 21, he argued that allowing finished implements of war to be shipped, instead of the materials permitted under the Neutrality Act, would generate employment for the millions still out of work since the Great Depression of 1932. He argued, moreover, that changing the law would increase the likelihood of peace. The government would insist that American ships keep out of the immediate battle zones.

As the Congress began to consider the neutrality revision, Roosevelt announced on September 22 that submarines, not American, had been seen 60 or 70 miles off Boston as well as off the southern tip of Alaska. To guard against belligerent activities, the neutrality patrol was now ranging from the farthest north United States coast down to and including the Caribbean and the Gulf of Mexico. After a bitter debate, the Congress approved neutrality revision, and a new measure, permitting shipments of arms on a cash-and-carry basis, was passed November 5. But the President still promised neutrality. In a radio address, October 26, he said that "America is neutral and does not intend to get involved in war." The change in the Neutrality Act, he said, did not mean abandoning neutrality.

That the President was out to mold American public opinion for war was quite obvious. In the view of *Time*,[5] he "deliberately set out to hasten the process" of moving public opinion to thinking in terms of a world struggle. In his message to Congress January 3, 1940, Roosevelt characterized as "wishfulness" and "pretending" the attitude of those who proposed to stay out of war by having the nation mind its own business. On May 15, while asking Congress for large defense appropriations, he attacked Midwest anti-war sentiment by picturing an enemy getting a foothold in South America and then, via Mexico and Cuba, sending planes over St. Louis, Kansas City and Omaha. Greenland could serve as a base of attack on New England, he suggested.

In his speech accepting the Democratic nomination July 19, Roosevelt said the nation faced the choice of freedom versus slavery, popular government versus dictatorship, religion against godlessness, justice against force, and courage to speak out and to act versus appeasement. Those who opposed his policies were branded as "appeaser fifth-columnists." Roosevelt seized the occasion of dedicating the Great Smoky Mountains National Park, September 2, to emphasize the dangers confronting the nation as an argument for a military draft. A war loomed, said the President, in which the people would be defending their homes, families and their way of life—a way already threatened. At Chattanooga, the President told his hearers they were "facing a time of peril unmatched in the history of the nations of all the world." A trade of fifty "over-age" United States destroyers to Great Britain in exchange for bases in the Atlantic, arranged in principle in July,[6] was revealed to Congress and the people the next day.

The preparedness program was buttressed by an appeal to the pocketbook. In June there had been nine million unemployed. Three days before the presidential election, Roosevelt pointed out that the vast and expanding effort had been accomplished by the addition of 900,000 persons to payrolls in August and September. When huge army orders that would relieve unemployment in depression-hit towns were placed, the news was sometimes publicized by as many as three government agencies.

In his election campaign speeches, the President denied flatly that he was leading the nation to war. On September 11, 1940, he said: "We will not participate in foreign wars and we will not send our army, naval or air forces to fight in foreign lands outside of the Americas, except in case of attack." In Boston, October 30, he told American fathers and mothers, "Your boys are not going to be sent into any foreign wars" and reminded them, "I have said this before but I shall say it again."

Two months after this promise, in early January, he sent Harry Hopkins, his alter ego, to London to bring Churchill quite a different message:

> The president is determined that we shall win the war together. Make no mistake about it. He has sent me here to tell you that at all costs and by all means he will carry you through . . . there is nothing that he will not do so far as he has human power.[7]

At an official dinner on this trip, Hopkins obsequiously pledged American support to Britain. According to Churchill's representative on the British Chief of Staffs Committee, Hopkins quoted from the Book of Ruth: "Whither thou goest I will go, and where thou lodgest I will lodge . . . here thou diest I will die."[8]

Ardent supporters of the Roosevelt policies afterwards admitted that the President engaged in outright deception. Robert E. Sherwood, Roosevelt's speech writer and compiler of the papers of Hopkins, Roosevelt's closest confidant, agreed that in the pre-war years the President did not speak the truth when he said he hoped and believed the United States would keep out of the war, and when he gave assurance and reassurance that every effort of the government would be directed toward that end. Says Sherwood:

> The inescapable fact is that this was what Roosevelt felt compelled to say in order to maintain any influence over public opinion and over congressional action.[9]

One sympathetic chronicler, who admitted frankly that Roosevelt repeatedly deceived the American people during the period before Pearl Harbor, defended the deception as follows:

> . . . If he was going to induce the people to move at all, he would have to trick them into acting for their best interests, or what he conceived to be their best interests . . . . But because the masses are notoriously shortsighted and generally cannot see danger until it is at their throats, our statesmen are forced to deceive them into an awareness of their own long-run interests. This is clearly what Roosevelt had to do, and who shall say that posterity will not thank him for it.[10]

With the November election won, Roosevelt moved toward war with plans for the Lend-Lease program. As finally passed, the act authorized the providing of war goods, with future payment or none at all, to any nation whose defense the President should decide was essential to the security of the United States. He proposed the idea in a press conference on December 19, and followed it ten days later with a radio broadcast in which he urged the stark necessity of the United States providing vastly more aid to Britain in order to save itself. The nation, he said, had never been in such danger. Attack need not be feared while a free Britain remained powerful on the Atlantic. But if Britain went down, enormous military and naval resources could be brought against the Western Hemisphere, and "all of us, in all Americas, would be living at the point of a gun." Great Britain and the British empire were the military spearhead of "resistance to world conquest." Lend-lease was to be "all-out aid to Great Britain short of war."

In his January 6 message to the Congress urging Lend-Lease enactment, the President painted a picture of noble aims and great dangers. The aim of the United States, he said, was "four freedoms" for people "everywhere in the world." These were freedom of speech, freedom of worship, freedom from want and freedom from fear. But imminent peril threatened such aspirations. The future and safety of the country and of democracy were "overwhelmingly involved in events far beyond our borders." Without the British navy, America would be invaded, although this time the President suggested it would be by the occupation of strategic points by "secret agents and their dupes." rather than by planes from South America. Those who hoped for peace negotiations were preaching the "ism of appeasement" and the nation should beware of them.

Lend-Lease was strongly opposed by anti-interventionist senators and representatives as a move to war, but spokesmen for the administration in both houses insisted it was a measure to ensure peace. Secretary of State Cordell Hull, urging passage of the bill at a House of Representatives Committee hearing, stated that the surest way to keep out of war was to prevent an invasion of the Western hemisphere. Secretary of War Henry L. Stimson told a Senate committee that Lend-Lease would buy time for the country to prepare for its own security. Secretary of the Navy Frank Knox testified before a Senate Committee that passage of the bill was the only way he could see to keep out of war.

Opponents charged that passage of the measure to provide war goods to Britain was in itself an act of war and that it would be followed by naval protection of the goods across the Atlantic. Secretary Knox agreed that such convoying would be an act of war, and said that he was opposed to it.[11] Secretary Stimson spoke outright for sending the goods in American ships and under convoy if necessary, claiming that such would not violate international law.[12] The bill was passed March 11, after provisions had been inserted stating that it did not authorize or permit convoying by United States naval vessels or the entry of American ships into a combat area in violation of the Neutrality Act of 1939.

2

The Secret War on the Atlantic

Even as Secretary Knox was denying, at a hearing on Lend-Lease, that convoying of ships carrying war goods was contemplated, plans for convoying were being made. United States and Britain staff talks had begun *sub rosa* in New York in January, with members of the British delegation in civilian clothes disguised as technical advisers to the British purchasing commission. General George C. Marshall, chief of staff, and Admiral H. R. Stark, chief of naval operations, urged the closest secrecy because disclosure to the American people might provide ammunition for the opponents of Lend-Lease and produce other possibly "disastrous" consequences.[1] The compiler of the Hopkins papers—himself a Roosevelt speechwriter—points out that had the plans "fallen into the hands of the Congress and the press, American preparations for war might have been well-nigh wrecked and ruined."[2] That is to say, Congress would have rejected Lend-Lease.

While the general plans drawn were to be used only in the event of war, it was agreed that convoying did not need to wait upon that. The navy was to begin escorting convoys as soon as the Atlantic fleet was in a position to do so.[3] Nine days after the passage of the Lend-Lease Act, Secretary Knox informed the President that the navy would soon be ready to convoy merchant shipping from North America to the United Kingdom.[4]

Rumors that the navy was already convoying filled the air. Roosevelt refused to answer press conference questions about it. A letter from Senator Charles W. Tobey to Secretary Knox, asking whether convoying was being engaged in or was contemplated, brought no reply. When Tobey wrote to the President, he was answered by the Senate majority leader, Alben W. Barkley, who said, on the authority of Secretary Knox and Admiral Stark, that no convoying was being conducted and added that in his conferences with the President there had been no intimation that convoying was being considered.

But public opinion was being prepared for the convoying operations already scheduled. Secretary Knox argued that the nation could not allow its goods to be sunk in the Atlantic, and must "see the job through." Secretary of State Hull, voicing the same sentiments, said "ways must be found to do this." The President was more cagey. Denying any intention of escorting convoys, he said that warships would travel anywhere in patrol work necessary to protect the hemisphere. This "reconnaissance," being to detect aggressor ships, was not convoying. But on May 6, in a speech which a White House secretary said had been previously discussed with the President, Secretary of War Stimson advocated convoys by direct implication, saying that Lend-Lease was not enough and that measures must be adopted to insure delivery of the goods to Britain.

Construction had begun in January on a base in Newfoundland for convoy support operations. American officers had secretly visited Britain in March and selected the site for a destroyer base and a seaplane base in northern Ireland. On March 20, Secretary Knox, who had denied to Congress that convoying was even contemplated, informed the President that the navy would soon be ready to convoy shipping to the United Kingdom[5]—a plan to be superseded in June by one to convoy ships only to Iceland, where the British would take over.

Moving to prepare the American people for belligerent operations on the Atlantic in support of Great Britain, the President on May 27 issued a proclamation of unlimited emergency, requiring all defenses be made ready "to repel any and all acts or threats of aggression directed toward any part of the Western Hemisphere." This was necessary, the proclamation said, because the objectives of the Axis belligerents included "overthrow throughout the world of existing democratic order and a worldwide domination of peoples and economies through the destruction of all resistance on land and sea and in the air."

In an accompanying speech, Roosevelt expanded on the thesis of the Nazis warring for world domination. European conquest could be but a step toward ultimate goals in all the other continents." Unless the advance of Hitlerism was forcibly checked now, "the Western Hemisphere will be within range of the Nazi weapons of destruction." If victorious, "Germany would literally parcel out the world, hoisting the Nazi flag on vast territories and populations." The Nazis "plan to treat the Latin American nations as they are now treating the Balkans. They plan then to strangle the United states and the Dominion of Canada."

The United States was mustering its forces "only to repel attack." But it could not afford to wait "until bombs actually drop in the streets of New York, or San Francisco or New Orleans or Chicago." To block such horrific possibilities, the neutrality patrol, Roosevelt said, had been extended further in both the north and the south Atlantic.

Greenland had already been included in the sphere of hemispheric defense. In June it was decided that the United States would occupy Iceland, relieving the British who had installed themselves there when Denmark was occupied by the Germans the previous year. On July 7, the President announced that navy forces had occupied that island. This move, placing the nation squarely in a belligerent zone, was explained as one in which the Icelandic government had amicably concurred, but actually the proposal had been accepted by the premier of Iceland only after much pressure had been applied by Prime Minister Churchill. Iceland's reluctant "invitation" to the United States did not come until the first occupation force was steaming into Reykjavik. "Invitation, acceptance and execution had to be announced simultaneously." The people of Iceland "did not accept the occupation with good grace."[6]

With Iceland occupied, the Atlantic Fleet in July was ordered to protect ships enroute to or from that island. Although the protection was ostensibly for United States vessels, others were permitted to join the convoys. The order actually spelling out the convoying of British ships to Iceland was sent out August 13, from the Atlantic Conference at Argentia, Newfoundland. Instructions were to "capture or destroy vessels engaged in support of sea and air operations directed against Western hemisphere territory, or United States or Iceland flag shipping." Lest there be any doubt, a further navy order explained that this meant "potentially hostile vessels actually within sight or sound contact of such shipping or of its escort."[7]

If naval operations on the Atlantic were resulting in hostile encounters, the government was not telling. On June 9, the Alsop-Kintner syndicated column reported that more than a month before, a United States destroyer, picking up survivors from another ship after an encounter with submarines, had attacked what was believed to be a German submarine. Secretary Knox denounced the story, refused to discuss the alleged incident, and served notice that henceforth he expected correspondents to print only such news of navy operations as his office considered proper. On July 2 he denied that naval vessels had engaged German craft while on patrol missions, and also that convoys were being escorted.

The Senate Naval Affairs Committee was not satisfied, and called Secretary Knox and Admiral Stark into a secret session July 11. More than two weeks later the story was confirmed. An American destroyer, picking up survivors of a torpedoed ship off Iceland, had dropped three depth charges on something believed to be a submarine—but which, it was carefully explained, might have been a large fish or a whale. Only years later did the public learn that the incident had occurred while the destroyer *Niblack* was conducting a reconnaissance of Iceland to ascertain its usefulness for destroyer and air bases.

The President told Churchill at the Atlantic Conference in August that American naval vessels would aggressively seek to create an incident which could serve as justification for declared hostilities. In pursuit of this aim, he did not hesitate to falsify naval incidents so as to arouse the war spirit. On September 4 the Navy Department announced that a submarine of undetermined nationality had attacked the U.S. destroyer *Greer* on its way to Iceland. Roosevelt, making this incident the occasion for issuing "shoot first" orders to American warships in the Atlantic, said the *Greer* had been attacked by a German submarine while on a legitimate mission in full daylight, carrying mail to Iceland.

"I tell you," said the President to the nation, "the blunt fact that the German submarine fired first upon this American destroyer without warning and with deliberate design to sink her." But when the Senate Committee on Naval Affairs finally elicited the true story from Admiral Stark, it found that the *Greer* had been trailing the submarine for three hours, reporting its position to a British plane which finally attacked with depth charges. The submarine had fired at the *Greer* only after the plane departed for its base to refuel and the *Greer* had actively continued the hunt alone. This information was not made public until late in October, but the "shoot first" orders stood, along with the emotion which the President's version of the incident had aroused.

An alleged attack on the USS *Kearny*, like the *Greer* incident, was presented deceptively to the American people and used to even greater propaganda effect in arousing their emotions. On October 17, the Navy Department announced that the *Kearny* had been torpedoed about 350 miles southwest of Greenland, and two days later it was learned that eleven members of the crew were missing and several injured.

In proclaiming an unlimited national emergency, Roosevelt had assured the nation that war preparations were "only to repel attack." Now, he claimed that attack had come. "We have wished to avoid shooting, but the shooting has started and history has recorded who fired the first shot . . . . America has been attacked. The USS *Kearny* was not "just a navy ship. She belongs to every man, woman and child in the nation." Dramatically naming, one by one, the home states of the *Kearny's* missing and wounded, he said that the German torpedo had been directed at every American.

Furthermore, according to Roosevelt, Hitler was not simply aiming at the United States. The President said he planned to conquer and rule all South America, also. To fuel further the fires of emotion aroused by the *Kearny* incident, the President claimed that he had gotten possession of a secret Nazi map of South America showing how that continent would be organized under Nazi rule. This alleged map—which was not exhibited—supposedly showed that the Nazis planned to eliminate all existing boundaries and rule the continent through five vassal states, one of which would include the Panama Canal.

The facts about the *Kearny* were found to be quite different from the President's account. They came out in two installments: first, a report by Secretary Knox admitted that the *Kearny* was on convoy duty and had gone to the aid of another convoy attacked by submarines. On reaching the convoy, the *Kearny* had dropped depth bombs, and became the target for three torpedoes, one of which struck her. But even this was not quite the whole story. The Senate Committee on Naval Affairs obtained from Admiral Stark the admission that not only was the *Kearny* on convoy duty at the time of the shooting but it had fought submarines for three hours before being hit. This information was not given to newspaper correspondents until early in December.[8]

The destroyer *Reuben James*, on convoy duty, was sunk October 30. But after the *Greer* and *Kearny* incidents, in which it had been revealed that the United States vessels were the attackers rather than the attacked, there was no expression of righteous presidential indignation. The navy—unknown to the public, of course— progressed from convoying of merchant ships to the actual carrying of British troops. In November, United States transports and destroyers met British troop ships outside Halifax, and transported 20,000 British officers and men to the Near East.[9]

Of the Atlantic convoy operations in 1941, the navy historian says:

"These officers and men were enduring all the danger and hardship of war; yet it was not called war, and for the most part they were escorting ships under foreign flags. Forbidden to talk of their experiences ashore, or even to tell where they had been and what they were doing, their efforts were unknown to the American people."[10]

Part II

The Great Deception

3

The Atlantic Charter versus Russia

The great deception of the war itself began with the decision to aid Russia when Hitler broke his partnership with Stalin and attacked the Soviet, June 23, 1941. To obtain popular support for this aid it became necessary to portray Soviet aims as similar to those of the West. The Soviet's actual goals, although expressed frankly to the West, were concealed from the American public under the cloak of the Atlantic Charter until, as the war progressed, they became a *fait accompli*.

When the attack came, Stalin and Hitler looked to most Americans like dictators of the same stamp. In partnership with Hitler, Stalin in 1939 had seized eastern Poland and the Baltic states—Latvia, Estonia and Lithuania. Stalin had liquidated his political enemies wholesale in the murderous purges of the late thirties. The Soviet Union had been expelled from the League of Nations in 1939 for its unprovoked attack on Finland, which Roosevelt himself had excoriated as an assault on a "small nation that seeks only to live at peace as a democracy." Everybody, he had said, "who has the courage to face the facts" knew that the Soviet Union was "run by a dictatorship as absolute as any other dictatorship in the world."[1]

Former President Hoover, in a radio address on June 29, said entrance of Soviet Russia into the war made a "gargantuan jest" of the interventionist argument that the United States should join the conflict to preserve democratic principles and ideals, as Stalinist Russia was "one of the bloodiest tyrannies and terrors ever created in human history." He predicted that, if the nation did join the war and won, "then we have won for Stalin the grip of communism on Russia and more opportunity for it to extend over the world."[2]

Many voices were raised in and out of the Congress, urging, as Senator Bennett C. Clark of Missouri put it, that Stalin was as "bloody-handed" as Hitler and the United States should tend to its own business and let the dictators fight it out. Senator Harry S.

Truman, later President, voiced his detestation of both dictators, saying that if Russia were winning help should be given to Germany, and if Germany were winning help should be given to Russia. Senator Robert M. LaFollette of Wisconsin accurately predicted the course that would be taken:

> The American people will be told to forget the purges in Russia by the OGPU, the confiscation of property, the persecution of religion, the invasion of Finland, and the vulture role Stalin played in seizing half of prostrate Poland, all of Latvia, Estonia and Lithuania. These will be made to seem the acts of a "democracy" preparing to fight Nazism.[3]

At the time of the break, American relations with the Soviet were so strained that Soviet diplomatic representatives had been restricted to the immediate vicinity of the District of Columbia, in retaliation for similar restraints on American personnel in Russia. The American ambassador in Moscow had advised Secretary of State Cordell Hull that it was impossible to create international goodwill with the Soviets. They were not affected by ethical or moral considerations, he said. Their psychology recognized "only firmness, power and force" and reflected "primitive instincts and reactions entirely devoid of the restraints of civilization."[4]

The Department of State, which had been anticipating the German attack, assumed that the United States would provide war aid to Russia, but it had not initially planned to whitewash the Soviet. A department policy memorandum, two days before the break, warned that such assistance should not be confused with approval of Russian communism:

> We should steadfastly adhere to the line that the fact that the Soviet is fighting Germany does not mean that it is defending, struggling for, or adhering to, the principles in international relations which we are supporting.[5]

When the attack came, Acting Secretary of State Sumner Welles set the stage for Russian aid in a statement which generally followed this line. Principles of Communist dictatorship and Nazi dictatorship, he said, were alike intolerable to the American people. Nevertheless, he said, Hitler had plans for universal conquest, the enslavement of all peoples, and the ultimate destruction of all free democracies. Consequently "any rallying of the forces opposing Hitlerism, from whatever source these forces may spring" would redound to the benefit of United States defense and security.[6]

Restrictions on exports to Russia were speedily lifted and a drive got underway for shipment of fighter planes, bombers, guns, and all types of war supplies and equipment. Harry Hopkins was sent to Moscow in late July to find out just what Stalin wanted and to assure him it would be forthcoming with no strings attached.

But it was apparent that picturing the ruthless Soviet dictatorship as fighting America's battle was not enough to generate widespread and wholehearted support for the vast assistance contemplated. It was necessary to portray Russia not merely as an iniquitous regime which had fortunately become an enemy of Germany, but as an admirable ally fighting for righteousness.

The Atlantic Charter formed a screen to hide Russian aims for three years of war. It was drawn up by Prime Minister Churchill and President Roosevelt August 11, at a secret meeting on American and British warships off Argentia, Newfoundland. At the conference, Churchill did his best to bring the United States immediately into war in both the Far East and Europe. He was unsuccessful in his efforts to get such a stern note sent to Japan that it would have been effectively a declaration of war, but he got from Roosevelt the statement that the United States would probably go to war against Japan, even if not attacked.[7]

Roosevelt was anxious to get into war against Germany as soon as possible. Three weeks before, Harry Hopkins had assured the British foreign secretary that the United States would come into the war, and asked that no secret commitments be made in the meantime.[8]

That Hopkins spoke precisely for the President is attested by Robert E. Sherwood, Roosevelt speechwriter and intimate, and compiler of the Hopkins papers: "Roosevelt could send him on any mission. . . with absolute confidence that Hopkins would not utter one decisive word based on guesswork as to his chief's policies or purposes. Hopkins ventured on no ground that Roosevelt had not charted."[9]

Returning from the Atlantic Conference, Churchill reported to the British War Cabinet, as quoted indirectly in the Cabinet minutes, that Roosevelt "obviously was determined" that the United States should enter the war. These minutes, opened after thirty years, quote Churchill indirectly as follows:

> If he were to put the issue of peace and war to Congress, they would debate it for months. . . . The President had said he would wage war but not declare it, and that he would become more and more provocative. If the Germans did not like it, they could attack American forces.

It had been decided, Churchill reported, that the United States Navy should operate a supply convoy across the Atlantic:

The President's orders to these [United States Navy] escorts were to attack any [German] U-boat which showed itself, even if it was 200 or 300 miles away from the convoy.
   The President made it clear that he would look for an incident which would justify him in opening hostilities.[10]

Orders went out from the conference which meant that the United States Navy was to convoy not only American ships but also British and neutral vessels. The American escorts were to be aggressive, according to Churchill's report. "Everything was to be done to force an 'incident.' "

Returning from the conference, Roosevelt disclosed nothing of what had occurred there except to say that the problem of Lend-Lease supplies for Britain had been examined and that steps to meet the Axis menace had been "made clear." Instead of facts, the public was given a high-sounding declaration signed by Roosevelt and Churchill which came to be known as the Atlantic Charter. It was in effect a joint statement of war aims, although the United States was not a declared belligerent. Roosevelt's signature to such a document, with the nation still ostensibly not at war, was "astonishing" to Churchill.[11]

The Atlantic Charter set forth the "common principles in the national policies of their respective countries" (the United States and Great Britain) upon which they proposed to base peace "after the final destruction of the Nazi tyranny." It contained a series of noble pledges. All peoples should have the right to choose their form of government. Self-government should be restored to nations deprived of it. All states, both victor and vanquished, should have access equally to the trade and the raw materials of the world. Aggressors should be disarmed. The seas should be free. Labor standards should be improved. That victory would not be used by the victors to seize territory was elaborated as follows:

Their countries seek no aggrandizement, territorial or other.
They desire to see no territorial changes that do not accord with the freely expressed wishes of the peoples concerned.

The President, according to Churchill, believed the declaration would "affect the whole movement of United States opinion,"[12] which, indeed, was its purpose, and Roosevelt made sure that it would be presented to the country in dramatic fashion. It was publicized while the President was still at sea, and to obtain maximum effect Roosevelt ordered that any details of the conference, including even the names of those attending, not be released until later. Roosevelt's instructions were that the declaration should "stand out 'like a sore thumb,' with nothing to detract from it or to cause any other discussion."[13]

This strategy was successful. The declaration of high moral aims for a just peace captured the front pages and the radio waves, obscuring the lack of information on what had actually occurred. It was greeted with fervor by supporters of an interventionist policy. Senator Alben W. Barkley, majority leader, said it would have the enthusiastic support of all who believed in freedom and democracy. Representative Sol Bloom, chairman of the House Foreign Affairs Committee, said it "crystallizes the aims and aspirations of freedom-loving people." The *Atlanta Constitution* compared it to the Magna Charta and the United States Constitution. The *New York Times* trustfully assured its readers that the die had been cast against dismemberment of nations as a means of maintaining peace.

The charter was assailed by anti-war senators and representatives as a move toward war. They charged that the President was running true to form by acting first and telling the Congress afterward, and that he had made some sort of alliance for which he had not authority. Senator Robert R. Reynolds, chairman of the Senate Military Affairs Committee, asked why no effort was being made to impose the "four freedoms" on Russia. The *St. Louis Post-Dispatch* said that if the conferees talked of peace they must also have talked of war. The *New York World-Telegram* asked how Roosevelt could participate in the affairs of another hemisphere and keep war from his own.

But in general the noble proposals of the declaration, as Roosevelt had anticipated, conditioned the American people toward believing that the war was a high-minded conflict in which victory would bring peace and justice to the world. In the view of the editor of the Harry Hopkins papers the effect of the charter was "cosmic and historic."[14] It became the American war banner, and its pledges were extolled as the actual results to be expected with victory.

From the start, however, the charter, with its solemn proscription of territorial aggrandizement and territorial changes against the wishes of the people concerned, was a fraud. Even invaded Poland planned territorial seizures, and the Department of State had been informed of its aims. Poland wanted to take East Prussia and expel the German population, a long-standing goal which had been soft-pedalled before the war for political reasons.[15] As for the Soviet Union, if the war were won, Russia would be a victor, and it had no intention of renouncing the territories seized in the 1939 pact with Nazi Germany. After the German attack, Russia, anxious for help, had signed an agreement with Poland, invalidating the territorial aspects of this pact, but the official Soviet press hastened to deny that this meant restoration of the pre-1939 boundaries. If this left Russian claims publicly equivocal, they had been made quite clear to the Department of State. The Russian ambassador in Washington on July 2 had let the department know that recognition of all the 1939 conquests was precisely what it expected.[16]

Authorization of aid to Russia, regardless of public sentiment, was easy, but payment for it was something else. Russia had some gold in the United States, and it was arranged that an exchange would be made for some Russian strategic materials, but these were drops in the bucket. It was obvious that the unlimited aid proposed could be provided only under the Lend-Lease Act. While the President could designate the nations to receive such aid, the Congress had to appropriate the money.

In August, an Associated Press dispatch reported that Congress would accept a bill authorizing Lend-Lease aid to Britain and China, but only if it were made clear that none of the money would go to Russia. The administration at first planned to make this promise,[17] but when the bill was laid before Congress on September 18, administration spokesmen instead said that there were no actual plans for such aid.

A campaign was begun to erase the Communist record, put a new face on Stalin, and convince the people that the Soviet had turned over a new leaf. It was no easy job. As Harry Hopkins in early September wrote to the British minister of information in a classic understatement:

We are having some difficulty with our public opinion in regard to Russia. The American people don't take aid to Russia easily.[18]

To generate popular support for aid to Russia it was necessary to obscure the ugly Soviet past by creating a new present. As a first step toward making the Soviet alliance palatable, it was necessary to get

Russia to subscribe to the noble expressed aims of the Atlantic Charter. This was achieved on paper, September 24, in London, when Russia joined with other nations fighting Germany in a formal declaration of adherence to the "common principles of policy" set forth in the charter. Great publicity was given to the new declaration which was repeatedly broadcast from London in many languages to all the world. In America, it was presented as proof that Communist Russia now sought only to establish peace and freedom everywhere.

All this was sheer deception on the part of the Western governments. Russia had signed the declaration with the private. stipulation that, so far as its own territorial smwere concerned, the principles of the charter were not to be applied. Specifically, as Churchill later reminded Roosevelt, "the basis on which Russia acceded to the charter" was that it keep "the frontiers she occupied when Germany attacked her"—that is to say, the spoils agreed upon in 1939 between Hitler and Stalin.[19]

The charter with this sham Soviet approval was held aloft as a beacon before the American people, and it carried such conviction to them that three years later, when its fraudulence was virtually admitted by the President, the *Washington Post* was to say that its provisions had been "imprinted in the hearts of mankind"[20] and the *Washington Star* that it had been widely accepted "in the literal sense as a charter of human freedom."[21] But from the start the USSR had privately made it plain: "This doesn't mean me."

Soviet public profession of noble war aims could not efface the obvious fact of Communist repression of liberty at home. The most difficult hurdle to surmount in prettifying the Soviet was the ban on religion. In Russia, worshipers were actively persecuted and anti-religious propaganda was conducted in the schools from childhood. Throughout the first half of 1941, the only foreign church in Moscow had been subjected to repeated robberies and desecrations which, in the view of the American ambassador, were part of an official plan to force its closing.[22] There was strong opposition to war aid to the USSR in the ranks of both Protestants and Catholics, the latter being especially affected by a 1939 papal encyclical enjoining them against collaborating with communism "in any undertaking whatsoever."

Russian official antagonism to religion was so well known in the United States that even when Welles had welcomed Stalin as a virtual ally, he had felt it necessary to admit the fact frankly:

39

This government has often stated, and in many of his public statements the President has declared, that the United States maintains that freedom to worship God as their consciences dictate is the great and fundamental right of all peoples. This right has been denied to their peoples by both the Nazi and the Soviet governments. To the people of the United States this and other principles and doctrines of communistic dictatorship are as intolerable and as alien to their own beliefs as are the principles and doctrines of Nazi dictatorship.

In many quarters the view was expressed that aid to Soviet Russia should be used as a lever to force relaxation of religious repression, but such proposals were given short shrift. When the American ambassador in Rome asked that aid be conditioned even on the stated "hope" that more humane and liberal policies would be adopted and religious and political intolerance abandoned, the idea was brushed aside. Undersecretary of State Welles replied that it might be deemed "pressure on the Soviet government to change certain of its internal policies."[23] Rather than using war aid as an instrument to ameliorate Communist policies, the administration chose to attempt to whitewash the policies.

Soviet religious persecution had been freely admitted and deplored by President Roosevelt on February 1, 1940, when he "heartily deprecated the banishment of religion" from that country. He now sought to erase such views. On September 11, according to Secretary of State Cordell Hull, the President explained to the Soviet ambassador the "extreme difficulty" of getting the necessary authority for Lend-Lease aid from the Congress because of "prejudice or hostility" toward the USSR, and proposed that the Soviets help with the propaganda. Roosevelt suggested that the Soviet constitution permitted religious worship, and urged as Hull wrote, that "if Moscow could get some publicity back to this country regarding the freedom of religion during the next few days . . . it might have a very fine educational effect before the next Lend-Lease bill comes up in Congress."[24] This the ambassador readily promised.

The President then set about further efforts to amend the record. Russia, welcoming the prospect of help from a Polish army to be formed from Poles taken prisoner or otherwise deported to Russia during the Stalin-Hitler honeymoon, had granted permission for the proposed army to have Catholic and Jewish chaplains. The President arranged for the Polish ambassador to report this formally to the Department of State so it could be given official publicity. On the day the Department of State published the Polish ambassador's letter, the President held a press conference at which he asserted that the Soviet constitution granted freedom of religion and hoped that the permission given to the new Polish army meant that "an entering wedge for the practice of complete freedom of religion is definitely on its way." He said the Russian position of freedom of religion and freedom to use propaganda against religion "is essentially what is the rule in this country, only we don't put it quite the same way."[25]

The President's statement aroused a storm in the press and pulpit. Religious leaders of all faiths, including those who favored aid to Russia, were incensed at the attempt to equate the known religious persecution in Russia with the religious freedom which existed in the United States. Newspapers which supported aid joined with those opposing it in castigating the idea. The *Philadelphia Bulletin*, an advocate of aid to the Soviets, expressed the prevailing reaction: "There is only one reason for aiding Russia, and that is the principle of assisting a wolf whose present fight is helpful to our cause. His home life is his own affair, but pulling a sheepskin over his shaggy ears will deceive no one as to his true character."[26]

The American embassy in Moscow was called upon for help. Secretary Hull informed the ambassador that "in view of the outstanding importance of this question from the standpoint of public opinion in the United States" the President "earnestly" asked for a pronouncement from highest Soviet authorities "at the earliest possible moment" which could be released to the press, confirming his press conference statement.[27] W. Averell Harriman, Roosevelt's roving ambassador who had arrived in Moscow to facilitate war aid, speedily obtained a promise that restrictions on religious worship would be reduced and that a public statement would be made "in a manner to obtain maximum publicity in the United States."[28]

But the resulting statement for American consumption consisted chiefly of quotations from Article 124 of the Soviet constitution, which *guaranteed* "freedom of conscience" and *recognized* "freedom of anti-religious propaganda." It was obvious that no actual change was contemplated. As Dr. Luther A. Weigle, president of the Federal Council of Churches, said, Article 124 really meant "that the right of propaganda is recognized for the forces that oppose religion but not for religion itself, which is robbed even of its proper means of defense."[29]

It was the strong Catholic opposition which bothered Roosevelt most. Myron C. Taylor, the President's personal ambassador to the Vatican, induced Pope Pius XII to issue an allocution which, while retaining the 1937 condemnation of communism, drew a distinction between communism and the Russian people. Aid to the Soviets could now be supported by Catholics without contradicting papal authority, and this was almost immediately reflected in the tone of the Catholic press and of diocesan pronouncements.

With opposition by religious groups somewhat worn down, the Lend-Lease appropriation bill was passed, the Senate acting October 13.

The President then sought to turn public attention away from the lack of religious freedom in Russia and focus it on religious repression under the Nazis. He had received a copy of a program drawn up by Alfred Rosenberg for a national church of Germany, which was sent to leading members of the Catholic hierarchy and other religious leaders and publicized by Assistant Secretary of State Berle in a speech before the National Council of the YMCA on October 25. Roosevelt followed this, in a Navy Day speech two days later, by informing the country that the plan sought to abolish all existing religions and substitute a new creed based upon *Mein Kampf* instead of the Bible, with the Swastika and sword supplanting the cross. Unable to convince the people that religious freedom existed in Russia, he linked the cause of religion with all who fought against Germany.

Harriman, who had sought to get Soviet religious restrictions lifted, had no illusions about what Stalin actually planned. Reporting to Secretary Hull after his attempt to get a Soviet statement for the American press which would support the President's press conference position, he said:

I leave with the impression that the Soviet government will give lip service and make a few gestures to meet the President's wishes, but is not yet prepared to give freedom of religion in the sense that we understand it.[30]

Of course, the American public did not get the benefit of these views.

In a subsequent confidential memorandum, Harriman expressed the belief that the Soviets would merely "create certain instances which would give an impression of relaxation without really changing their present practices." The Polish refugees and army were to be allowed "some" priests; two had been released from confinement for the purpose and more were to follow. But unless Stalin was willing to compromise his entire Communist philosophy, religious worship would be tolerated "only under closest GPU scrutiny with a view to keep it under careful control like a fire which can be stamped out at any time . . . . The Communists will unquestionably continue anti-religious education. Religious worshipers will be restricted in economic or political advancement even if they are no longer persecuted. Priests or clergymen will be closely watched as will everybody with whom they have intimate contact."[31]

In short, while the administration was doing its utmost to persuade the American people that the Soviet was changing its stand on religion, its own diplomatic representatives recognized the move as a fraud.

On November 7, the President stated his finding that defense of the Soviet Union was vital to the defense of the United States, thus enabling him to order that shipments to Russia be made under Lend-Lease.

During this period of de facto American belligerence on the Atlantic, the President lost no opportunity to promote the idea that Germany would force war on the United States. In his Navy Day speech, he announced he had secret proof of German plans to carve Latin America into five vassal states. Actually, Hitler, who had no desire to add the United States to his declared enemies, had been leaning backward to ignore the fact of American belligerence on the Atlantic. As Admiral Harold R. Stark, chief of naval operations, put it in a memorandum for Roosevelt at the end of September: "He has every excuse in the world to declare war on us now, if he were of a mind to."[32] But American hostile actions were increasing, and open war was obviously only a matter of time. When Japan attacked Pearl Harbor, December 7, Hitler admitted the fact of war by a formal declaration.

With the beginning of declared war, a new statement of aims was drawn up, entitled the "Declaration of the United Nations," to be signed by all the nations allied with the United States. It incorporated the Atlantic Charter, and the fraudulence of the charter's pledges were underlined with the new document.

The charter itself had not mentioned religious freedom, one of the "four freedoms" enunciated by Roosevelt the preceding January as an aim of the United States for all the world, and this omission had been widely commented upon and laid to fear of giving offense to Stalin. For the proper effect on public opinion, it was deemed necessary to get religious freedom into the new document.

There had been no actual change in Soviet policy. Indeed, even as the declaration was being drafted, the American chargé in Moscow reported to Secretary Hull his belief that any promise of religious freedom would only be "lip service," as Harriman had predicted. Nevertheless, for propaganda purposes it had to go in. The Soviet ambassador flatly balked at such a promise, but offered to accept the meaningless phrase, "freedom of conscience." Roosevelt finally got "religious freedom" in the declaration only by assuring the ambassador that the two disparate expressions meant precisely the same thing.[33] To do this, according to Churchill, he had to exert his "most fervent efforts."[34]

Thus the original Russian adherence to the Atlantic Charter was only with the private reservation that the Russians would not adhere to the clause barring territorial aggrandizement; the Russian signing of the Declaration of the United Nations was with the understanding that "religious freedom" meant only the right to have a conscience. The declaration was given to the world January 1, 1942. The charter and the declaration, banners for the American people in a great crusade of righteousness, were both bogus, but the deception must be laid mostly to the West, not Russia.

4

A Tight Lid on Soviet Aims

The Declaration of the United Nations, with the bogus Soviet adherence to its stated aims, was made public January 1, 1942, with great fanfare, as evidence of the noble objectives of the war. All the signing nations, said President Roosevelt, had subscribed to the purposes and principles of the Atlantic Charter, and would employ their full resources against the enemy "to defend life, liberty, independence and religious freedom, and to preserve human rights and justice." Secretary of State Hull hailed the declaration as proof that "law-abiding and peace-loving" nations could unite in war to preserve "liberty and justice and the fundamental values of mankind."

Victory for the allied nations, Roosevelt told the Congress January 6, meant victory for democracy, for "the ideal of family, the simple principles of common decency and humanity." The United Nations' objectives were not only the smashing of militarism but "establishing and securing freedom of speech, freedom of religion, freedom from want, and freedom from fear everywhere in the world." The fight was "not only for ourselves but for all men and all generations." The aim was "to cleanse the world of ancient evils, ancient ills."

Along with these noble aims went fearful warnings. America was in great danger, he told a press conference on February 17. The enemy could "come in and shell New York tomorrow night under certain conditions," and they could probably even drop bombs on Detroit. At this time when the nation was physically threatened, aid to Russia, he said, could be measured "in terms of dead Germans and smashed tanks." Those who questioned large Soviet aid, fearing that Russia might be too powerful after the war, were lumped with what he termed an American "Cliveden set"[1] of Washington.

While admonishing the nation about its great peril, the President held the Atlantic Charter, to which Russia had subscribed on paper, as its moral shield. In a February 23 broadcast, he again stressed that the United Nations were agreed on the broad principles of the peace which was sought. "The Atlantic Charter," he said, "applies not only to the parts of the world that border the Atlantic but to the whole world; disarmament of aggressors, self-determination of nations and peoples, and the four freedoms—freedom of speech, freedom of religion, freedom from want and freedom from fear."

As this was spoken, Roosevelt and others high in the administration knew that Stalin had no intention of establishing freedom of speech, freedom of religion or freedom from fear in any Soviet-controlled territory unless the Soviet departed totally from its existing practices. As to territorial seizures, Stalin had followed his specific reservations to the Atlantic Charter's pledge by laying the Russian territorial demands on the line to Anthony Eden, British foreign minister, in early December.

Eden, in Moscow seeking a Russo-British treaty of alliance, had been told flatly that Stalin's price was eastern Poland and part of Finland, together with Estonia, Latvia and Lithuania. East Prussia would be transferred to Poland. Rumania was to give the USSR special facilities for bases and would be compensated by territory taken from Hungary. These arrangements Stalin proposed to be put in a secret protocol of the treaty. Later, he was induced to lower his asking price for the treaty to recognition of the seizure of the Baltic states and part of Finland, with other demands temporarily held aside.

The Department of State knew all this. It "had at no time been in doubt" that Stalin would seek British acquiescence in territorial claims which would make the Soviet Union "the dominating power of eastern Europe if not of the whole continent."[2] Before Eden left for Moscow, Secretary Hull, citing the Atlantic Charter, had asked that no specific commitments be made "at this time."[3] This stand against the territorial clauses in the proposed treaty was maintained strongly while the British-Russian discussions went on, but the qualification "at this time," was always present; the demands, although assailed in Department of State papers as contrary to the Atlantic Charter, were not refused permanently. A memorandum by Secretary Hull to President Roosevelt, dated February 4, said such an agreement "at the present time" would have an unfortunate effect upon the attitude of small countries everywhere. The integrity of the Atlantic Charter would certainly be affected by recognition of Soviet claims to the Baltic states "at this time."[4] As Hull put it, "later arrangements" could be discussed "at the proper time" with no commitments to individual countries "at this time."[5]

But the British government, according to the editor of the Harry Hopkins papers, had always regarded the Atlantic Charter with its noble pledges as "not much more than a publicity handout."[6] From the Atlantic Conference Churchill had telegraphed his cabinet that Roosevelt was determined on its promulgation because of its prospective effect on American public opinion, and it would be "most imprudent on our part to raise unnecessary difficulties."[7] He was now quite ready to forget the charter's pledges to get the Russian treaty, and reminded Roosevelt that "the basis on which Russia acceded to the charter" was that it keep the frontiers occupied when attacked by Germany.[8] Foreign Secretary Anthony Eden, three weeks later, also reminded Under-Secretary Welles that the "understanding" that had accompanied Soviet adherence to the charter meant that "consequently the Baltic states were a part of Russian territory."[9]

But Roosevelt, although he had been willing to acquiesce in secret "understandings" undermining the charter, was dead set against an immediate treaty which openly incorporated them. He tried to divert Stalin from pressing these objectives by emphasizing his plans for a second front, which, Harry Hopkins told Eden, should "take the heat off" the demands upon England.[10] Eden finally got Stalin to drop all references to territories except for the Baltic states. On these, Stalin was adamant.

Faced with the prospect of a flat negation of the territorial clause in the Atlantic Charter by both Britain and Russia, Roosevelt proposed a face-saving compromise. He suggested a "reciprocal exchange of populations" for the Baltic states and Finnish territory, by which the inhabitants who did not wish to live under communism could leave those territories with their properties and belongings.[11] They could take communism or get out.

The proposal, as characterized in a Department of State memorandum, with which Welles agreed, amounted to a mass exile of populations with no place to go, and "whose only crime is that they exist." But Welles suggested to the British ambassador that the treaty with this clause would be more nearly in accord with the "spirit" of the Atlantic Charter than without it, and the arrangement would make it easier for American public opinion to "tolerate" the transaction.[12]

Stalin ignored the scheme. His demands, always frankly stated (although kept secret by the West), were set, and the British went ahead with plans to sign a treaty in May on the Soviet's terms. The continued strong resistance of the United States at last succeeded in excluding mention of the planned territorial seizures from the treaty, but as has been seen, these objections were only to the making Of such settlements "at this time." The façade of the Atlantic Charter was served temporarily, but the substance of the Russian demands was not refused, and remained unaltered throughout the war. The President recognized that the territorial question would present itself eventually. There would be a "proper time" but "this was not the moment."[13] Until this "proper time" the Atlantic Charter banner could wave.

The expectation that Stalin, if strong enough, would have these territories after the war, is backhandedly admitted by Secretary Hull. Had approval of the seizures been incorporated in a treaty with Britain, he said, they would be used by Stalin "at the peace conference in case the war should end with a weakened Soviet Union not occupying the territories he was demanding."[14] Obviously Hull considered there would be no question if Russia was already occupying these territories, which would doubtless be the case with victory.

Widespread distrust of the Soviet Union existed, despite the government's efforts to erase it from the public mind. This distrust was shared by some in the government closest to the picture. The assistant chief of European affairs in the Department of State on April 9 proposed caution in permitting Soviet citizens to become permanent residents. Such persons, with their relatives treated as hostages, were required to act as Soviet agents. The American Communist Party, he said, although supporting the war to the extent that the Soviet Union was helped, was still working for a Communist dictatorship. He urged that secret Soviet agents not be permitted to enter and carry on their activities in the United States.[15]

But the attitude of President Roosevelt was quite different. Representative Martin Dies, chairman of the House Committee on Un- American Activities, which was trying to get Communists out of the administration, was told by Roosevelt that he did not believe the findings of the committee. Indeed, he said that a tolerant, if not protective, attitude should be taken toward Communists in the United States.[16] Vice President Henry A. Wallace, chairman of the Board of Economic Warfare, suggested that Dies would do less damage if he were on Hitler's payroll, when Dies attempted to obtain dismissal of board personnel affiliated with Communist front organizations.[17]

Roosevelt's own actions reflected the attitude he urged upon Dies.

He protected Communists in key posts. A notable instance was his insistence that Communist radio operators be retained on American merchant ships—an action that did not become known until long after the war ended. Japanese, Nazi and Fascist operators were eliminated by a special board headed by Rear Admiral Adolphus Staton, but when the board went after Communist operators it was blocked by the White house. On May 19, Secretary of the Navy Knox read to the board a memorandum from the President, specifying that no action be taken against Communist operators.

Rear Admiral S. C. Hooper, responsible for communications at sea, who had set up the board, expressed the view that a temporary military alliance was "no reason to condone the establishment of Communist party cells in the United States." But Knox said it was "an order which must be obeyed without mental reservations," and the Communists stayed. The following year, Staton was ordered by the White House not to testify before a congressional committee investigating the Federal Communications Commission. The activities of the board in rooting out subversives ceased after the Roosevelt memorandum. Staton was returned to the inactive list, and Hooper was given a post outside Washington and then retired for physical disability.[18]

In a radio speech of April 28, Roosevelt called critics of aid to Russia "bogus patriots who use the sacred freedom of the press to echo the sentiments of the propagandists in Tokyo and Berlin." They were "noisy traitors—betrayers of America, betrayers of Christianity itself—would-be dictators who in their hearts and souls have yielded to Hitlerism and would have this Republic do likewise." Commentators on the radio and in the press who questioned Russian political aims were charged with hurting the war effort.[19]

Vice President Henry Wallace compared Russian "democracy" favorably to that existing in the United States. In a New York speech, he hailed the "economic democracy" of the Soviet Union and said that the "political or Bill-of-Rights democracy" of the United States led to "rugged individualism, exploitation, impracticable emphasis on states' rights and even to anarchy." But Russia and the United States, he said, were working toward a common middle ground. The chief difference between the economic organization of the two countries was that in Russia it was almost impossible to live on income-producing property. Russia, he said, had probably gone farther than any other nation in practicing "ethnic democracy."[20]

Whatever effort was exerted to improve the Soviet image,

propaganda had to stay sharply away from any definitive discussion of political war aims, with Russia as an ally. The firmly expressed territorial intentions of the Soviet made it impossible to meet an increasing demand for enlightenment on political dispositions in Europe, once the war was won. Any statement which agreed to the Russian claims would have had an incalculably adverse effect on public opinion, while one which took issue with them would have brought sharp Soviet rejoinder and torn a gaping hole in the Russian alliance.

With Russian territorial demands kept out of the Soviet-British treaty in May, the pretense of mutually-held noble aims could be preserved. The President brushed aside questions about political dispositions to follow victory in Europe and dwelt upon the promises of good for all men. June 14 was designated "United Nations Flag Day" to celebrate the January signing of the United Nations Declaration, with its adherence to the Atlantic Charter. On that day, Roosevelt not only pledged the "four freedoms" as the rights of men everywhere, but specifically suggested that they also applied to Germany: "We ask the German people whether they would rather have the mechanized Hell of Hitler's 'new order' or, in place of that, freedom of speech and religion, freedom from want and freedom from fear." In July, Secretary Hull assured the nation that although the "aggressors" would be kept down by a United Nations force, all war political settlements would be guided by the pledges of the charter.

The President restated adherence to the Atlantic Charter in a message to Prime Minister Churchill on August 14, 1942, the anniversary of the promulgation of that declaration: "We based, and continue to base, our hopes for a better future for the world on the realization of these principles set down a year ago. This declaration is known as the Atlantic Charter." Since then, nations and groups of nations in all the continents had united and had formed "a great union of humanity dedicated to the realization of that common program of purposes and principles set forth in the Atlantic Charter, through worldwide victory over their common enemies . . . . We reaffirm our principles."

In a September 3 speech, the President repeated the battle cry of the charter and the "four freedoms," and said they augured a world of freedom, equity and peace. Critics who did not believe such promises would be carried out were termed "puny prophets," men who "play petty politics in a world crisis."[21]

That the eneny was not excepted from the protection of the charter

50

was again affirmed emphatically on October 27, when Roosevelt told the press that the charter applied to all humanity, as he and Secretary Hull had already made "perfectly clear."

While the charter was thus held high and the Russian territorial intentions kept carefully submerged, the government propaganda machinery sought to deflect attention from political war aims by stimulating discussion of plans for peace. Care had to be taken, however, that such discussion did not build too specifically upon the charter's pledges and thus disturb the Soviets. The approach to this dilemma is best shown by the guidelines sent to editors by the Magazine Division of the Office of Facts and Figures and the Book and Magazine Section of the Office of War Information, into which the former agency was merged during the year.

Editors were urged to emphasize the aim of religious freedom as part of the peace to be won. But as no such freedom had existed in Russia for many years, and everyone knew it despite the President's efforts to gloss it over, the topic had to be handled with circumspection. It was suggested that articles be published showing what life would be like without religious freedom, with the assumption that winning the war would ensure it. The OWI provided material showing how religious freedom had been restricted in Germany, while preserving a discreet silence on the situation in Russia.

Territorial matters had to be kept off limits. "All discussion of actual boundary lines of countries" was to be avoided in articles on the coming peace. Articles should deal with the anticipated postwar world in terms of gains in the fields of health, housing, education, foreign trade and other such subjects, but not with "actual terms of the peace treaty, particularly with reference to map making." This, it was cautioned, might disclose "minor disagreements" among the United Nations. How "minor" these disagreements were, the people were yet to learn.

The first part of 1942 had been disastrous, But with the naval victory at Midway in June, the initiative in the Pacific had passed to the United States. North Africa had been invaded. By November 4, Rommel was beaten at El Alemein. The Russians had held at Stalingrad and taken the offensive, soon to result in the capitulation of the Sixth German army. The tide of battle had turned when the year ended, but improvement in the fortunes of war inevitably brought nearer the day when the hollowness of the charter's pronouncements would become plain.

Already Britain had been willing to accede to the Russian claims and Roosevelt had set forth a plan to turn the Baltic states over to Russia if necessary. Within three months the President was to agree secretly with Eden that the Russians would have to have the Baltic states, and to acquiesce in the Russian claims on Poland, and was to add his own proposal for giving Poland German territory and forcibly uprooting millions of people from their homelands. A few months after that—at Teheran—he was to express his approval of the Russian claims to Stalin personally, again in secret. Within three years, he was to say publicly that the Atlantic Charter was a mere memorandum. But the lid was to be kept closed on Pandora's box as long as possible, and the Atlantic Charter was held before the people as expressing the aims for which they were fighting and which were expected to prevail.

5

The Charter Secretly Abandoned

The year 1943 began with the Germans firmly resisted at
Stalingrad, the Russians increasing their pressure on Poland for
territory, and the Atlantic Charter well on its way to extinction,
although the American people did not know it. During the 1942
British-Soviet treaty discussions, the United States had merely refused to put its stamp on the Soviet demands "at this time." In
December, the President had declined the request of Prime Minister
Sikorski, of Poland, for a statement opposing the Russian territorial
claims, and a month later gave him a letter consisting of generalities.
He had assured Sikorski, however, of his sympathy for Poland's plan
to seize part of Germany.[1] In March, Roosevelt was to agree
specifically, although secretly, to the emasculation of the charter,
with its pledge against territorial seizures.

But there was no diminution in lip service to that document. On
January 1, the anniversary of the promulgation of the Declaration of
the United Nations, the President said the United Nations were
bound together by the charter's "universal ideals". Their "eternal
spiritual values" outweighed even their overwhelming military force.
The "sacred principles of life, liberty and the pursuit of happiness"
would be restored as the cherished ideals of mankind. On the same
day, reporters attempting to reduce these rhetorical ascents to
specifics were told that the most important war objective was to
maintain peace. The President brushed aside questions on how this
was to be done as just "details."

Roosevelt held up the four freedoms in a speech to Congress
January 7, and said that the basic issue of the war was between
"those who believe in mankind and those who do not . . . between
those who put their faith in the people and those who put their faith
in tyrants." Peace could be maintained by preventing rearmament by
Germany, Japan and Italy "or any other nation which seeks to
violate the Tenth Commandment . . . 'Thou shalt not covet.' " Of

course, none of the United Nations coveted anything, being "bound together in solemn agreement" against acts of aggression or conquest.

But it was only a question of time until the fraudulence of such protestations would become apparent. Disclosure of the hollowness of the Atlantic Charter, although some time off, was inexorably drawing nearer. Something would have to fill the void eventually. Instead of political aims, the nation was given the slogan of "Unconditional Surrender."

This mouth-filling catch phrase was adopted at a conference of Roosevelt and Churchill at Casablanca, which Stalin declined to attend. Not a part of the planned official statement, it was announced by Roosevelt at a subsequent press conference, January 24. As the President described it, "and then suddenly the press conference was on, and Winston and I had not time to prepare for it, and the thought popped into my mind that they had called Grant 'Old unconditional Surrender,' and the next thing I knew I had said it." Roosevelt's son quotes the President as saying it would be "just the thing for the Russians . . . Uncle Joe might have made it up himself."[2]

Just why Roosevelt chose to describe unconditional surrender as an impromptu declaration is not known. The notes of Harry Hopkins show that the President spoke from carefully prepared material, consulting it as he talked. The biographer of Hopkins says the announcement was "very deeply deliberated."[3]

According to Churchill the unconditional-surrender slogan had actually been discussed before Roosevelt announced it, but Churchill assumed it had been superceded by an agreed statement in which it was not mentioned.[4] Years later, in July 1949, he apologetically told the House of Commons: "I was there on the spot and had to rapidly consider whether the state of our position in the world was such as to justify me in not giving support to it . . . I did support it, but it was not the idea I had formed in my own mind." Four months after that, in November 1949, Churchill admitted to the House of Commons that he had been mistaken—that he had telegraphed the British Cabinet for approval five days before the announcement was made.

Regardless of how long the actual unconditional-surrender phrase had been in Roosevelt's mind, there is reason to believe that the attitude had been burgeoning in both the United States and the British governments that they must enter Germany as conquerors, not merely as victors. It is indicated by the reception accorded efforts of the underground Hitler opposition to get cooperation from the West in their plans to overthrow Hitler and set up a new and democratic

German government. This movement included high military officers, state officials, churchmen and labor leaders throughout Germany. All their activities were at the risk of death if caught, and they repeatedly sought assurance from the West as to what kind of new government would be acceptable if they were successful.

In June 1942, Louis P. Lochner, formerly Berlin correspondent of the Associated Press, acting for the underground movement, had sought an interview with Roosevelt to lay the opposition's plans before him. Roosevelt refused repeated requests for an interview and finally, in response to a letter from Lochner, told him to desist from his quest, terming it "embarrassing."[5] In the same month, Dr. George Bell, bishop of Chichester, who had met in Stockholm with churchmen who were leaders of the underground, endeavored to get cooperation of the British government. The underground leaders proposed a democratic government which would repeal the Nuremberg race laws, restore Jewish property, withdraw from all occupied territory, and pay reparations for damages. They asked whether the West would be willing to negotiate with such a government. Anthony Eden, foreign secretary, was more courteous to Dr. Bell than Roosevelt had been to Lochner, but the answer was the same: no reply.[6]

Whether the underground would have drawn enough support to overthrow Hitler if buttressed by encouragement from the West can be only speculation; when an attempt was finally attempted in 1944, Hitler escaped and the planned revolution fell through. But it is significant that the West was not interested in the possibility of a successful outcome. Fighting across Europe to unconditional surrender was apparently preferred.

At any rate, the West now was saddled with a war objective which military historians generally agree prolonged the conflict by nerving the enemy to desperation, and which cost countless lives. All possible peace negotiations, even if they offered a victorious settlement with the overthrow of the Hitler regime, were rejected in advance. In the words of General J.F.C. Fuller, the British military historian,". . . .the Western allies could offer no terms, however severe. Conversely, their enemy could ask for none, however submissive." Unconditional surrender meant "that because no great power could with dignity or honor to itself, its history, its people and their posterity comply with them (the Casablanca terms), the war must be fought to the point of annihilation."[7]

Neutral European countries had hoped for some kind of concrete statement of allied peace aims rather than a vindictive slogan. Disappointment in Switzerland, according to the Bern correspondent of the *Washington Star*, showed "how much this continent would welcome an elaboration of the Atlanitc Charter." But the press in America was fervently enthusiastic. The *Boston Post* said that America "stands mute in awed admiration" of the bravery and valor of the President. The *Minneapolis Tribune* opined that "the meeting will rate as one of the greatest victories of the war." Walter Lippmann, the widely read columnist, likened the unconditional surrender agreement to a "gale of fresh air"; it was a "cleaning and invigorating wind" that blew out of Casablanca.[8]

To the *Detroit Free Press*, the conference was a "towering milestone." The *Cleveland News* found it "the opening shot of the greatest battle ever fought for human freedom." The *Philadelphia Bulletin* praised the President's personal courage because he had "shared the danger" by making the trip and asserted the conference had well served to advance "the dawn of a better day." The *New York Times* said Roosevelt's Casablanca trip was "one of the most brilliant episodes of his career; a journey which brought the breath of . . . democratic enthusiasm into three continents."

A few were not so enthusiastic. The *Providence Journal* questioned the absence of the Russians and the Chinese, suggesting that the United Nations were not nearly so united as they should be. The *Chicago Tribune* said acidly that the fortunes of the allies would be promoted better if Roosevelt and Churchill left military affairs to military men. The *New York Daily News* said the meeting had simply produced "another catchword or rallying cry" and averred with prescience that "the first ally to march into Berlin will be Russia."

The unconditional surrender slogan was given an effective boost in the mass mind—always affected by what it believes to be majority opinion—by misleading presentation of a Gallup public opinion poll, February 6. Headlined in the *Washington Post* as "Unconditional Surrender Policy Upheld By Public In Overwhelming National Vote," the report said the poll revealed "an almost unanimous opposition in this country to a compromise peace." Actually, the poll mentioned neither unconditional surrender nor a compromise peace. The question asked was: "If Hitler offered peace now to all countries on the basis of not going further, but of leaving matters as they are now, would you favor or oppose such a peace?" That is, did the people favor permitting Hitler to keep his gains. Ninety-two percent of those questioned naturally said no. "Unconditional surrender" had not been coined when the poll was taken, and the people did not even know the Casablanca conference was in progress. But it was accepted as the battle cry.

At Casablanca, a vast air offensive had been planned, the objective of which was not merely striking at military and industrial targets, but "the undermining of the morale of the German people." In other words, an extension of mass bombing of civilian populations, already under way by the Royal Air Force. With this in prospect, and with no peace acceptable other than by unconditional surrender, a vast effort to increase hatred of Germans had to be set in motion as a war spur. This campaign was to prove effective, but while it was getting under way reliance had to be placed on the noble aims of the Atlantic Charter to create a new world.

The war to unconditional surrender was still to be a war for the principles of the charter. Roosevelt again held up that document in a speech on February 12. True, there was a hint that the charter no longer applied to all peoples, as once had been pledged; the right of self-determination which it proclaimed did not carry the right of any government to "commit wholesale murder" or make slaves of its own people or any other people. Still it was the "unalterable purpose" of the United Nations to restore to conquered peoples their "sacred rights." And on February 21, in a letter to the *St. Louis Post-Dispatch*, Roosevelt reaffirmed that the nation was fighting for freedom "for all people everywhere."[9]

Administration spokesmen eulogized the pledges of the charter as pledges that would be kept. Joseph C. Grew, special assistant to the secretary of state and former ambassador to Japan, in a nationwide broadcast January 31, called the conflict a war for freedom which was "already the subject of solemn understandings in the Atlantic Charter and the Declaration of the United Nations." John G. Winant, ambassador to Britain, in a Princeton address January 30, promised that the United Nations would "carry the Four Freedoms to the peoples of the earth."

Assistant Secretary of State Adolph Berle, before the American Hungarian Association January 31, held up the Atlantic Charter as promising freedom from fear for all nations. Under-Secretary of State Welles, on an OWI broadcast February 12, hailed the fact that 31 nations had subscribed to "the great principles established in the Atlantic Charter," and quoted specifically the clause barring enforced territorial changes. Again at Toronto on February 26, Welles asserted that the United States and Canada sought attainment of the objectives of the charter.

Unconditional surrender, which was supposedly to make possible the effectuation of the charter pledges, was upheld by dire warnings of what would happen without it. Grew, in Cleveland February 5, said the only alternative would be a stalemate which would mean the "doom of civilization!" Unless so beaten, he said, "the Germans and the Japanese will fight their way here—literally here"— and would subject the inhabitants of Cleveland to oppression. In Baltimore April 1, in a nationwide broadcast, Grew said that only the British and American air forces had prevented that city from becoming a heap of ruins.

While Roosevelt and administration officials were publicly upholding the charter, Roosevelt privately had been moving in a quite different direction. Three weeks after he had assured the nation that he was fighting for freedom "for all people everywhere," he secretly acquiesced in the prospect of turning the Baltic states and eastern Poland over to communism, and in the awarding of large German territory to a truncated Poland, itself soon to be doomed to Communist rule.

This was done in a March 14 conference with Anthony Eden, British foreign secretary, in Washington. At this meeting, the life of the Atlantic Charter was effectively extinguished. It was not buried, however. For nearly two years more, it was kept on exhibition, like the body of Lenin in Moscow, but with the difference that the American people did not know the charter was dead.

Roosevelt agreed with Eden that Russia should have Bessarabia and the Polish territory approximately east of the Curzon line. Poland would be given east Prussia, and the President himself proposed removal of the Prussians from their land. As to the Baltic states, the President said the Russian armies would be occupying them when the war ended, and nothing could be done about it, but, in view of American sentiment, he proposed to "urge" that the Soviet conduct plebiscites there to supplant the ones claimed to have made in the days of Stalin-Hitler cooperation. Reminded by Eden that there was little chance of the Kremlin agreeing, Roosevelt proposed that the absorption of the Baltic nations by Russia be used as a "bargaining instrument" for concessions elsewhere.

The later furor over Soviet refusal to permit a democratic government in Poland following the Yalta conference contrasts strangely with the secret views of Roosevelt in 1943, as expressed to Eden.

58

When the latter said Russia would be satisfied with a Polish border along the Curzon line if the right kind of people controlled the rest of Poland, Roosevelt's only question was whether, after the war, a "liberal" Polish government satisfactory to Russia could remain in office.[10]

All this was kept secret. After Eden conferred off-the-record with congressional leaders, they told newspapermen he had urged that such details as boundaries were best left until after victory. The *Washington Post* said: "The impression was general, however, that delicate issues were for the most part avoided, while several congressmen reported that Eden had made equivocal replies concerning Russia's territorial aims in Poland . . . ."[11]

The President told the nation the talks with Eden were only exploratory, but that he and Eden had agreed 100 percent and there was "95 percent agreement" among all the nations fighting Germany. The public assumption was that this meant agreement according to the pledges of the charter.

It was even reported in London that Roosevelt and Eden had agreed on the desirability of restoring the old Polish frontiers. When Secretary Hull disclaimed any knowledge of this, a Washington dispatch to the *New York Times* (April 15 and 16) said diplomatic circles viewed it as "a reaffirmation of this government's policy of not making any territorial commitments during the war." Evidencing the general lack of suspicion that territorial dispositions had already been decided upon, *Fortune* magazine, two months later, conducted a public opinion poll in which it asked whether it was believed that Russia would make demands "that we can't agree to."[12]

A few days after the Roosevelt-Eden meeting, General Sikorski had again appealed apprehensively to the President for support against Russian demands on Poland, citing the Atlantic Charter. He had to wait nearly a month for an answer. Roosevelt finally assured Sikorski he was keeping the Polish problem "constantly in mind" in order that "I may decide what course of action would be most helpful to pursue in the interests of Poland and of all the United Nations."[13]

The secret Roosevelt-Eden agreement on European dispositions did not affect the Department of State façade that no territorial dispositions would be made until the expected peace conference. This façade was maintained to diplomatic representatives as well as to the people. On June 16, Undersecretary Welles wrote to the ambassador to the London-based Polish government-in-exile, "We are quite firm . . . in our determination not to be a party to any discussion of future frontiers at the present stage of the war." On July 10, Secretary Hull wrote to Ambassador Standley in Moscow that liquidation of boundary differences, unless done "amicably," should wait the termination of the war and be included in the general settlement.[14]

Popular distrust of Russia was still a problem. It had diminished only slightly. A public opinion poll in January 1943 revealed that only 46 percent believed the Soviet could be trusted for postwar cooperation. This was better than the 39 percent so responding in a poll a year earlier, but it was apparent that more selling of the Soviet had to be done. Joseph E. Davies, former ambassador to Russia, adviser to Roosevelt and soon to be his personal message bearer to Stalin, met criticism of Stalin's absence from Casablanca by explaining that he had to stay home to direct his armies. Davies said suspicion of Soviet intentions after the war only played into Hitler's hands, and that Russia wanted only to see that the smaller countries were to determine their own government without any coercion from the outside.[15]

How far such propaganda could be from the actual beliefs of the propagandist is indicated by a private conversation which Davies subsequently had with an official of the Department of State. His public statement, he admitted frankly, was not borne out by known facts and was contrary to the facts of the past. He had been "whistling by the graveyard" to create a favorable public opinion toward Stalin, which he felt was incumbent upon him.[16]

Russia itself gave little help to pro-Soviet propaganda. Stalin's absence from Casablanca was only one sign of the lack of Soviet collaboration. It had been very difficult for the American and British military to get technical information from the Russian front. Military missions were not encouraged, and only rarely had military observers been welcomed. Truculence, amounting sometimes almost to belligerence, had been the reward to the United States for its large war aid. Ambassador Standley reported March 10 that the more military successes the Russians achieved, the less cooperative they became.[17]

President Roosevelt took every opportunity to stroke Stalin's fur. On February 4, he fulsomely congratulated Stalin on the victory of Stalingrad, "the city which has forever honored your name." The message, according to an inspired United Press Washington dispatch, "was viewed as further evidence of the increasing cooperation between the two leaders and their countries in the fight against the common enemy and was calculated to silence critics who deplored the fact that Stalin was not a participant at Casablanca." But it brought from Stalin only polite thanks, and a veiled reference to his continuing demand for an immediate second front.

On the twenty-fifth anniversary of the Red Army, February 23, there were even more fulsome encomiums from America. Roosevelt said the Red Army's achievements were "unsurpassed in all history." Hull hailed the Red Army as "backed by the self-sacrificing devotion of the men and women of Russia." Mrs. Roosevelt, Secretary of the Treasury Morgenthau and Harry Hopkins were among those who sent congratulatory messages to Stalin.

At a New York celebration on Washington's birthday, a representative of the War Department even drew a parallel between the Red army and the army of George Washington as both having been born in revolution. Senator Elbert D. Thomas of Utah saw similarity in the tyrannies against which both had fought. In the new Russia, men, women and children had "tasted freedom." Senator James E. Murray said the Russian people had risen to "defend the cause of mankind" at a time when civilization was "threatened with extinction." Former ambassador Davies said the Russian defense had relieved men everywhere of the fear that our civilization, "based upon the ideals of goodwill, altruism and brotherhood," faced destruction.

But Stalin was impervious to honeyed words. In a speech to the Soviet army he made no mention of the United States, Britain or the United Nations, and said that in the absence of a second front Russia alone was bearing the whole weight of the war. He ascribed purely to Russian efforts the increase in equipment which had brought war successes and made no mention of the large aid given by the United States or Great Britain. In the words of a Department of State internal memorandum, Stalin's speech stood out "sharply against the background of generous and unstinted praise which American and British officials, including the king and the President," had sent to the Soviet government on the same occasion.

Soviet refusal to make public recognition of the vast and growing United States war assistance was causing increasing discussion, and the administration became concerned as the time approached for consideration of Lend-Lease aid for the coming fiscal year. Apprehensive of possible adverse action in Congress, the President asked Ambassador William H. Standley to obtain some kind of public Russian admission of the help received.[18] Repeated attempts brought no results. Finally, on March 8, Standley frankly told newspaper correspondents that the Soviet authorities seemed to be "trying to create the impression at home and abroad that they were fighting the war alone, and with their own resources."

The undiplomatic statement created a commotion in Washington. Acting Secretary of State Welles assured the press that it had been made without prior consultation, and that complete trust and understanding existed among all the United Nations. Standley's frankness was likewise derogated by the chairmen of the Foreign Relations Committees of both houses of Congress. But it got results when diplomatic efforts had failed; news of American aid at last began appearing in the Soviet press. The official Russian history of the war refers to Lend-Lease supplies made available to the Russians both before and after the battle of Stalingrad as wholly negligible, and attributes Russia's difficulties to "the sabotage of the Second Front."[19]

The effort to improve the Soviet image received something of a jolt in March, when it was learned that the Russians, three months before, had executed two Polish socialist leaders, Wikto R. Alter and Henryk Ehrlich. The two had been kept in prison since their seizure by the secret police in December 1941, on the charge that they were Nazi spies. Eleanor Roosevelt, wife of the President, and William Green, president of the American Federation of Labor, were among the prominent persons who had tried vainly to obtain their release.

But such incidents did not bother the Vice President of the United States, Henry A. Wallace. In public addresses he implied or directly stated that much anti-Soviet feeling arose from sympathy to fascism. He expressed concern that the nation might "double-cross" Russia rather than be adversely affected by Russian objectives. Domestic disaster and even another world war was threatened if "fascist interests, motivated largely by anti-Russian bias," got control of the government.[20]

Former Ambassador Grew assured nationwide radio listeners on April 1 of "the reality of our common cause with the Soviet Union," and said, "whoever fights Germany is . . . deserving of our respect, confidence and trust." In a broadcast on April 4, Assistant Secretary Berle called Soviet Russia one of the "four great freedom-loving powers" of the world, and said a strong and victorious Russia was "necessary to the United States."

While the administration was trying to paint a picture of harmony with the USSR under the banner of the Atlantic Charter, the Soviet attitude toward Poland was hardening as military successes mounted. In the Stalin-Hitler honeymoon of 1939, more than a million and a half Polish citizens, in addition to 180,000 prisoners of war, had been deported to Russia. After the German attack, the Polish government-in-exile had been permitted to conduct relief activities among these hapless people. In late 1942, as Poland stubbornly refused to cede territory, such activities were progressively harassed. Poles in Russia were subjected to widespread persecution. Some who had been forcibly deported from their own homes were imprisoned because they could not show legal entry papers. Others were charged with spying and various other crimes. In November 1942, sixteen welfare delegates of the Polish embassy in Moscow were even being held on charges of spying for Great Britain and the United States.

In early 1943, Stalin dropped any pretense of amity toward the London Polish government. He announced in effect that all persons deported from eastern Poland were Soviet citizens. Relief agencies were closed, food distribution halted, and directors of schools, orphanages and hospitals replaced by Russians, on the familiar accusation of espionage. Fantastic diatribes were issued against the Polish government, and in late February 1943 an article in the Soviet Embassy's Washington information bulletin called flatly for the annexation of eastern Poland, followed on March 2 by a Soviet statement foreshadowing the breaking of relations unless demands were met.

The Polish ambassador in Washington, appealing to President Roosevelt for some kind of assistance to the Poles in Russia, reported that they were being beaten, starved and ejected from their dwellings for refusing Soviet citizenship. The National Committee of Americans of Polish Descent urged the nation in newspaper advertisements to "hold the moral line" of the war and insist that the Poles be brought out of Russia. It argued that, with millions of dollars of Lend-Lease goods going into Russia daily, surely this could be done "before the stigma of guilt blots our conscience." Ambassador Standley, who previously had felt that it was inadvisable for the United States to approach Russia on behalf of the Poles, on April 3 came to the conclusion that the situation called for Western intercession. "I realize," he wrote Secretary Hull, "what a harmful impression the revelation of the true facts concerning the situation of the Poles in the Soviet Union would have upon world opinion and our united effort."[21]

But there was to be no intercession. The price of relieving the Poles in Russia was agreement on territorial demands, and the Polish government-in-exile would not budge. Ambassador Standley had informed Secretary Hull on March 9 of his belief that the Soviet had decided to force the issue by any "bludgeon tactics" necessary. On April 9, a Department of State memorandum suggested that Russia might be seeking an opportunity to break with the London Polish government in order to set up a Moscow controlled "free Poland."

A colorable pretext was needed, and it came soon. In mid-April, the Germans announced the discovery near Smolensk, Russia, of mass graves containing the bodies of thousands of Polish officers, with all evidence indicating that they had been barbarically murdered by the Russians while the Soviet had held that territory. The Poles asked for an investigation by the International Red Cross, on which, with a show of high indignation, the Soviet severed diplomatic contact. The reception accorded to news of this massacre reveals the extent to which the United States was willing and eager to occlude the brutal facts about its Communist ally in a war supposedly for an Atlantic Charter peace.

6

Covering Up Soviet Atrocities

On April 13, 1943, the German radio announced the finding of mass graves of thousands of Polish officers in the Katyn forest near Smolensk, Russia, territory that had been occupied by Soviet troops until the summer of 1941. The men, wearing heavy, fur-lined field coats, their hands tied behind them, had been killed by pistol shots in the back of the head, and it appeared that some had been buried alive. Newspapers, letters and diaries found on the bodies, the German radio said, identified many of the men and fixed the time of their death as not later than April or May 1940. The Germans charged the men had been murdered en masse by the Russians and offered to produce proof found in the graves.

Everything pointed to Russian guilt. Prime Minister Churchill wrote long afterwards that he had believed from the first that the Russians were guilty. Indeed, the British ambassador to Poland, Owen O'Malley, reported when the discovery was made that he was convinced the Russians had committed the murders. "We have, in fact, perforce used the good name of England to cover up the massacre," he wrote in another report.[1] But such views could not be admitted to the people in wartime, and O'Malley's messages were kept secret until the official records were opened thirty years later. The governments of Britain and the United States proclaimed at the time of the German discovery that it was all a monstrous lie. In the United States, most of the press joined in an effort to suppress, color or explain away the evidence so that the people would not know their ally had perpetrated one of the most barbaric atrocities of history.

This chapter is concerned with the way the massacre was covered up in America rather than with the atrocity itself, the facts of which have been extensively published. Nevertheless, a brief résumé of events prior to and surrounding the discovery is necessary in order to show how the facts were denied.

When the Russians had occupied eastern Poland, in cooperation with Hitler, they had imprisoned hundreds of thousands of Poles.

Proceeding with customary Communist policy of liquidating or suppressing potential opposition leadership, they had separated from other prisoners 15,400 army officers, government officials, clergy and other civilian leaders, and had imprisoned them in special camps in Russia. After the Hitler-Stalin break, when the Russians were driven from Poland, the Soviet had hastily resumed relations with the London Polish government-in-exile, and had welcomed the proposed formation of an army from Poles in Russia to fight alongside the Soviet, under the leadership of General Wladyslaw Anders, himself just released from 20 months in a Russian prison. Anders immediately set out on a far-reaching search for the mission officers, but only 400 had been found at the time of the Katyn discovery. They had been detached from the others after extended examination, and had been sent to a special camp for Communist indoctrination, from which they were released in September 1941. These men had been permitted to correspond with their families during imprisonment, but not a word had been heard from the others since May 1940.

Repeated Polish appeals to the Russian general staff, the Russian foreign office and the Russian secret police had brought no news of the mission officers. Stalin had told Anders in December 1941 that they had escaped to Manchuria. Three months later, he suggested they had fled and had become dispersed when the Germans invaded Russia. To the Poles, this did not ring true because they knew the Russians kept detailed prisoner lists, and the men could not have been lost with no record.[2]

When the bodies were found, the Polish government asked for an investigation by the International Red Cross, domiciled in Switzerland. The Germans seconded the request, offering full cooperation, and the Red Cross agreed to act if requested also by the Soviet. Russia angrily rejected the proposal, and on April 26, with a menacingly vituperative blast, abruptly broke off relations with the Polish government. The Soviet now changed its story again about the disappearance of the men, and for the first time said the Germans had captured the Polish officers and put them to death. The Poles, it said, were in league with the Germans, and the request for a Red Cross inquiry was aimed "to please Hitler tyranny."

Until the German disclosure, the American people had not even known that the officers had disappeared. The U.S. government, however, had long been in possession of facts indicating a high probability that they had been liquidated by the Russians. In the spring of 1942, the whole story of the disappearance of the officers had been laid before the Department of State by the American embassy in Moscow,[3] and subsequently the department received further details from the Poles, with appeals for help in finding the missing men. The Russians were not cooperative. An American army officer named as liaison officer with the two million Poles deported to Russia, with the specific assignment to ascertain what had happened to the officers, was refused a Russian visa.[4] Efforts of Ambassador Standley to find out something were fruitless, and in September the Soviet let him know that no interference by the United States was welcome.[5] The President and the Department of State "ignored numerous documents from the ambassadors in London and Moscow and to the Polish goverment-in-exile which strongly pointed to Soviet perfidy."[6]

With the Russian rejection of a Red Cross inquiry adding corroboration to the apparent German evidence of Russian guilt, the United States government first tried to ignore the whole affair, although within the Department of State a policy memorandum was circulated which clearly conveyed doubts of Russian innocence. The memorandum called attention to the Polish government's long attempts to find the missing men and to the efforts of the American ambassador to assist in the search. It advised against taking any definite stand because of the "extremely delicate nature of the question" and the "various conflicting contentions."

The Department of State, along with the President, blanketed itself with silence, but Roosevelt was determined to believe—or to appear to believe—in Russian innocence. German radio broadcasts were monitored especially for him with the assistance of a former Nazi press chief, Dr. Ernst F. S. Hanfstaengl, who had fled Germany before the war. Hanfstaengl, able to appraise German propaganda from intimate experience, became convinced that the German broadcasts on Katyn were truthful. This was reported to Roosevelt and to Elmer Davis, director of the Office of War Information, and Undersecretary of State Welles by John Franklin Carter, who made regular reports to the President under a Department of State contract. In Carter's words, the reaction was that "they didn't want to believe it, and that if they had believed it they would have pretended not to."[7]

Prime Minister Churchill was secretly convinced that the Russians were guilty. Years later, he wrote that Prime Minister Sikorski had presented him with a "wealth of evidence" to that effect, but neither the British nor the American people learned this at the time. Of the

Russian story that the Germans had committed the murders, Churchill wrote:

> This version to be believed involves acceptance of the fact that nearly 15,000 Polish officers and men, of whom there was no record since spring of 1940, passed into German hands in July 1941, and were later destroyed by the Germans without one single person escaping and reporting either to the Russian authorities or to a Polish consul in Russia or to the underground movement in Poland. When we remember the confusion caused by the German advance, that the guards of the camps must have fled as the invaders came near, and all the contacts afterwards during the period of Russo-Polish cooperation, belief seems an act of faith.[8]

The British ambassador in Moscow was likewise convinced that the Russians had perpetrated the massacre. When the Soviet broke relations with Poland, the British ambassador in Washington informed the Department of State "in strictest confidence" of the Moscow ambassador's view that it had been done to cover up Soviet guilt for the murders.[9] But U.S. Ambassador Standley, in Moscow, received no request from Washington for any information—"none whatever."[10]

Despite his belief in Russian guilt, Churchill on April 24 promised Stalin that "we shall certainly oppose vigorously" any Red Cross investigation.[11] Roosevelt sent a secret message to Stalin expressing confidence that Prime Minister Churchill would find a way of prevailing upon the Polish government in London in the future "to act with more common sense."[12] Churchill found a way. Pressure was put on General Wladislaw Sikorski, prime minister of the Polish government-in-exile, and in another message to Stalin April 25, the next day, Churchill could report that as a result of this pressure Sikorski had agreed to withdraw the request for the inquiry. The Poles, he wrote on April 30 to Stalin, had "accepted our view."

Unable to get an international Red Cross investigation, the Germans organized a commission for the purpose composed of leading medical men and scientists from twelve neutral and occupied countries, including Switzerland, Finland, Belgium, France, Denmark and Italy. Present at the inquiry were representatives of the Polish underground and a twelve-man Polish medical team. The state of the corpses and other physical evidence, and the diaries and letters found on the bodies, confirmed that death had occurred in April 1940. Microscopic analysis of trees placed over the graves showed that they had been planted in 1940, whereas the Germans did not arrive until 1941.

The conclusion, made public April 30, was unanimous that the massacre had been committed while the Russians held the territory. To the extent that it was mentioned at all in the American press, excepting a few newspapers, it was presented simply as German propaganda. Elmer Davis, who reported to the President and also wrote speeches for him, finally took notice of the massacre in a broadcast on May 3, in which he called the whole thing a hoax. The German story, he said, provided a good example of Hitler's dictum that it was easier to make the people swallow a big lie than a little one. Davis derided what he termed "suggestions" of an international Red Cross inquiry, carefully avoiding the fact that such an inquiry had been blocked only by a Russian rejection.

This official attitude continued throughout the war and afterward. Every effort was made to prevent the public from questioning Russian innocence. Most of the American press, though under no totalitarian rule, slavishly adopted the same line. Most newspapers printed nothing about the discovery until it was forced into the news by the Russian break with the Polish government. Then, in remarkable concert, most of those which mentioned the massacre at all sought by slanted presentation or outright argument to convince the people it was a lie. Nearly a decade later, when exhaustive congressional investigation clearly and unanimously established Russian guilt, some of these journals admitted soberly that the circumstantial evidence alone should have been enough to convince them of the truth in 1943.

The news of the finding of the bodies was first published April 16 by the *New York Times*, which gave it exactly two sentences near the bottom of the fourth page, under a tiny headline which merely said "Nazis Accuse Russians." The *Times* story on this momentous discovery follows in full:

London, April 15—The latest German attempt to sow discord between Allies is a story of the alleged finding of graves of 10,000 Polish officers in a forest near Smolensk. In broadcast accounts the Germans suggested these officers, taken prisoners during the invasion of Poland in the winter of 1939-40, had been shot in the spring of 1940.

The dispatch omitted actual mention of the Russians, and only in the press of Switzerland and other neutral countries could one read that all evidence found on the bodies showed the men had been murdered in the spring of 1940 when the Russians controlled the territory. So far as this writer has been able to ascertain, only the *Times* carried anything at all.

The following day, however, the Polish government made public the full story of the missing officers and asked for an inquiry by the International Red Cross, to which the Germans at once agreed. The Associated Press gave the news only three paragraphs and coupled it with a Moscow assertion that it was all "a monstrous lie," adding as a further neutralizer "a report from Polish refugees in Stockholm" that the Germans had shot several hundred Polish peasants.

Most of the press continued to ignore the massacre. The *Chicago Tribune* carried the AP story, and the *New York Times* and *New York Herald-Tribune* had special pieces from their correspondents. In numerous other leading newspapers surveyed by this author, there was not a line. In the nation's capital, the *Washington Post* and the *Evening Star* printed nothing. On the following day, it was discussed in the *Washington Herald* in a general account of Polish efforts to obtain an investigation of Russian atrocities to prisoners. On April 19 the *Washington Daily News* carried a *Pravda* diatribe against the Poles for requesting the inquiry, referring vaguely to the German charge "that the Russians have killed 10,000 Poles," and giving no further explanation.

When, on April 23, the Associated Press reported from Berne that the Red Cross was willing to organize an inquiry if requested by all parties concerned, but had been blocked by Russian refusal, the *Chicago Tribune* was one of the few papers giving space to the story. The United Press, the second largest press association, took its first notice. It referred to the Polish "dispute" with the Soviet Union over the "alleged" disappearance of the Polish officers which "has been used by the Berlin radio for propaganda purposes. The Germans claim the men were killed." This dispatch appeared in the *New York World Telegram* and the *New York Journal-American* and was the first time the story had been touched upon in either paper. There was no mention of the alleged discovery of the bodies in a mass grave, no mention of a proposed Red Cross inquiry or the Russian refusal, no mention of the Germans' proposal to submit their evidence.

The *Washington Herald* returned to the story with an article by Frank C. Waldrop which discussed the mystery of the missing men in detail and cited the evidence of Russian guilt. But the *Washington Post* and the *Washington Star* would have none of it.

Throughout the country, the newspapers sought to quash the story. In Atlanta, as one of many similar examples, the *Journal* did not mention the massacre until a week after the discovery, when the Red Cross agreed to an inquiry if requested by Russia. Having printed nothing previously, the *Journal* was forced to insert a brief explanation of what the proposed inquiry would be about, but even then it was careful to avoid mentioning that the Germans had charged the Soviets with the murders. In Chicago, the *Sun* kept the story from its columns until on April 20 it could display prominently a *Pravda* charge that the Poles were supporting Nazi aims, and that the massacre was the work of the Germans. When, on April 24, it finally published a Polish statement that more than 8,000 officers imprisoned by Russia had disappeared, the *Sun* coupled this with another *Pravda* blast terming it German propaganda.

The weekly news magazine *Time* reported the finding under the heading "Good for Goebbels," and used invidious quotes, calculated to persuade the reader it was a lie without actually saying so. "These unfortunate men, purred Berlin, had been murdered by the Russians in the spring of 1940." *Time* said invidiously that the Polish government-in-exile "promptly remembered" that the men had been missing for three years. There was no mention of the long, disheartening search which the Poles had made for their leaders, no mention of the mass graves or of the evidence found on the bodies. The Germans, said *Time*, had "planted" the story.[13]

Newsweek contented itself with five sentences relating that the Germans claimed to have found 10,000 officers in mass graves, slaughtered by the Russians, and that the Polish government had asked the Red Cross to investigate. There was no mention of the German claim that evidence found on the bodies had fixed the approximate murder date as during the period when the Russians still occupied the territory.[14]

But the story would not just go away. When Russia broke relations with the Polish government-in-exile, with the Katyn discovery as an excuse, the press generally had to take at least enough notice to explain what Russia was talking about. The Associated Press on April 26 carried a dispatch from Moscow, near the end of which were inserted a few lines telling of the German charge. It merely said that soon after the Germans announced the finding of the bodies at Katyn, the Polish government-in-exile had charged that 15,000 soldiers and civilians captured by the Russians were missing, and that it had been unable to get a satisfactory explanation. The brief note reported the willingness of the Red Cross to organize an inquiry if asked by both sides, but that since no "invitation" had come from

Russia such an inquiry appeared unlikely. These few facts were sandwiched in the middle of a story filled with Russian charges against the Poles, and constituted the entire account carried by the Associated Press for afternoon papers and in a rewritten form for the morning papers the next day. This was the first account carried in the *Washington Evening Star* and the *Washington Post*.

The *Christian Science Monitor* first mentioned the discovery April 23, in a news account which said the "affair" had been "ventilated" by the Germans as part of their anti-Bolshevik propaganda, the story having been "produced" to divide the United Nations. On April 27, a second article derogated the evidence found on the bodies as "only circumstantial and full of gaps." Moreover, it said, extermination of conquered peoples was a Nazi custom to which the Russians had not been addicted in the current war.

News efforts to defend injured Russian innocence were paralleled on the editorial pages. The question of Russian guilt must not even be asked, said the *Washington Post*. "The assumption of all loyal members of the United Nations must be that they were killed by the Germans."[15] Furthermore, said the *Post*, the Polish government-in-exile was dominated by persons "predominantly reactionary and feudal," an assertion which not only had no bearing on the issue of Russian guilt but was also substantially untrue, as most of the members of the Polish government-in-exile had labor or peasant backgrounds.[16]

The *Washington Star* did not even discuss it. The *Christian Science Monitor* on April 27 said the German story was "concocted with diabolical cunning." No inquiry would prove anything and the allied nations should refuse to be "diverted by sensations." The *Atlanta Constitution* marshalled all the arguments it could think of to show the German charge false, and glossed over the Russian rejection of a Red Cross inquiry by dogmatizing that it would prove nothing.[17] The *Atlanta Journal* called it a trick to split the camps of the Allies.[18]

To the *New York Times* editor also, the affair was a "trick" the Germans had played on the Poles who, with the Russians, had fallen into a "Nazi trap."[19] Ann O'Hare McCormick, foreign affairs commentator and member of the *Times* editorial board, said there was not even proof that the officers had been killed, and if so there was no proof that the Germans had not been the executioners. It was "beyond the bounds of credulity" that it had taken the Germans so long to find the graves, or that the victims would be recognizable.[20]

The *Times* gave first-page position to a Washington dispatch asserting that the Nazis had early made a "specialty" of displaying slaughtered bodies to correspondents, although it was impossible to determine who they were or who had murdered them. "Now they have played the same trick on the Poles, themselves."

In Chicago, the *Sun* condoned the Russian rejection of a Red Cross inquiry with what had become a stock phrase—"obviously no investigators could conduct an objective investigation in German-occupied territory."[21] The *Chicago Tribune*, however, on April 28, spoke plainly:

> The extreme violence of the Russian declaration is easy to explain. The commissars know that their conduct in the past had made it easy for the world to believe the story. . . . As the Bolsheviks have murdered millions of their own people, including many hundreds of revolutionary comrades, there is no inherent reason to believe that the man who ordered all these executions would hesitate on humanitarian grounds to kill a relatively small number of Polish leaders.

The Russian declaration, said the *Tribune*, "springs from a sense of guilt. . . ." But the *Tribune* was alone.

The syndicated columnists, to whom newspaper editors had increasingly abdicated their function, descended upon the story with unrestrained zeal in defense of the maligned and innocent Russians. Dorothy Thompson on April 30 devoted her widely-circulated column to explaining why it was a German fabrication.[22] "Experts," she said, had told her that identification after three years would have been impossible. She dismissed the fact that three-year-old trees had been found growing on the graves, showing the men had been buried in 1940, with the assertion that the trees could have been transplanted. Trees would not flourish in the clay soil of Katyn, she said, and anyway, if the Russians had committed the murders they would have chosen another region for burial. It was just a "tall tale." As to a Red Cross inquiry, no "valid investigation" could be conducted.

This insistence that an objective Red Cross inquiry would prove nothing had become the party line of the columnists generally. It was adopted by Ernest Lindley in the *Washington Post*,[23] and other papers. Glossing over the Russian refusal of an inquiry, he asked, "What good would come of it?" even if the German charge were proved true. William L. Shirer[24] said it was suspicious that the Germans had "waited" nearly two years before discovering the mass grave, and said that "to fall for German propaganda" seemed "a good way of trying to lose the war." Samuel Grafton, in the *Chicago Sun* and other newspapers,[25] devoted an entire article to the value of the story to the Germans as anti-Soviet propaganda of the Polish government-in-exile and in effect warned the nation to beware of that government.

Walter Lippmann, the widely syndicated commentator on foreign affairs, ignored the story entirely. On April 29, he achieved the feat of discussing the Russian break with Poland in detail without ever mentioning the gruesome discovery which the Russians had used as an excuse.

If newspapers tried to hush up the story, it was by their own choice. With the radio it was different. Broadcasting stations operated under licenses which were granted and renewed by the Federal Communications Commission. Since 1942, pressure had been applied to stations employing broadcasters critical of the Soviet. If recalcitrant, they would find themselves in trouble in getting their licenses renewed. The pressure was increased as commentators on Polish language stations in Buffalo and Detroit reported facts indicating that the Russians had committed the massacre. In the case of a Detroit commentator, the OWI and the FCC arranged a meeting with the Wartime Foreign Language Control Committee, consisting of owners and managers of stations. The presence of the FCC representative was effective. The committee saw to it that the offending commentator was restricted to repeating news items as they came from the press. By indirect pressure, the OWI and the FCC "accomplished their purpose, namely, keeping the full facts of the Katyn massacre story from the American people."[26]

The Russians, who had regained the Smolensk territory in January 1944, put on an elaborately staged show to try to establish their innocence. Seventeen news correspondents were invited, along with Kathleen Harriman, daughter of the ambassador, and John Melby of the American embassy staff. No bodies were removed from graves by direction of the correspondents. One letter, supposedly written by a Polish prisoner two days before the Germans came in but unmailed, was exhibited in a glass case, with other alleged evidence. The "investigation" consisted chiefly of statements by Russian officials.

The *New York Times* correspondent reported the fact that some bodies were in heavy field overcoats lined with fur, strange garb for August or September, the months in which the Russians charged the

Germans with committing the murders. The Russian explanation had been that the nights were cold. The *Times'* story was noncommittal, as were others. Henry C. Cassidy, chief of the Associated Press Moscow bureau, later testified before the House Katyn investigating committee that the newspapermen were not convinced, but that he reported no conclusions because he knew anything adverse would anger the Russians and would not get past censorship anyway.

The reports of Melby and Miss Harriman to the embassy were curiously suggestive of an attempt to reach a desired conclusion. They admitted that the witnesses were well-rehearsed, the evidence was minute and petty, there were many unanswered questions and doubts, and that they were expected to accept statements as true just because Soviet officials made them. Despite all this, both dutifully gave their opinions that the Germans were guilty, and Miss Harriman cited as the most convincing evidence "the methodical manner in which the job was done." Ambassador Harriman's confidential report to the President, giving the opinions of his emissaries, referred to "German Shooting of Captured Polish Officers in Katyn Forest," although he admitted therein that the evidence and testimony were "inconclusive."[27]

In May 1944, George H. Earle, former governor of Pennsylvania and the President's special emissary in Turkey and the Balkans, brought evidence of Russian guilt directly to Roosevelt, but got nowhere. Earle had photographs which had been taken at the graves and affidavits from officials of the Bulgarian and Rumanian Red Cross organizations, testifying that they had personally inspected the bodies at Katyn and that there was no doubt that the Soviet was responsible. The President's response was that it was "entirely German propaganda and a German plot."[28] Earle insistently continued to send evidence of Russian guilt to Roosevelt, and finally, on March 22, 1945, told the President that he would publicize the facts unless ordered not to do so. Roosevelt forbade him, and Earle, who held a naval commission, was sent to Samoa.[29]

Official efforts to prevent the American public from learning the truth about the massacre extended to the military. In 1943, shortly after the bodies were found, two U.S. army officers, prisoners of the Germans, were taken to Katyn to see the evidence for themselves. Both became convinced of Russian guilt. The senior of these officers, Col. John H. Van Vliet, was released from imprisonment in April 1945. In Washington, on May 22, he handed a written report to

Major General Clayton Bissell, army assistant chief of staff in charge of Army Intelligence. It was suppressed and kept secret, and Van Vliet was given a written order not to discuss it. After the war, as official attitudes toward Russia changed, rumors of the suppressed report became current. Finally the army searched, but it had disappeared. In 1950, Van Vliet prepared a second report.

General Bissell later testified he had classified the first report as "top secret" because he saw in it "great possibilities of embarrassment." Questioned at length, Bissell said he thought the report had been sent to an official of the Department of State, but that official denied receiving it. No receipt for its transmittal—an ironclad aspect of procedure with such documents—could be found. An independent investigation conducted by the army's inspector general in 1950 concluded that there was nothing to indicate the report had ever left Army Intelligence.

The conclusion of the House of Representatives investigating committee was unequivocal: the Van Vliet report "was either removed or purposely destroyed in Army Intelligence." According to the testimony of officers who were stationed in Army Intelligence during the war, there was a pool of pro-Soviet civilian and military personnel who exerted great efforts to suppress anti-Soviet reports. Top-ranking officers who were too critical of the Soviets were bypassed.

At the Nuremberg trials, the Soviet made a weak attempt to fasten Katyn guilt upon the Germans. One witness gave apparently prepared answers to questions by the Russian prosecutor. Another repeated the findings of the 1944 Russian "investigation." A third was a Bulgarian member of the international commission which had found the Russians guilty, and who, after imprisonment by the Soviet, and with the prospect of being returned to Communist-controlled Bulgaria, had repudiated the earlier verdict. The American and British prosecutors were in possession of voluminous evidence gathered by the Poles which showed Russian guilt, and the Katyn massacre was simply dropped.

It was not until the United States found itself fighting a war in Korea against an army trained, equipped and supplied by Russia, that an official effort was made to reveal the facts of Katyn. At long last, the whitewash was to be stripped away. A House of Representatives inquiry into the massacre was initiated in September 1951. A bipartisan committee consumed two years in the investigation, during which time it heard 81 witnesses—including one eyewitness—and took depositions in both the United States and Europe.

Its conclusion was unanimous. The Poles had been murdered by the Soviet not later than than the spring of 1940.

Only 4,143 bodies had been found in the Katyn forest graves. Testimony showed that the approximately 15,400 prisoners had been placed in three camps. Those murdered in the Katyn forest were the prisoners from a camp at Kozielsk, where the majority of high-ranking army officers and hundreds of doctors who were army reservists had been held. Noncommissioned officers and peacetime political and education leaders, also reservists, were imprisoned at Starobielsk. Poland's frontier guards, home police and public officials of eastern Poland were imprisoned at Ostashkov. Religious leaders were imprisoned in all three camps. Nothing has ever been heard of the prisoners of the latter two camps. Testimony before the investigating committee indicated that the Starobielsk prisoners had probably met their death somewhere near Kharkov in the same manner as the Katyn victims, and that the Ostashkov prisoners had probably been murdered by being placed on barges in the White Sea, which were then sunk by artillery fire.

When the committee's reports were issued, some of the newspapers which had done their best to mislead the public at the time of the discovery had nothing to say. Others were penitent in varying degrees. Most were inclined to blame the government for their own attempts to convince their readers that the whole thing was a fraud.

The *Washington Star* agreed that the OWI, the FCC and government officials from the President down "ignored evidence that the Germans were right." It did not hesitate to criticize "the part played by our government in concealing the facts from the American people." But it made no mention of the fact that nearly all newspapers, including the *Star*, had lent themselves fully to that concealment.

The *Washington Post*, which at the time of the massacre had insisted that German guilt "must" be assumed, was a little more forthright. When the interim report of the investigating committee was issued, July 22, 1952, the *Post* said remorsefully:

It is now painfully plain that the suspicion of the western governments and press concerning the Russian version of the Katyn story . . . should have been aroused when the Kremlin refused to permit an investigation by the International Red Cross, as was requested by the Polish government-in-exile.[30]

On the issuance of the committee's final report, December 22, 1952, the *Post* said:

One reason that many American newspapers were content to accept the Russian story was that it had apparently been accepted in official quarters. In our opinion this does not wholly exonerate the press, which should, as a matter of principle, be always distrustful of official motives, and should draw its conclusions independently from such evidence as is available.

Explaining why there was no powerful defense of radio commentators forced off the air by the OWI and FCC, the *Post* added:

> . . . resistance to the government in such a matter in time of war would have necessitated a much higher degree of civic courage than is required to condemn the government nine years afterward for having applied the pressure. And it is mainly this absence of civic courage, the reluctance to risk the odium of dissent when the cry is for unity, that enables the policy makers and propagandists to compound such blunders as were made in the aftermath of the Katyn episode.[31]

But in 1943, Russian guilt in such a heinous crime could not be admitted without giving the lie to the nation's own pro-Soviet propaganda, which most of the press, under no totalitarian rule, had been implanting in the mass mind—of which it had become a part.

7

On to Teheran

The whitewashing of the Russians when the Katyn Forest massacre was discovered was but a manifestation of the swelling tide of pro-Soviet propaganda in 1943. Most of the press, the radio and the movies had already gotten behind the official effort to create a new Russian image. A notable instance was the issuance by *Life* magazine on March 29 of a special 116-page edition devoted entirely to gilding the Soviet. Colorful illustrations of Russian scenes, portraits of Russian officials, and appealing pictures of farmers, workers and children sought to create a sympathetic and approving attitude.

A capsule history of Russia was provided which ended conveniently before Stalin's notorious purges of the late thirties. The Stalin-Hitler pact of 1939 was explained as necessary to gain time to prepare for a German attack after the democracies' refusal to support a policy of collective security. The Soviet was described as working for collective security against fascism after being admitted to the League of Nations, but the fact that it was later expelled from the League because of its 1939 attack on Finland was not mentioned. In an article by former ambassador Joseph E. Davies, Russian territorial demands were defended and Poland was charged with raising controversy. Readers were assured that Russia would go as far as any nation in "a high-minded and altruistic effort" to cooperate in creating a stable world.

Film makers, working closely with the Office of War Information, vied to glorify the Soviets. Davies' book, *Mission to Moscow*, which represented the 1937-38 purges as destroying a German "fifth column," was made into a pretentious picture, with the production supervised by the author. Opening in New York two weeks after the disclosure of the Katyn Forest massacre, it broke all records for the theater. Backed by a huge advertising budget and a tremendous promotional push, the film was shown in every hamlet. The National Council of American-Soviet Friendship presented certificates of appreciation to Davies and the producers in a big New York rally at which a United States senator expressed the "immeasureable debt" which the United States owed to Russia.

The film was so fulsome in its praise of the Soviet Union and President Roosevelt, and so filled with historical distortions, that even many sympathetic reviewers confessed to misgivings. Fifty-two American educators, historians, writers and trade union leaders issued a statement terming it "the first full-dress example of the kind of propaganda hitherto confined to totalitarian countries . . . . It falsifies history and glorifies dictatorship." Even the Writers War Board, which had been formed at the instigation of Secretary of the Treasury Morgenthau, and which was itself very active in the effort to promote trust in the Soviet Union, felt impelled to denounce the picture because of its falsification of facts and unrestrained acceptance of the supposed merits of Russian communism.

Nevertheless, when a special preview was held in Washington under the auspices of the National Press Club, with a packed house of newspapermen, diplomats and government officials, the *Washington Post* reported: "There was a deep and almost reverent silence through most of the showing . . . . At the end there was a great burst of applause which ended only when the theater orchestra drowned it out with the finale."[1] In contrast, it may be added, at the end of a private showing for Stalin the Russian dictator walked out without a word or look for anyone. American newspapermen were told that changes would have to be made before the film could be shown in Russia.

The North Star, a big propaganda film, pictured German cruelty against the backdrop of a Russian agricultural commune where life had been just one happy idyll, filled with music and rollicking gaiety. The children on walking trips happily sang of themselves as the "future generation"—with lyrics by Ira Gershwin. The villagers, wrote the gagging reviewer of the *New York Times*, might be "light-hearted peasants in musical comedies set in mythical foreign lands." When they gathered for a sociable evening it was like a scene from *Oklahoma.* The film, he said, was in "startling contrast" to the Russia of fact. But the *Times'* weekly magazine gave the film a full-page picture display entitled "Peasant Epic of Russia" and *Time* called it a "milestone."

Actors who objected to taking part in pro-Soviet propaganda productions sometimes found life difficult. Washington influence was exerted to prevent Robert Taylor, a leading actor, from entering the navy until he had starred in *Song of Russia*, glorifying Soviet institutions and ideologies. Lowell Mellett, motion picture coordinator of the OWI, came to Hollywood and blocked his attempt to get out of the cast, according to Taylor.[2]

Communist propaganda was not confined to overt pro-Soviet films. Hollywood was infested with Communists and sympathizers, and non-Communist producers found it difficult to weed out propaganda because of the insidious way in which it was inserted. Although in a numerical minority, Communists controlled the Motion Picture Writers' Guild and were engaged in a constant effort to get control of the Screen Directors' Guild. Their influence was such that anti-Communist writers had to "play ball or else." Numerous screen writers, questioned in 1947, refused to tell a House of Representatives committee whether they were Communists.[3]

While the public was thus being fed pro-Russian propaganda and the evidence of the Katyn massacre was being brushed aside, President Roosevelt was trying to arrange a personal meeting with Stalin which he had sought repeatedly since 1941. Churchill also desired such a meeting, including himself, and had so told a joint session of Congress, May 1, while in Washington for a conference with Roosevelt. But this wasn't Roosevelt's idea at all. He wanted a tête-à-tête with Stalin without Churchill. Even as the Prime Minister was addressing Congress, Roosevelt was engaged in correspondence with Stalin, without Churchill's knowledge, trying to work out a meeting for just the two of them. In a letter to Stalin, May 5, Roosevelt proposed to take with him only Harry Hopkins, an interpreter and a stenographer. Roosevelt told Stalin that they did not need staffs from the armed services to discuss military and naval matters.

The President was in frequent communication with Stalin through the usual channels, but the exclusion of Churchill rendered the invitation highly delicate, and he advanced his proposal in a letter carried personally to Stalin by former ambassador Davies. Roosevelt did not want to go to Russia, and, with Churchill barred, the site of the proposed meeting was a ticklish question. He pointed out to Stalin that, without Churchill, British territory had to be rejected. Likewise, he ruled out the possibility of Iceland, because it would be "quite frankly difficult" not to invite the Prime Minister to a place so near Britain. He suggested somewhere near the Bering Straits, in either Alaska or Siberia.[4]

Stalin at first agreed to attend such a meeting in July or August. The Prime Minister learned of the plan a month after it had been presented to Stalin, and voiced most vigorous objections to such a conference with Britain left out. But Stalin had grown so caustic about the failure of Britain and the United States to establish a second front in 1943 that Churchill withdrew his objections and agreed any meeting would be beneficial, "if you can get him [Stalin] to come." Stalin, however, backed off, and on August 8 informed Roosevelt that it would be impossible to attend even in the autumn, and proposed instead a lower-level conference of the three nations. Not until Roosevelt and Churchill assured him after the Quebec conference that a large-scale build-up was under way for an invasion the following spring, and that Anglo-American operations in the Balkans would be strictly limited, did Stalin finally consent to attend a meeting—with Churchill to be there also. It was to be preceded by a conference of foreign ministers including China, the site for which, on Stalin's insistence, was to be Moscow.

While the stage was thus being set for the Teheran conference, at which the territorial seizures which Roosevelt and Eden had secretly agreed on in March were to be defined to Russian satisfaction, the President continued to preserve the public façade that any such dispositions had been deferred until after the war. On July 28, in a speech praising Russian sacrifices under the leadership of Stalin, he derogated the discussion of "details of the future." Time, he said, should not be taken out "to define every boundary and settle every political controversy." His informal agreement with Eden of the preceding March, granting Soviet demands and allowing the Poles to seize German territory, was kept strictly under cover.

Roosevelt still displayed the Atlantic Charter as his standard. On August 14, the second anniversary of its signing, he pointed out that all the United Nations had "subscribed to the purposes and principles" of that document. Before the Canadian Parliament, August 23, he said those who did not believe the pledges of the charter would be put into effect would have sneered at the Declaration of Independence, laughed at the Magna Charta, and derided Moses when he came from the mountain with the Ten Commandments.

But when the president of Poland sought to have these generalities translated into specific protection of Polish territory, Roosevelt was cagey. In a note to Roosevelt on August 31, the fourth anniversary of the German attack on Poland, the Polish president affirmed that his country was still sustained by its "unshakeable faith" in the charter and of the Four Freedoms—"proclaimed by you." Roosevelt in return praised the gallant stand of the Poles, but avoided any return mention of the charter or the Four Freedoms.

In the light of political developments, mere affirmation of the Atlantic Charter was becoming steadily less effective as a substitute for a stated foreign policy. If there was a policy, nobody knew it. Recognizing the widespread "profound concern" that was being expressed, Secretary Hull sought to allay it in a radio broadcast, September 12. The paramount aim of foreign policy, he told the people, was to defeat the enemy as soon as possible. He again cited the Atlantic Charter and the Declaration of the United Nations, and called for an international organization "based on rules of morality, law and justice," in which the "peacefully-inclined" nations would restrain the "aggressors."

But the secretary of state answered none of the questions that were being asked. An editor of *Harper's Magazine* thus described the public desire for information:

> Every editorial page, every magazine, every publisher's list reveals how widespread, earnest and intent the debate is . . . . It seems too bad that it has to be conducted in total darkness. What are the principles and policies of the government? On what are they based? What are the controlling facts? Who speaks for the government? What does the government want? Who is it trying to avoid? . . . There is simply no way of knowing. We have some resounding phrases like "unconditional surrender". . . . We have some brave abstractions like the Four Freedoms. . . . What I am afraid of as a civilian, as an American citizen, is that we are going to be asked to ratify *faits accomplis*. . . . [5]

It had been generally expected that at the coming Moscow conference of foreign ministers, set for October 18, exigent territorial questions which were disturbing the American people would be a prime subject for discussion. But a few days before the opening, Stalin, with a sharp attack by *Pravda*, let it be known he had no such intention. "The Soviet Union's borders," as *Pravda* put it, "can no more be a topic of conversation than, for example, the borders of the United States or the status of California." At the conference, the Russians flatly rejected any consideration of Poland or the Baltic states. The objective of the Russians was a speedy cross-channel invasion of the continent by British and American troops. On this, according to Foreign Secretary Eden, they were completely and blindly set, and it was the only decision in which they took an absorbing interest.[6]

With territorial plans barred from discussion, the invasion promised, and plans for it set forth, harmony prevailed. At the conclusion of the conference, a declaration of unity was issued. It was a defeat for the West and a victory for Russia at every point where principle was involved, although the public, of course, was not told this. The Russians agreed to act jointly in matters relating to surrender and disarmament of the enemy, but not as to occupation of enemy territory or enemy-held territory. They refused to agree to act jointly in maintaining peace and security pending the reestablishment of law and order, and they refused to agree that military forces would not be employed in other states except by agreement of all the victors. On these matters they would only "consult." But they were willing to cooperate in an international organization to preserve peace, which would cost them nothing.

The conference results, however, with the Russians agreeing to join an international organization, were presented to the American people as a magnificent achievement in establishing "unity"—indeed as a diplomatic "victory." The "American view" had prevailed. Acclaim was general. Washington dispatches referred to Hull as "returning in triumph" from Moscow, "where he played a leading role in laying the foundations for a durable peace." He had brought with him "an agreement of momentous importance to the future of the world." The President called the conference a tremendous success. The *New York Times* editorially said the "American formula" had apparently been accepted verbatim at Moscow, and "the historic task he [Hull] has accomplished is a triumph for his country and the world because it lays the cornerstone of the structure of peace." Senator Harry F. Byrd of Virginia said Hull had "achieved a diplomatic success nearly beyond measure" and urged that a joint session of Congress present him with the Congressional Medal of Honor. Hull's own view, as expressed later to Secretary Morgenthau, was that he had gotten along so well with the Russians because he assured them that he wanted to "hold a secret trial before which I would bring Hitler and his gang . . . and I would shoot them all, and then I would let the world know about it a couple of days later."[7] The "success" of the meeting brought Senate approval of a resolution favoring participation in an international organization to preserve peace.

The conference had actually been a dismal failure. Harry Hopkins, the President's most intimate adviser, said of it privately, "we are prostrate." When the Polish ambassador asked why, then, was such enthusiasm being fed to the American public, Hopkins replied: "Perhaps because we want to show the Soviets that we harbor no suspicions of their conduct."[8]

Even Hull privately expressed some disillusionment. He admitted to the Polish ambassador that the Russians were determined to regard the Polish boundary question as solved in their favor.[9] They had determinedly opposed his suggestion of western Allied forces at the Russians' side in the liberation and occupation of countries bordering on Russia. He could not draw any final optimistic conclusions from the meeting but wanted to believe the Russians were sincerely desirous of collaboration with the western Allies in postwar settlements.[10]

The Moscow conference declaration had said that "after the termination of hostilities they [the allied nations] will not employ their military forces within the territories of other states except for the purposes envisaged in this declaration and after joint consultation." The public did not know that the Russians had refused to accede to a requirement for *agreement* on such action, but the weasel-wording of the clause was apparent. "Consultation" effectively meant nothing. Uneasiness grew as to what had actually transpired at Moscow. On November 13, the Catholic bishops of the United States said the Moscow conference had failed to dispel "the fear that compromises on the ideals of the Atlantic Charter are in prospect." On the same day, the Soviet ambassador in Mexico City stated plainly that Russia was going to take eastern Poland.

Had the United States agreed to this in Moscow? At a November 15 press conference, Hull refused to comment on the statement of the Soviet ambassador to Mexico or to permit direct quotation at all. He said there had been no discussion at Moscow of the Baltic states or Poland, but did not reveal that such discussion had been firmly rejected by the Russians at the outset. The discussions, he said, had been based on the doctrine that every nation in Europe would have the right by a free plebiscite to select its own form of government.

But if Russia could keep its forces in a conquered country by mere "consultation" with the other victors, what would a plebiscite amount to? Asked whether a military organization in an occupied country would supervise a promised plebiscite, Hull said weakly that it would not be "supposed" to do so. He assured reporters that the principles of the Atlantic Charter had not been compromised, but admitted vaguely that some questions had been reserved for treatment through diplomatic channels.

The next day, Hull held another press conference to qualify his statement about plebiscites. While plebiscites would be held in liberated areas, he said certain territorial settlements would have to be made before one knew what these plebiscite areas were, and the settlements would not be made until the end of the war. Furthermore, the promise of plebiscites would not apply directly to boundary disputes, but only to choosing forms of government.

In other words, the right of self-determination was to be exercised by the "liberated" peoples only after the victors had established themselves in the territories claimed, and the plebiscites would very likely be conducted by the occupying military forces. The fears of the Catholic bishops had been confirmed. A leading Protestant organ, *Christian Century*, said: "Mr. Hull has paid for his 'general international organization' with the scuttling of the Atlantic Charter."

But Hull on November 18 assured a joint session of Congress, where he was given a tremendous ovation with thunderous applause, that at the end of the war the United Nations would have a common interest in "the principles and spirit of the Atlantic Charter and the Declaration of the United Nations." The four-power declaration of unity issued after the conference assured the world that there would no longer be need for spheres of influence, alliances or balance of power.[11] On the same day, former Ambassador Grew, before a New York audience, placed the charter and the Moscow declaration side by side as the two "great cornerstones" for an invulnerable and enduring edifice of world peace.

Prime Minister Stanislaw Mikolajezyk of Poland, who had taken office upon the death of Sikorski in July, attempted vainly to see Roosevelt in advance of the coming Big Three conferences. The Moscow Declaration had obviously meant that the Soviet military command would take over exclusively the administration of occupied Polish territory, which to the Poles meant immediate and complete sovietization.

The Poles tried unavailingly for an opportunity to seek direct assurance from the President that the Atlantic Charter actually would apply so far as their own territory was concerned. Roosevelt, asked by Prime Minister Mikolajezyk in October for a Washington meeting, waited three weeks to reply and then suggested delaying it until the middle of January. The Polish ambassador was unable to see Secretary Hull or even his adviser on political relations. Poland, the invasion of which by Hitler had been the original *casus belli*, was now a troublesome embarrassment to relations with Stalin, Hitler's former ally. The course was set for Teheran, where the President was to offer to Stalin his secret, outright approval of virtually everything Stalin wanted.

8

Teheran—Secrecy Until the Election

At Teheran, the President of the United States and the Prime Minister of Great Britain put their stamp of approval on the territorial dispositions which Roosevelt and Eden had secretly agreed upon in March. Stalin was given everything he had demanded, and came out even better than when dividing territory with Hitler. But the American people were told nothing of all this.

The conference was Stalin's, from first to last. Even the site was chosen on his insistence, despite Roosevelt's urgent requests for a place more accessible. Urging the necessity of being where he could act on bills passed by Congress, the President pleaded that the conference be held nearer Cairo, where a preceding meeting with Generalissimo Chiang Kai-shek of China had been set. Until the last, Roosevelt insisted he could not possibly go to Teheran and on November 5 wrote Churchill he was "begging" Stalin to meet him at a nearer point. But the Soviet dictator was adamant. It was Teheran or nothing, and Roosevelt yielded.

Other than by press rumors, the people did not even know the meetings were being held. At Cairo, photographers were permitted on the leash, but at Teheran the press, as Roosevelt had proposed to Stalin, was "entirely banished." First confirmation of the meetings came in a Lisbon dispatch to a British press agency, December 1, reporting the fact of the Cairo parley and saying that Roosevelt and Churchill were enroute to somewhere in Iran to see Stalin. Actually, the Teheran conference had ended.

At Teheran, Soviet seizure of eastern Poland was endorsed. As to Lithuania, Latvia and Estonia, Stalin declared these countries off limits for discussion; they had already "voted," while occupied by Soviet troops, to join the Soviet Union. The West acquiesced. Support was given to Tito, the Communist chief in Yugoslavia. It was agreed in general that Germany should be dismembered, with a large part going to Poland as compensation for the Soviet seizures. With Roosevelt supporting Stalin, Churchill's desire for a drive into the

Balkans—which might deter Russian expansion in Central Europe—was quashed.

All these decisions were kept secret. An official communique, issued from Moscow on December 6, consisted of generalities. A "common understanding" had been reached. The conferees had "shaped and confirmed our common policy" and left the meeting "friends in fact, in spirit, and in purpose." The German military power was to be destroyed, and the peoples of all countries devoted to the elimination of tyranny, slavery, oppression and intolerance were to be welcomed into a world family of democratic nations.

The American people never at any time received from their President any facts on the principal Teheran agreements. Roosevelt secretly committed himself to the Soviet territorial acquisitions and the Polish seizure of German lands in private conversations with Stalin, with Churchill absent. He likewise approved Russian annexation of Lithuania, Latvia and Estonia, while casually suggesting a face-saving plebiscite "some day" to satisfy "world opinion."[1] He assured Stalin he was confident these people would choose to join the Soviet Union in such a vote.

Roosevelt explained frankly to Stalin that his approval of Russian demands had to be kept secret until some time after the 1944 election. According to the official minutes of the meeting, the President said "there were in the United States from six to seven million Americans of Polish extraction, and, as a practical man, he did not wish to lose their vote." He further hoped Stalin would understand that "for political reasons" he could not participate in any decision at Teheran or even the next winter on this subject, and that "he could not publicly take part in any such arrangement at the present time." As to Russian absorption of the Baltic states, there were also in the United States "a number of persons of Lithuanian, Latvian and Estonian origin," and "it would be helpful for him personally" if Stalin would publicly declare an intention to hold elections there.[2] Stalin would make no promise.

In an official session, Roosevelt proposed the dismemberment of Germany into five countries, plus two regions to be placed under international control. But when the proposed Russian and Polish seizures of territory were discussed, Roosevelt, having already committed himself in private conversations with Stalin, merely sat in, while Churchill carried the ball. The Soviet was to get part of East Prussia and the eastern territories of Poland, which nation in turn was to get German territory west to the Oder. As the conference ended, the Prime Minister was to offer to the Poles a "reasonable formula" substantially meeting the Soviet demands, but not describing it as a Russian proposal. If the Poles refused, Great Britain "would be through with them and certainly would not oppose the Soviet government under any conditions at the peace table."[3]

An incredible self-delusion determined Roosevelt's attitude toward Stalin. Among those who warned him against appeasement of the Russian dictator was William C. Bullitt, who had been the first ambassador to Russia after the Soviet regime was recognized. "Bill," replied the President, "I don't dispute your facts, they are accurate. I don't dispute the logic of your reasoning. I just have a hunch that Stalin is not that kind of a man. Harry [Hopkins] says he's not and that he doesn't want anything but security for his country, and I think that if I give him everything I possibly can and ask nothing from him in return, *noblesse oblige*, he won't try to annex anything and will work with me for a world of democracy and peace."[4]

Roosevelt had persuaded himself that the Soviet butcher of the thirties, the erstwhile collaborator with Hitler, was in reality an admirable fellow. He remarked to Frances Perkins, his secretary of labor, that Stalin had once studied for the priesthood and asked, "doesn't that explain part of the sympathetic quality in his nature which we all feel?"[5] He went to Teheran "prepared to like Stalin and determined to make himself liked."[6] Making no apparent gain with the Soviet dictator at first—"although I had done everything he asked me to do"—Roosevelt tried the tack of shining up to Stalin by crudely baiting the embarrassed and reddening Churchill about his personal habits for Stalin's amusement, until Stalin finally broke into a hearty guffaw. "I kept it up until Stalin was laughing with me and it was then that I called him Uncle Joe. He would have thought me fresh the day before, but that day he laughed and came around and shook my hand . . . . From then on, our relations were personal. . . ." Stalin, in Roosevelt's view, "had an elegance of manner that none of the rest of us had."[7]

Roosevelt told his son, Elliott, "It's a pleasure working with him [Stalin]. There's nothing devious." The big job of the United States would be "making sure that we continue to act as referee, as intermediary between Russia and England."[8]

At his first tête-à-tête with Stalin, the President volunteered the prospect of turning over to the Soviets a part of the American-British merchant fleet after the war. He approved giving one-third of the captured Italian fleet and merchant ships to Russia. Roosevelt took it upon himself to suggest that Stalin not discuss postwar India with Churchill because the latter had no solution, while proposing his own "solution" of turning India towards communism—"reform from the bottom, somewhat along the Soviet line." He agreed with Stalin "100 percent" that France—French divisions were then serving under General Eisenhower in North Africa—should be "punished" by not getting back Indochina; furthermore, he proposed that no Frenchmen over 40, and none who had ever taken part in the existing government, be allowed to return to position in the future.

The conference was presented in the United States as a great accomplishment because "agreement" had been reached with Russia. Typical was a propaganda release on December 7, a photograph showing Roosevelt and Stalin together, under the caption "No Difference of Opinion." The accompanying text read: "This photo is symbolic of the understanding reached between the United States and Russia at the three-power conference in Teheran. Marshal Joseph Stalin and President Franklin D. Roosevelt smile amiably as they sit together." The text was misleading. Roosevelt, true, was smiling—even laughing—jovially toward the Russian dictator at his side; but Stalin, unsmiling, was looking straight ahead, like an old dog ignoring a puppy.

Eulogistic speeches were delivered in Congress, to great applause. Representative (later Senator) William Fulbright said the conference "demonstrated that this time we have the leadership to organize a peaceful world." The majority leader of the House acclaimed the President's "outstanding courage." and the "historic results" of both Cairo and Teheran. Not all the legislators were so enthusiastic. Senator Robert Taft said the statement was of a very general nature and revealed little. Others said it was significantly short of direct language. But such discordant voices counted little against the popular will to believe that something of great good had been accomplished.

Most newspapers, knowing as little as the Congress, were equally eulogistic. The *New York Times* said the Cairo and Teheran conferences had "laid the foundation for a new and better order in the world. . . ." But on the same day, a dispatch from Cairo reported that at Teheran, Stalin had demanded all the territory seized in cooperation with Hitler, with "compensation" for other states. "Fortunately," commented the *Times* with remarkable naïveté, "the principles of the Atlantic Charter and the Declaration of Moscow, Cairo and Teheran provide against misuse of power and assign their rightful role to all nations, large and small."

With the ink on the Moscow and Teheran declarations scarcely dry, Stalin, without consulting the West, signed a treaty of alliance with President Eduard Beneš, of the Czechoslovakian government-in-exile, which would enable Russia effectively to dominate central Europe. Highly disconcerted by this unilateral action, Secretary of State Hull refused to comment. When a State Department spokesman solemnly assured skeptical reporters the treaty was "not to be understood to be in conflict with the general framework of worldwide security," they roared with laughter.

Other than the flowing official statement issued at the end of the conference, the President gave the country no information on Teheran. In a Christmas Eve radio broadcast he voiced only generalities. The conferences had discussed "international relationships from the point of view of big, broad objectives, rather than details."

More evidence soon came from Moscow that any Teheran harmony had been at the expense of America's presumed war aims. Wendell Willkie, defeated Republican candidate for President, in a magazine article naively praising the Moscow and Teheran conferences because of their "pledges of good will," mentioned the question of Soviet intentions toward Finland, Poland and the Baltic and Balkan states.[9] *Pravda* sharply gave notice that the Baltic problem was an internal affair of the Soviet union. A "democratic plebiscite" had already settled matters there. As to Finland, Poland and the Balkans, the Soviet Union could make the "necessary arrangements" without outside help.

With the Polish seizure approved in substance at Teheran, Stalin saw no reason for pussyfooting. On January 11, American newspapers carried a Soviet broadcast announcing the intention of taking Polish territory west to approximately the Curzon line, with Poland to get German territory as compensation, and suggesting that Poland join the Soviet-Czech mutual assistance pact.

Roosevelt, making his state of the Union address to Congress the same day, ignored the Soviet broadcast. He told virtually nothing about the conference except that military plans for victory had been concerted, and asserted flatly that there had been "no secret treaties or political or financial commitments."

But the Teheran communique had said "we have shaped and formed our common policy." If this was a fact, either Roosevelt's statement to Congress was substantially false or the USSR had broken away from that policy. The nation generally chose to believe the latter . A *Washington Post* editorial piece said "Russia is now revealing that in matters that concern her directly she insists on playing a long hand." The *New York Times* complained that "so far as is publicly known" Russia did not take up the matter with the United States or Britain, but simply laid down an ultimatum.

On January 26, Anthony Eden, British foreign secretary, assured the House of Commons that his government stood by the principles of the Atlantic Charter and did not intend to recognize any territorial changes unless they took place with the free consent and good will of the parties concerned. But at the same time the press was given to understand "on highest authority" that the statement did not suggest British backing of Poland's boundary stand against Russia. Furthermore, in answer to persistent questioning in Commons, Eden said the charter's territorial pledge did not apply to enemy countries.

Eden's statements brought increasing calls on both sides of the Atlantic for full information on whatever arrangements had been made at Teheran. Roosevelt, in an election year, as he had pointed out to Stalin, remained silent; but Churchill held office at the pleasure of Commons, and the longer the concealment the greater the political risk stored up for the time of inevitable disclosure. Pressure which Churchill had persistently applied to the Polish government in London, as promised at Teheran, had not brought acquiescence in the Russian demands, and on February 22 he publicly approved the Soviet claims as "just." He admitted, furthermore, that it had been agreed for Poland to obtain German territory in both the north and west as compensation.

The Atlantic Charter did not apply to the enemy, he said. Unconditional surrender meant that the victors could make such territorial changes as they wished in enemy countries, bound only by their own consciences. Churchill hailed Tito, the Communist guerrilla chief in Yugoslavia, as an "outstanding leader, glorious in the fight for freedom," and promised him support. As to General Draja Mikhailovitch, the anti-Communist who previously had been supported as an ally, Churchill charged that his commanders had made deals with the enemy.

The Prime Minister's speech met the harshest criticism in the House of Commons, where he was accused of being a ventriloquist's dummy for Stalin and of making agreements with Russia that he was ashamed to reveal. What was the position of the United States? Roosevelt said nothing at all. From State Department sources, Washington correspondents wrote it was "believed" the United

States would agree to denying Germany the protection of the Atlantic Charter. It was "gathered officially" that, if *Churchill* obtained a settlement on Poland, even by handing over German territory, "there was no reason to expect the United States would dissent." Whatever the Polish deal, no responsibility was ascribed to Roosevelt; it was all Churchill's. The *Washington Post*, referring to a suggestion by Churchill that the "Big Three" needed to meet again to clear the air, said it would pose a dilemma for Roosevelt if the President refused to accept the "Anglo-Russian" thesis on Poland.

But if a "common policy" had been confirmed at Teheran, then, despite Churchill's studied omission of any mention of the United States in his revelations, Roosevelt also must have approved. The managing editor of the *New York Times* wrote: "No doubt that is Mr. Churchill's position. But does the United States agree that Russia should take slices off Poland to the east? Does Washington agree that East Prussia and part of German Silesia should be given to Poland? Who knows?"[10]

Certainly Congress did not know. On February 29, a member of the House of Representatives[11] raised these questions of Teheran: "What if anything tangible was accomplished? What decisions were arrived at? To what future foreign policy has Mr. Roosevelt committed us, or possibly to what future policy has Mr. Churchill inspired us? Is it not about time that Mr. Róosevelt gave us the answer to these questions? Or has he nothing tangible and of future benefit to report to us? The American people have a right to know."

The first bit of real information on Teheran—and, indeed, the only one—which the President gave to the country came March 3, when Roosevelt at a press conference offhandedly confirmed a rumor that the Italian fleet was to be divided equally among Russia, Britain and the United States. He put aside questions on foreign policy and the Atlantic Charter by directing attention to the necessity of winning the war. But the questions remained. As the *New York Times* artlessly put it on March 4, "Recent developments have cast some doubt on whether the principles of the Atlantic Charter and subsequent pronouncements are valid or not. And for that reason it appears essential that the voice of America should be raised again in unmistakable fashion to clarify that point, lest leadership slip from American hands entirely."

The suspicion grew that unsavory Teheran agreements approved by Roosevelt were being withheld until after the fall election. If the President openly admitted that Russia was to get Polish territory, there would be an adverse reaction among Polish-American voters, especially numerous in several cities, including Buffalo, Detroit and Chicago. Other national groups who, like the Poles, had hitherto been strong Roosevelt supporters, would also resent Russian subjugation of the Baltic republics. And voters of German descent, however opposed they were to Hitler, would be disheartened and antagonized by approval of Polish seizures of German territory with the forcible expulsion of the population. On March 9, Arthur Krock, Washington correspondent of the *New York Times*, referring to concealment of foreign policy pending the election, said it appeared that Russia would dominate the postwar structure "because of the fog that masks our policy and has produced diplomatic inaction (so far as the record shows)." Krock's addition of the pointed parenthetical phrase exemplified the suspicions of presidential dissembling held by most of the press with access to Washington sources.[12]

The American people still tried to cling to their faith in the Atlantic Charter. Archbishop Francis J. Spellman, in a broadcast to American soldiers in Africa, assured his hearers the charter was still alive. On March 21, Secretary Hull in a 17-point statement on policy said the organization of "peace-loving" nations for which foundations had been laid in Moscow would provide peace and security according to the charter pledges. Avoiding direct reference to Churchill's frank statement that the charter did not apply to the enemy, he left an oblique opening in this direction by saying that its pledges implied an obligation not to settle disputes by force. The whole thing was so vague that the Chicago *Sun,* a strong administration supporter, termed it "Mr. Hull's 17-point mumble."

It is possible that Hull actually did not know enough about the Roosevelt commitments to say anything specific. He was not taken to Cairo or Teheran, although the British foreign secretary was present. Hull later wrote plaintively, "I learned from other sources than the President what had occurred at the Casablanca, Cairo and Teheran conferences." Hull said that Roosevelt was prompt, "with few exceptions," to answer his questions on secret matters.[13]

More than a mumble came from London. A large group of members of the House of Commons demanded that the status of the charter be cleared up. The day after Hull's statement, Churchill said the charter was primarily a "declaration of spirit and purpose" and reaffirmed that the enemy, when vanquished, would not be permitted to invoke it against any seizures of territory the victors might propose. "Further clarification" of Britain's position under the charter was needed. Politically embarrassed by American silence on Teheran, he nevertheless did not mention the United States directly, but again urged that consultation among the principal Allies was necessary.

"What both the British and the American people wish to know," said the *New York Times*, "is whether the Atlantic Charter still applies, and, if not, what takes its place as a standard of conduct and a frame of reference for the organization of victory."

Members of the Senate Foreign Relations Committee spent two hours in secret session with Hull, unsuccessfully trying to find this out . All they could get was that the most important factor in foreign policy was the necessity of winning the war, and this might require "expedience" in other phases.[14] A group of members of the House of Representatives, meeting with Hull, likewise got nowhere. One representative reported that "silence is still the settled policy of the State Department." Another said, "We were told that our comments showed no knowledge of the facts, and yet we are denied the facts."[15]

Indications mounted that Stalin would do as he pleased on other matters besides Poland. The December treaty of alliance with Czechoslovakia had been followed in January by a blast from the Soviet embassy in Washington clearly implying the intention of communizing Rumania. In March the Soviet, in a sudden, unilateral action, recognized the Badoglio government in Italy, which was supposedly still functioning as a temporary arrangement that might or might not be made permanent by the victors. Department of State radio broadcasts with the announced purpose of informing the people on foreign policy continued to hail the "unity" achieved at the Moscow conference as averting the certainty of a third world war and eulogized the plans for an international organization to keep down aggressors. But they gave no answers to the exigent questions being asked.

The President attempted to divert attention from Russia and focus it on the misdeeds of the Hitler regime by issuing a statement excoriating the persecution of the Jews. As for war objectives, he said, "the United Nations are fighting to make a world in which tyranny and aggression cannot exist, a world based upon freedom, equality and justice, a world in which all persons regardless of race, color or creed may live in peace, honor and dignity." Reporters who persisted in asking questions about foreign policy were told to read this document.

The people in general just would not believe the charter was dead.

Soldiers, too, took it seriously. United States servicemen in the British Midlands presented a church with a stained glass window depicting its signing by Roosevelt and Churchill on the deck of a battleship.[16] But the *Christian Century*, on April 5, put its finger on the domestic political aspects of Teheran secrecy:

> Suddenly, all over the country, Americans are awakening to the fact that they really know very little about the purpose for which their government is fighting. . . . And they begin to fear that no enlightenment will be offered them until the President is free from the dread of losing Polish or Lithuanian or Italian votes in November. They begin to suspect that no clear expression of his European policies can be extracted from Mr. Roosevelt until he is certain that his fourth term ambition will not be imperiled.

Secretary Hull went on the air again April 9 to try to reconcile the charter with Soviet and British statements. The charter, he said, was "an expression of fundamental objectives," including the "prevention of aggression and the establishment of world security." But it did not prevent any steps, including those relating to enemy states, which were necessary to achieve these objectives. He doggedly preserved the Teheran façade: "As the President has said, neither he nor I have made or will make any secret agreement or commitment, political or financial."

While thus dealing ambiguously and even falsely with the people, the Department of State was exerting influence on the British government to suppress dispatches on European political developments. When this was charged by Governor Dewey of New York, Secretary Hull denied it; whereupon the London correspondent of the *New York Times* cabled flatly that there had been repeated instances, although the dispatches had been passed in regular routine through the British censorship.[17]

As the American press continued to criticize Russian statements and actions as contrary to the Atlantic Charter, Stalin's increasing irritation was reflected in the ugly tone of the Soviet press. On May 7, *War and the Working Class* savagely attacked those in England and America who contended that the charter barred the seizure of Polish territory or the dismemberment of Germany. But Stalin continued to defer to Roosevelt's request for secrecy about his commitments.

In May, the President endeavored to quell public restiveness with two inspired articles by Forrest Davis in the *Saturday Evening Post*. It was learned that the articles had been read at the White House before publication.[18] The President's major preoccupation, said Davis, had been "reassurance" of Stalin. Roosevelt had shown a "tough-minded" determination to enroll Stalin as a sincere collaborator in postwar settlements, as the center of his "great design." But Davis had been advised "in the highest American quarters" that no agreement was reached on the disposition of a defeated Germany or on any major postwar issue. The Reich "was not even mentioned at Teheran." The situation was kept "as the President puts it, fluid. If Stalin wished to present the Kremlin's point of view regarding its boundaries and the attitude of the [Polish] government-in-exile, he had a hearing, plus free discussion, but no assent by the others. . . ."

If these articles were accurate, the actions of Russia since Teheran would appear to be in utter defiance of the harmony which supposedly had been achieved at Moscow and Teheran. As the *Post* itself said editorially:

> Since Teheran, Stalin has cut Russia in on the Italian fleet; made it plain that he intends to produce his own solution of the Polish problem; intervened in Italy to the confusion of the other Allies; made it plain that Russian troops will control whatever part of Germany they occupy without regard to Anglo-American plans for the rest of Germany; persuaded us to get tougher with the helpless Finns; changed Allied policy toward Yugoslavia. All of this has been accepted without known objection on our part.

Prime Minister Churchill reckoned it was time to lift the veil further. The war had become "less ideological," he told the Commons on May 24. He delivered a panegyric on the "profound changes" that had taken place in Russia, with "the Trotskyite form of communism" having been completely wiped out, with a "remarkable broadening" of Soviet views and with religion enjoying a "wonderful rebirth." General Mikhailovitch in Yugoslavia was no longer being supplied with arms, and full support was now being given to the Communist leader, Tito, who, Churchill said, had "largely sunk his Communist aspect in his character as a Yugoslav patriotic leader." As to Poland, over which Britain had gone to war, the cornerstone of policy had become the Anglo-Russian treaty of alliance of 1942. Churchill reaffirmed that the protection of the Atlantic Charter—which remained a "guiding signpost"—nevertheless applied only to the victors, who might dismember Germany if they so decided.

In Congress, even prewar supporters of the Roosevelt interventionist policies termed the President's silence, in the face of the Churchill revelations, embarrassing and humiliating. Addressing the President from the Senate floor, Senator Styles Bridges of New Hampshire said: "Mr. Stalin speaks and you are silent. Mr. Churchill speaks and you are silent. . . . If a military victory is to be the only issue settled. . . . quite obviously this was not and is not our war."

The soldiers, too, were asking such questions, and the army attempted to answer them in a guidebook for information officers, editors and instructors of orientation courses. The war aim was set forth as simply "the total defeat of the Axis powers." There was "no room for discussion of anything short of total military victory over the enemy. Peace feelers do not interest us."

Much of the advice to those forming opinion among the soldiers was addressed to the glossing over of Communist Russia. Although "we do not agree with their political ideas (and they do not believe in ours) we believe utterly in the defense of the principle for which they are fighting." This principle, the guidebook set forth, was the right to determine how they should be governed. The 1939 Russian attack on Finland, which President Roosevelt at the time had bitterly assailed, was backhandedly defended; it was a "military fact" that if the Russians had not so acted "the Allied cause would be weaker today."[19]

How lost were any rational war aims was indicated by a private communication about the Balkan situation from Churchill to Secretary Eden in May which did not see the light of day until the Prime Minister's memoirs were published. "Broadly speaking," wrote Churchill, "the issue is: Are we going to acquiesce in the communization of the Balkans and perhaps of Italy?"[20] Acquiescence as to the Balkans came soon—secretly of course—in an off-the-cuff agreement which Churchill negotiated with Stalin with Roosevelt's approval, giving the Russian dictator "90 percent" predominance in Rumania and 75 percent in Bulgaria, the British getting 90 percent in Greece. Influence in Yugoslavia and Hungary was supposedly to be divided 50-50; but with Western support already thrown to the Communist regime in the former, and Soviet penetration of eastern Europe making communization of the latter inevitable, the agreement effectively provided for a Communist regime there also. Later, Churchill was to insist he meant this only as a temporary arrangement.

Still avoiding specifics about Teheran agreements or war aims in an election year, the President turned to phrase-making, and proposed that the conflict be given the name of "The Tyrants' war." But, asked the Washington *Times-Herald*, "Which Tyrant?" Other newspapers reminded Roosevelt that even a war against a tyrant ought to have a political objective. When Roosevelt was renominated for a fourth term by the Democratic Party in July, the press renewed its urging that he speak out frankly on war aims, with no result. *Life* magazine[21] voiced a general complaint when it said that the President should have reached some fundamental agreements with Stalin in 1943, if not 1942. That such agreements in effect had long since been reached, was as much a closed book to this influential publication as it was to the man in the street.

Stalin had turned in July to the job of seeing that the new Poland, to include seized German lands, would be Communist-controlled. He had set up at Lublin a Polish Communist "Committee of National Liberation," which agreed to the cession of the eastern territories to Russia, and which was to administer the territory to be retained by Poland as the Germans were driven out. He then had moved against the non-Communist Polish underground. With Soviet forces just outside Warsaw, radio broadcasts in Polish from Moscow called upon the Poles to rebel against the Germans. Expecting Russian help, the underground on August 1 rose against the occupiers. The Soviet then not only halted its forces but barred help from the west by refusing to permit British or American planes to land on Russian fields after dropping ammunition in Warsaw—a refusal finally modified when it was too late. After a fierce sixty-day battle, the remnant of the Polish fighters surrendered. As Stalin in 1940 had liquidated much of Poland's non-Communist leadership in the Katyn massacre, he now had effectively destroyed the non-Communist home resistance.

Meanwhile, approval of the Tito Communist regime in Yugoslavia was bearing fruit as Tito ordered the British and American military missions out of territory which he controlled. He required of the United Nations Relief and Rehabilitation Administration that its supplies could be distributed only by the local (Communist) authorities. "The British," said *Newsweek*, "are desperate in their desire to save face and explain their Yugoslav failure to public opinion."[22] A stony silence met Churchill's discussion of Yugoslavia in Commons. Roosevelt, the election two weeks off, said nothing.

The general administration attitude toward Russia was privately and pithily expressed by James Forrestal, secretary of the navy, in a September letter to a friend: "I find that whenever an American suggests that we act in accordance with the needs of our own security he is apt to be called a goddamned fascist or imperalist, while if Uncle Joe suggests that he needs the Baltic provinces, half of Poland, all of Bessarabia and access to the Mediterranean, all hands agree that he is a fine, frank, candid and generally delightful fellow who is very easy to deal with because he is so explicit in what he wants."[23]

In October a vast publicity campaign was begun by the Department of State on the promised international organization to preserve peace, for which plans had been laid at a conference at Dumbarton Oaks, in Washington. The international organization of itself was to be worth the war. But this was pie-in-the-sky to voters of Polish extraction. Normally Roosevelt supporters, their restlessness had been growing throughout the year. As early as January, the Polish National Council in New York had flatly asked whether the principles of the Atlantic Charter had been abandoned as to the countries within reach of Soviet military power. If so, said the council, "the Atlantic Charter is nothing but a propaganda trick devised to induce these people to continue their resistance against Germany on the basis of false pledges."

In May, the American Polish Congress, formed to represent the various regional groups, had sought a meeting with the President, but had been ignored. Not until Governor Thomas Dewey of New York, the Republican candidate for President, was asked to be the chief speaker at the New York Polish-American celebration of Pulaski Day, October 8, did Roosevelt give the Poles a hearing. A committee then asked the President to insist that "neither an alien nor a puppet system of government" be imposed on Poland, and that none of its population be disposed of against the freely expressed will of the people, as the Atlantic Charter had pledged.

Roosevelt received the delegation before a large map of Poland showing boundaries as of before the war, which was taken by some as promising restoration of the old Poland. But Roosevelt's actual words were only glowing generalities. Rumblings of Polish-American disillusionment became so loud that the President was impelled to seek a second meeting with the spokesman of the White House conference, Charles Rozmarek, head of the Polish National Council. It was held in the President's private car, in Chicago, on an election trip in late October. According to Rozmarek, the President was more specific this time,[24] saying he would uphold the principles of the Atlantic Charter and that these principles included the integrity of Poland. Rozmarek thereupon gave his pledge of support in the election, which was immediately publicized by the Democratic National Committee,[25] and widely quoted in Polish-language newspapers and the press generally just before the election.

Churchill meanwhile had brought representatives of the Polish government-in-exile to Moscow to try to obtain agreement on the cession of territory to the Soviet and the setting up of a new Polish government. With Roosevelt—who had never admitted the facts of the Teheran agreements publicly—facing the polls November 4, the possible political danger to the President was obvious. On October 16, Churchill informed his king that he was "wrestling" with the London Poles, and that if a settlement was not reached "we shall have to hush the matter up and spin it out until after the [American] presidential election." It soon became apparent that if an agreement was reached, the political liability might be even greater, for Stalin insisted not merely on the territorial seizure but on Communist control of the government of an altered Poland. With the election only two weeks off, Churchill promised Roosevelt he would cable any agreement to him and keep it temporarily secret if the President desired. Roosevelt on October 22 replied he wanted the option of keeping it secret for two weeks if advisable, adding significantly, "You will understand."[26]

As it turned out, the necessity of hiding an adverse Polish-Soviet settlement from American voters did not arise, for there was no settlement. The President was elected for a fourth term. Churchill, who had rigorously observed silence on Roosevelt's commitments at Teheran, now expected a clear pronouncement from Washington but none was forthcoming. The Prime Minister refused to wait longer and, on December 16, laid Teheran bare. He announced that if Poland did not cede to Russia voluntarily all territory east of the Curzon line, Britain would support Russia's demands. Poland was to get East Prussia and could take a large additional part of Germany. German inhabitants of lands to be taken by Poland were to be "expelled" without concern for the ability of shrunken Germany to absorb them. These dispositions, he said, did not constitute merely a British-Soviet agreement. They had been discussed at Teheran, he said, and had been a subject of discussion ever since, and Roosevelt had been kept informed at every stage both by British and by his own diplomatic advisers. Ambassador Harriman had been present at virtually all the post-Teheran Moscow discussions and the United States had raised no disagreement. Churchill found "difficulty" in discussing these matters because the United States had not seen fit to disclose its position publicly.

Congress, the press and the public demanded that the facts as stated by Churchill be denied or admitted. On December 18, the new Secretary of State Edward Stettinius issued a statement to the effect that, while the United States stood unequivocally for a strong, free and independent Poland, it would not object to the delineation of Poland's frontiers by agreement. If this should result in Poland desiring to "transfer" national population groups, he said, the United States government would assist.

But the President himself tried to keep silent. At a press conference a few days later, he dismissed a barrage of questions on foreign policy, saying that it was already on the record. Finally, asked to explain how the principles of the Atlantic Charter could accord with the Churchill revelations, the President in effect disowned the charter. Although both he and Churchill had agreed to its wording, the President said, the charter itself—whose status he had once ranked with that of the Ten Commandments—was only a "scribbled thing" for the ship radio operators. It was "one of the things that was agreed to on board ship, and there was no formal document."

This characterization of the charter diverged sharply from the facts. Undersecretary of State Sumner Welles, who worked with Roosevelt on the several drafts of the charter, later wrote that the President "considered and discussed every word." It was issued as a press release, Welles said, only because of the circumstances under which it was agreed upon. "It was exactly what it purported to be," a notice to the world by the heads of the two governments that "the two great nations which they represented would adhere to the principles set forth in the declaration."[27] Churchill, in a letter to Roosevelt, August 9, 1942, pointed out that "we considered the wording of that famous document line by line together. . . ."[28]

The reporters did not have the advantage of these firsthand accounts of the drawing-up of the charter, but it was obvious that the President was trying to cover up the abandonment of its noble war pledges by denying they had ever been formally made. They reminded Roosevelt that however "scribbled" the charter might have been originally, it had been given official status in the Declaration of Washington the following January.

In answer, the President took pains to de-emphasize the official character of the Declaration itself by what he termed an "amusing" story of the informal way in which one of the signatories had adhered. Pressed on the fact that the official communique had said the Atlantic Charter statement was signed by both Roosevelt and

Churchill, the President replied: "Oh, I think it's probable in time they will find some documents and signatures." Then a reporter put the basic question point-blank:

"Whether or not it was signed, you promulgated and stood for it, and you stand for it now?"

Roosevelt did not answer.

The President himself termed his statements amazing, and the public agreed. From the start there had been numerous skeptics, but the mass of the people and of the press had believed it to be an expression of actual war aims and of promises for the peace. They had endeavored to preserve this confidence despite Russia's actions, Churchill's progressive admissions, and Roosevelt's silence. Only a month before, 103 bishops and archbishops of the Catholic Church considered the charter to be sufficiently alive to call for its acceptance "without equivocation." Public reverberations were so great that in a succeeding press conference, Roosevelt attempted a retrieval. The principles of the charter were still sound, he said, but now and then someone comes along with something better, and he believed that some day someone would come forward with something better than the Atlantic Charter. Referring vaguely to documents throughout history that had affected public thinking toward objectives for a better world, he said the Atlantic Charter stood for such objectives.

The *Washington Star* pointed out that the charter "has been 'sold' to the United States and to most of the world as a solemn statement of the high purposes of the Allied nations in fighting this war. It cannot now be 'unsold' without disillusioning millions of men and women who have accepted it in the literal sense as a charter of human freedom."

Nevertheless, the charter had to be "unsold" as a statement of specific purpose and reinterpreted as a kind of pious homily. The task was taken up by the Office of War Information, which had previously held the charter high before the people as a beacon. The OWI director, Elmer Davis, in a nationwide radio broadcast, now told the people "nobody ever said it could all be put into effect day after tomorrow or even at the end of the war."[29]

9

The Deceptions of Yalta

The pattern of deception which had continued all through the war was followed at Yalta. The American people were deceived in what they were told, and much was not told. Secret protocols were agreed upon which provided for Soviet domination of Manchuria and other aggrandizement in the Far East, and for the use of forced German labor by the victors after the war. The revealed results were portrayed as a victory for free government everywhere, whereas they actually amounted to accepting communism in Poland and a spreading Communist control in Central and Eastern Europe.

Roosevelt locked the secret protocols in the White House safe. They did not see the light of day until long after his death, and even when they were revealed by Moscow, not Washington. The secret agreement on the Far East was disclosed by Russia in January 1946. The protocol on forced German labor—the existence of which Roosevelt denied—was laid bare by Russia nearly two years after Germany surrendered.

As 1944 ended, it appeared that the war would be over in a matter of months, and a new conference had been planned to wrap up the political package arranged at Teheran. The disposition of Germany had to be decided, and the awards of Polish territory to Russia and German territory to Poland had to be formally defined. The most exigent problem was Poland. The real issue was no longer one of territory, for Churchill had in effect forced the Poles to bow to the inevitable, as promised to Stalin at Teheran. The issue was the freedom of the new Poland, including the German territory to be given to the Poles, and the Poles insisted that it must not be Communist-controlled. But for months such an outcome had been only a desperate hope. Stalin had let Churchill know in October that he expected the Polish Communist puppet committee which he had set up in July to have a majority in the new government. He underlined his stand in late December, when the Yalta conference was already in the works, by recognizing as the government of Poland a regime which this committee had set up at Lublin as the Russian forces occupied Polish territory. Stalin brushed aside Roosevelt's plea that action be delayed until the conference, which had been secretly set for February 2. His action was advance announcement that no non-Communist government would emerge from the conference.

Yalta, on the Russian coast of the Black Sea, was chosen as the site for the meeting on Stalin's insistence. He obdurately rejected Roosevelt's efforts to select a site not on Russian soil. As Yalta approached, the political results of the war were everywhere becoming more apparent. Rumania and Bulgaria were occupied by Soviet forces and Hungary and Yugoslavia lay in the Communist shadow. Churchill had no illusions. "I think the end of this war may well prove to be more disappointing than was the last," he wrote to Roosevelt privately, January 8.[1]

But to Roosevelt the political outcome of the war was a secondary consideration. Primary was the establishment of an international organization to preserve the peace, which presumably was to be made later. In the words of James F. Byrnes, present at the conference as an adviser and later to be secretary of state, "our chief objective for the conference was to secure agreement on the Dumbarton Oaks proposals for the creation of an international organization."[2] With the earlier altruistic war aims long since lost, a permanent United Nations would be the substitute, and it was necessary to obtain this at all costs. The Russian territorial seizures, the scheduled truncation of Germany, Stalin's evident intention to communize the new Poland, all international political matters took a minor place beside this goal.

Roosevelt, as Yalta approached, had nothing to say on any stand the United States might take on political settlements. Instead, he hailed the "principles" of the Atlantic Charter, which he had just finished relegating to the status of a press release. In the words of *Time* all problems were labeled "Do Not Open Until Peace."[3] Even the once-acclamatory liberal press joined in widespread harsh criticism of the lack of information on American objectives as the approaching conference was rumored. One journalist wrote:

Mr. Roosevelt's expediences and compromises, his postponement of questions and evasion of issues are coming home to plague him in a dozen places. Yet still unrepentantly he wisecracks, he postures, he ducks, he does everything but come clean and tell the country what he is up to. . . .[4]

The day before the opening of the Yalta conference—still officially a secret, but generally known—the managing editor of the *New York Times* wrote:

> . . . .To bring it right home, let us say that President Roosevelt has consistently abstained from informing the American people of what he did in their name at these famous meetings. Is the American public going to get the news of what happens from Mr. Roosevelt or from other sources? Of course, there will be a joint official communique. In all likelihood, it will tell as little as most such statements tell. . . . [5]

It was a prescient question. One secret Yalta protocol gave the Russians control of the Manchurian railways and the port of Darien, a naval base at Port Arthur, and ownership of the Kurile Islands and southern Sakhalin. Flat provision for the postwar use of German forced labor, in defiance of the Geneva convention, was included in a secret protocol on reparations. Another secret agreement, of little substantive importance and which was soon ferreted out by the press, provided for three Soviet votes in the anticipated United Nations organization.

A joint communique issued after the conference stated that Russia was to be given Polish territory west to approximately the Curzon line and that Poland in turn was to be given German territory to a line to be fixed at a "peace conference." The Communist regime set up by Russia was to be the government of Poland, "reorganized on a broader democratic basis with the inclusion of democratic leaders from Poland itself and from Poles abroad." Free elections were to be held as soon as possible.

The communique did not reveal that Stalin had been deaf to all efforts of the West—primarily Churchill—to obtain a Polish regime at the outset that would not be dominated by Communists, and that he had stonily insisted that the Communist puppet group be the nucleus. Nor did it reveal that the West, well aware of what "free elections" under a Communist regime amounted to, had unsuccessfully tried to get Stalin's consent to three-power supervision to insure their fairness. All Stalin would permit was that the West send observers with no authority except to consult and report.

The communique said that Germany was to pay reparations "in kind," but said nothing about forced German labor, although it was spelled out in the secret protocol. This protocol was not an offhand product. The Russian intention of using millions of German prisoners, possibly including women, for a period of ten years had been stated to Ambassador Harriman in Moscow, January 20, and the American position papers for Yalta had approved the plan. Roosevelt gave his specific approval at Yalta, telling Stalin he wanted the Soviet to get all the manpower it could without starving Germany. The details were left to be worked out by an allied Reparations Commission to be set up in Moscow.[6]

A "Declaration of Liberated Europe" said the three powers would concert their policies to help liberated countries set up governments of their own choosing, "reaffirming our faith in the principles of the Atlantic Charter." The statement was hollow. On Soviet insistence, consultation to effect such concert was to take place only when all three considered it necessary. If the Soviet demurred, there would be no consultation before action, as events soon proved.

But Yalta was hailed as a great achievement because "harmony" had been established. The Polish question had been "settled." Agreement had been reached with the Russians on the use of the veto in procedural matters, which since Dumbarton Oaks had been an obstacle to the proposed international organization. It now appeared possible to organize a permanent United Nations, which by now had become the only visible objective of American policy other than military victory, and a conference to achieve that end was set for April 25 in San Francisco.

While the President was still enroute from Yalta by sea, a carefully-planned campaign was begun to paint the conference results in glowing colors. James F. Byrnes, director of mobilization and reconversion, had been dispatched from Yalta early to get it under way, and upon arriving in Washington he issued a statement fulsomely praising the results of the meeting and especially the effects of Roosevelt's participation.

"Every American," he asserted, "should be proud of the role played by the President." Byrnes credited Roosevelt with the "solution" of the Polish question[7] and with obtaining agreement on the formula for voting procedure in the proposed world organization, which was held up as a remarkable achievement. His "great skills, tact, patience and good humor" had more than once "brought about decisions." This panegyric looked peculiar a few months later when, as the new secretary of state, Byrnes found himself seeking from the White House information on secret Yalta protocols of which he knew nothing. As he later wrote, "I wanted to see how many IOU's were outstanding."[8]

The Department of State, through Acting Secretary Grew, found special gratification in the "reaffirmation of our faith in the principles of the Atlantic Charter." Most of the press followed. The praise of the conference was equalled only by the praise of the President for his part in it. A *New York Times* headline proudly announced, "Roosevelt Shaped 2 Yalta Decisions." Editorially, the *Times* said the Yalta agreements "justify and surpass most of the hopes" of the meeting which had shown the way not only to an early victory in Europe, but "to a secure peace and to a brighter world." The *New York Herald-Tribune* said the conference had provided "another great proof of Allied unity, strength and power of decision." *Time* magazine said "all doubts about the Big Three's ability to cooperate in peace as well as in war seem now to have been swept away." To the *Philadelphia Record*, Yalta was "the greatest United Nations victory of the war." In the *Washington Post*, Sumner Welles, former undersecretary of state and close confidant of Roosevelt, called Yalta an "outstanding achievement" and eulogized the declaration on liberated countries, with its promise of helping them to achieve free government.

There were some discordant voices, among them being the *Wall Street Journal*, which asked, "have we reached the stage where almost any settlement at all is becoming acceptable to a great many of us?" But the *Journal* was in the minority. Yalta was generally proclaimed a famous victory for democracy and peace.

Acting Secretary of State Grew in a broadcast February 17 said the San Francisco conference would give the United States and other "peace-loving nations" the chance to bring about permanent world peace.[9] Assistant Secretary of State Archibald MacLeish the next day told the nation that criticism of the government as having no foreign policies came from "people with special motives," who were laying the foundation for disparaging the administration of the nation's allies. From Mexico City on February 22, Secretary of State Edward Stettinius lauded the proposals for a world organization as "based squarely upon the principles of the Atlantic Charter and of the United Nations Declaration."

In a broadcast February 24, Stettinius again fulsomely praised the agreement on voting procedure in an international organization as contributing mightily to the prospects for world peace. Assistant Secretary Dean Acheson told the nation by radio that the Yalta conference was "a good example of foreign policy reflecting national purpose," and held up the agreement on Poland as a notable step toward a free government there. MacLeish, on the same broadcast, said the important thing was that the United States was going to take its "full share of responsibility in building the peace, everywhere in the world," which, Acheson added, would be "a good guarantee that we are not fighting this war for nothing."

The President told Congress on March 1 that Yalta spelled the end of unilateral action, exclusive alliances, spheres of influence and balances of power. "Never before have the major allies been more closely united—not only in their war aims but in their peace aims." The "solution reached on Poland," he said, was an "outstanding example of joint action by the major allied powers in the liberated areas." The President said he did not agree with all aspects of the Polish boundary arrangements, which were "quite a compromise." Actually, as has been seen, he had agreed broadly to the boundaries as early as March 1943. His chief dissent at Yalta had been a request that Poland get the city of Lwow, which Stalin firmly refused, despite Roosevelt's plea that there were six or seven million Poles in the United States and that he hoped Stalin would "make a gesture in this direction."[10]

Giving no inkling of the secret agreement on forced labor as reparations, the President spelled out reparations "in kind" as meaning such things as plants, machinery, rolling stock and raw materials. Unconditional surrender, he promised, did not mean enslavement of the German people.

But the known intention of Soviet Russia was to use millions of Germans at forced labor for many years. At a press conference the next day, reporters pressed Roosevelt for information as to Yalta decisions on the question. Reporters were not permitted to quote the President directly, but on important matters they endeavored to use his words precisely. A *New York Times* correspondent wrote: "Mr. Roosevelt replied that the matter of German labor had not been discussed as part of the reparations question, but that after seeing the devastation wrought by the Germans at Yalta he did not think it would be a bad idea to get some German soldiers, some German ex-soldiers, to go in there and clean things up."[11] Actually, as in his denial of "treaties" after Teheran, the President was splitting a semantic hair to cover up his commitment. He had *agreed* specifically to German forced labor and had signed the reparations protocol which flatly included it, but there had been no *discussion* of details. The transcript of this evasive press conference is omitted from *The Public Papers and Addresses of Franklin D. Roosevelt.*[12]

In general, the press eulogized the labors of the President at Yalta, accepting the assumption that they were a great success. Said Walter

Lippmann of Roosevelt's Yalta efforts, "there is no tonic like doing the right thing boldly and finding that it succeeds."[13]

Even as Roosevelt spoke, the Declaration on Liberated Europe was dead. On February 27, the western Allies had been rebuffed by the Soviet in an effort to "consult" on formation of a democratic government in Rumania. The day before Roosevelt's appearance before Congress, the Soviet had demanded that the king of Rumania install a Communist-dominated regime. To Foreign Secretary Anthony Eden, writing long afterward, the Soviet move in Rumania "instantly showed up the hollowness of the declaration."[14] But Undersecretary of State Grew, two days after the Communist move, asserted in a nationwide broadcast that the declaration "points the way toward close cooperation by the big powers." Two days after that, the Rumanian Communist regime took over.

On March 17, the Soviet bluntly rejected an American proposal of a joint committee in Bucharest to safeguard the principles of the declaration. Reports appeared in the press that Americans had been thrown out of both Rumania and Bulgaria. Nevertheless, on the same day, the Department of State promised the nation that consultation among the big powers would assure democratic institutions in these countries. James C. Dunn, assistant secretary of state, explained away Communist moves in central Europe by saying "of course full democratic processes cannot begin until the end of the military operations period. . . . What you read about in the liberated countries is hardly more than our peacetime business regulations and our wartime controls."

Observers from the west were barred from Poland. The Soviet insisted that the Yalta agreement provided merely for adding some other Poles to the existing Communist regime, which indeed it did. Now, only Poles recommended by that regime were to be invited to consult on forming a broadened government. To Churchill, the Soviet plan was clear. He wrote to Roosevelt on March 13 that Russia was blocking the setting up of a new government "so that the process of liquidation of elements unfavorable to them and their puppets may run its course."[15] The Prime Minister repeatedly urged Roosevelt to join in putting the issue squarely up to Stalin, but the President counseled delay.

While the Yalta façade was cracking, the first secret agreement leaked out. On March 29, the Washington correspondent of the *New York Herald Tribune* revealed that Roosevelt and Churchill had agreed to give the Soviet Union three votes in the assembly of the proposed world security organization, representing the Ukraine and Byelorussia as separate republics. The next day, the White House admitted this to be a fact, but asserted that, as part of the bargain, the United States had also reserved the right to ask for three votes.[16]

Embarrassed and red-faced, Stettinius faced a volley of pointed questions from newspaper reporters the next day. Why had the arrangement been kept secret? Had the members of the United States delegation to the coming San Francisco conference been told? And were there other secret agreements? Stettinius had no answer and lamely voiced confidence that the San Francisco conference had not been endangered, based, as a reporter quoted him, on his faith "that what we went to war about was not in vain." A few days later, in a formal statement, he said flatly that there were no other Yalta secret agreements except those relating to military matters, initial membership in the international organization, and territorial trusteeships.

The Department of State, which in its publicity had repeatedly emphasized the promise to keep the public informed on foreign policy, sought to repair the damage to confidence. Assistant Secretary MacLeish and Michael McDermott, press assistant to the secretary, explained in a radio broadcast that the secret Russian vote agreement had been a complete surprise to them, and attempted to minimize its significance as a "furore in the press room." But the disclosure had done more than agitate the press. The entire nation had been shocked by the fact of a secret protocol. That others of far greater importance were still to be revealed was widely suspected.

Although discord was apparent, the public was not aware of the full extent of the dissension between the West and Russia. On March 8, an effort had been made by a German officer, through American intelligence in Switzerland, to arrange to negotiate a surrender of the German forces in Italy. The Russians had been informed, but they choose to assert bad faith on the part of the West. Acrimonious charges by Russia were capped by a note from Stalin to Roosevelt on April 13, so insulting that Roosevelt, in reply, expressed his "bitter resentment" against what he termed Stalin's "informers" for such vile misrepresentations." Foreign Secretary Eden wrote long afterward that it had become obvious that "collaboration between the great powers was already displayed in failure."[17] But if a permanent United Nations was to be set up at San Francisco, such views could not be publicly admitted.

The rift widened as the West rejected the Russian demand that the

Warsaw Communist regime, as it stood, represent Poland at the San Francisco conference, whereupon the Soviet announced that its delegation would be headed by the ambassador in Washington rather than its foreign minister, V. M. Molotov. The possibility of postponing the conference was widely discussed, but by now a permanent United Nations had become the sole fruit to be obtained from the war other than sheer victory. A dispatch to the *New York Times*, April 3, reported that, despite pronounced uneasiness in Washington, the feeling was that the nation must go through with the conference to prove its "good faith."

Secretary Stettinius, on April 4, assured the nation that "temporary difficulties of a political nature" would not stand in the way. Yet how could an organization, for whose very existence it was necessary to turn over a large part of Europe to communism, be an effective instrument of democracy, peace and justice? How could an organization of the victors preserve peace when the victors themselves could not agree on what the peace should be? The secretary of state answered such questions over the air with an ingenious argument: despite differences, the world organization had to be created before a peace was arranged in order to enable it to deal with conflicts arising from the peace settlements themselves.

On the death of President Roosevelt, April 12, Stalin made the gesture of rescinding his refusal to permit Molotov to attend. Although Stalin was adamant that there should be no Polish representation except by the Communist puppet regime, the gesture was the signal for another wave of roseate predictions of world harmony that would result from San Francisco. Former Secretary of State Hull said the conference would be "one of the great turning points of history." Some of the press was cynically pessimistic, but more of the nation's newspapers adopted a tone of determined hopefulness. Those who took a critical view of the coming conference were freely characterized as rejecting the only hope of permanent peace. Typical of this attitude was a *Nashville Tennessean* cartoon labeled "If Ye Break Faith," which pictured the heads of Roosevelt and a soldier beside a kind of monument entitled, "San Francisco, Lasting Peace."

While the public was being so deluged, the Americans and British were working frantically behind the scenes in a last-minute effort to get Stalin to agree to a Polish government with some claim to democracy so that the San Francisco façade would not be marred. But Stettinius and Eden got nowhere in repeated sessions with

Molotov that sometimes lasted far into the night. On the eve of the conference, ignoring the West's appeals for postponement, Stalin concluded a treaty with the Polish Communist puppet regime. The nation over which Britain had gone to war was not to be represented in building the organization for peace.

Despite all this, the conference opened with "trust Russia" as the keynote. The press gave large space to an article in the Soviet army publication, *Red Star*, urging trust among the major allies. President Truman urged "continued cooperation" of the nations fighting the axis. Stettinius hailed the assembled delegates at San Francisco as representing nations that "loved peace and freedom." Molotov called for a strong security organization of "peace-loving" nations. The fact that he also truculently suggested that nations of Europe had been reluctant to prevent the war and asserted that Russia had "saved European civilization" did not prevent the speech from drawing loud applause.

So that a gloss on Russia could be preserved until the peace organization was set up, the West had kept secret a most sinister Soviet development. A group of Polish non-Communist underground leaders, including some of the West's likely candidates for democratic representation in the Polish government, had disappeared in March after revealing themselves to confer with Soviet officials. Eden and Ambassador Harriman in Moscow had tried unsuccessfully to learn their fate. Holding down the lid of secrecy proved impossible. On the day the conference opened, the fact of their disappearance was revealed in press dispatches from London.

At first the newspapers, filled with fanfare of the conference, minimized the ominous affair. The *New York Times* printed only fifty words on an inside page under a tiny, one-line heading. But as more details were ferreted out by London correspondents, it assumed large proportions in the press, and on May 3, Molotov finally admitted that the men were in a Russian prison. Conversations on constituting a Polish government were suspended. Two days later, while Molotov was acclaiming the principles of justice, peace and freedom for all in a speech to the conference, the Moscow radio announced that the Poles would be tried for high treason.

In desperation, Harry Hopkins, always notably sympathetic to Russia and persona grata to Stalin, was drafted to leave a sick bed for a personal appeal to the Russian dictator to save the conference from the rocks. Stalin refused to release the imprisoned underground leaders, but agreed that four of the ministries in the Communist

Polish government could go to non-Communist Poles. A group of Poles from London was chosen to go to Moscow to confer with the Communist puppet regime. But even as they began conferring, the Soviet subjected them to obvious pressure by putting the imprisoned underground leaders on trial. Originally charged with illegal possession of the radio sending sets which had been their means of communication with the London government from Poland, the prisoners were now charged with murdering Russian officers and planning a Western bloc to contain communism.

As was usually the case in Soviet trials, the accused "confessed." They had been held in solitary confinement for weeks and questioned day and night under glaring electric lights. Twelve were sentenced to prison terms ranging from four months to ten years. Two years later, after Poland had become completely a Communist state, they were released. While they were "confessing" a new government was set up with a two-thirds Communist majority, which by means of coercion, intimidation and executions eventually became airtight Communist rule.[18]

Nevertheless, Stalin had promised that the Communist Polish government would later hold "free elections," and with this weak façade on Poland, the San Francisco conference went ahead. The United Nations, to preserve peace, freedom and justice for all the world, was constituted in a cloud of euphoria. Poland was officially handed over to communism on July 5, with recognition of the Communist puppet government. When the Yalta-promised elections were finally held in 1947, any remaining effective non-Communist influence had been extinguished by terrorism and murder.[19]

When the European war ended with Germany's surrender, on May 7, the two principal secret protocols remained locked in a White House safe. While the Japanese surrender was being negotiated in late August, the Soviet occupied the Kuriles, along with southern Sakhalin and islands adjacent, and on September 2, Stalin announced that they all now belonged to the Soviet Union. Secretary of State Byrnes, who had succeeded Stettinius, said that the United States would not oppose the move, but denied that any commitment had been made on the Kuriles.

The following January, Acting Secretary Acheson told reporters he understood there had been no final territorial decision on the Kuriles at Yalta, but cautiously warned that he might be wrong. The Moscow radio promptly spoke up: The USSR had been specifically given the Kuriles, with no strings attached, as well as southern

Sakhalin and the nearby islands. Byrnes then admitted this to be true, explaining that the deal had been made after he left Yalta and he had not even heard of it until after the Japanese surrender. The American copy had been kept in the White House as a top military secret, and Byrnes had learned of its existence from the official Yalta interpreter, on September 2. He knew it dealt with the Kuriles, southern Sakhalin, Port Arthur, Dairien and the Manchurian railways, but even then he had apparently not seen the document, as he told reporters he was not certain whether the protocol also dealt with other subjects. President Truman said he had learned of the agreement before the Potsdam conference in July.

The Department of State, with the reluctant acquiescence of Britain, then published the protocol. It specified that "the Kurile Islands shall be handed over to the Soviet Union." Not only had President Roosevelt promised Stalin to "take measures" to insure China's consent, but "the heads of the three great powers have agreed that these claims of the Soviet Union shall be unquestionably fulfilled after Japan has been defeated."

Military security was given as the reason for secrecy, inasmuch as at the time of Yalta Russia had not entered the war against Japan. But the Japanese war had ended September 2. Apparently it was then considered safe to let the secretary of state know something about it. How long the agreement would have been kept secret, except for Moscow, can only be guessed.

The agreement on the use of German forced labor, which was part of the secret protocol on reparations, was not be to revealed until the spring of 1947. When the Western allies and Russia got into a reparations quarrel, Stalin published the full text of the secret reparations protocol. Among other things, it specifically provided for "use of German labor." Thus the American people learned from Moscow, not Washington, that their President had approved forced servitude for the soldiers of their conquered enemy, flatly contrary to the Geneva convention providing for the return of war prisoners as soon as possible after the cessation of hostilities.

For more than a decade, German soldiers were held in captivity to work in the mines and forests of Russia. It is estimated that more than one million died. The conditions under which they labored in France were so harsh as to bring about United States intervention, but nothing could be done about their condition in Russia. In 1947, England was using the labor of 350,000 and in France, to which the United States had turned over approximately 440,000 prisoners, more than 300,000 were still held. In Russia, more than 3,000,000 were at forced labor. The Americans had freed all their prisoners by August 1947, and in March, France, yielding to American pressure, had begun sending prisoners home at the rate of 20,000 a month. Britain returned the last of its prisoners in July 1948. The Russians claimed to have returned the last of their military prisoners in 1955. The *New York Times* reported on February 22, 1959, that 180,000 German civilians who had been deported between 1944 and 1949 were believed to be still held in Russia. Eight hundred thousand German civilians had been taken to Russia, and 400,000 of these had died.

Part III

With Hatred Toward All

10

The Build-Up

The preceding chapters have dealt with some of the principal specific deceptions of the war: the concealment of hostile actions on the Atlantic while the nation was ostensibly not a belligerent; the representation of the Atlantic Charter pledges as actual war aims while Soviet aims rendering these pledges a fraud were kept hidden; the secret dispositions of Teheran; and the Soviet protocols of Yalta.

But even if the people could be persuaded that all nations allied against Germany had noble objectives, and actually proposed to abide by the pledges of the charter, glorified war aims were of themselves not enough to animate a gigantic war conducted in Europe. As in all mass wars, hatred was also essential. The shooting war had to be supported by a home campaign to inflame passions against the enemy.

Hitler's record of political and racial persecutions and murders had aroused deep repugnance in the American people long before 1939. After the outbreak of hostilities in Europe, animosity had grown as fear of Germany was promoted to justify increasingly un-neutral policies in aid to Great Britain. But in December 1941, when the de facto war became a declared conflict, hatred was still aimed chiefly at Hitler and the Nazi leaders rather than the entire German people. The attitude of many Americans in 1941 toward Germans in general was expressed by Norman Cousins, editor of the *Saturday Review of Literature*, when he called upon American writers to draw a distinction between German culture and Hitler's barbarism. "Of course, there is a distinction—a distinction Americans must recognize and respect if we are to avoid falling victim to the same excessive feeling of superiority that has obliterated—only for the moment, we hope—the warmth and richness of the cultural side of the other Germany."[1]

Even after a year of declared war, Dr. Albert Bushnell Hart, internationally known emeritus professor of history at Harvard, decried the idea of general German iniquity. "I know the stock," he said. "I lived among them. . . . They are just like friendly families down in Maine. . . . If we are realistic we must admit that the peace after the First World War failed because Germany was trampled upon to the extent that the embers of unrest among the people were easily fanned into flame by Hitler."[2]

Such views had to be eradicated or smothered. The people had to be indoctrinated with the belief that their very existence was threatened by a wholly iniquitous foe. The battle had to be a holy Armageddon, where total good fought total evil. A massive campaign of propaganda fixed this doctrine in the minds of a large part of the American people. How hatred swelled is illustrated by the position, in 1944, of the editor of the *Saturday Review* whose 1941 temperate view was cited above. He now found it impossible to draw any distinctions between "good" Germans and "bad" Germans. The "good" Germans were all dead or shattered in mind and body by forced labor or imprisonment. There was no longer any "other Germany,"[3] he said. Belief in the iniquity of the entire German people not only brought mass attitudes to a point of frenzy in wartime but continued long after the enemy was conquered, resulting in an occupation policy of such vindictiveness that it almost prostrated Europe before being reversed.

The ideas which came to form the basis for building a frenzy of anti-German hatred were those of Sir Robert Vansittart, British diplomatic counsellor and chief hate propagandist. In a series of radio broadcasts of fantastic fury in 1941, Vansittart laid to the whole German people a train of evil and viciousness that extended back two thousand years.

Vansittart went back to Julius Caesar to buttress his proposition that Germans as a people did not consider robbery infamous, and quoted Tacitus to prove that they hated peace. Charlemagne had the "lust for world domination." The rise of Hitler was only the current expression of the desire for war inherent in the German character. The Germans, he said, had made five wars in the past seventy-five years, and if they had had their way there would have been a war twice as often.

Their lust for world conquest, he said, had made the Germans the exponents of every imaginable variety of "dirty fighting and foul play." They "have pledged no word without breaking it, have made no treaty without dishonoring it, have touched no international faith without soiling it." German literature, medicine, music and philosophy were but "sideshows." German heroes had always been "offensive persons according to the standards of everyone else." The Germans, he said, methodically obliterated from the air defenseless towns and villages in order to drive refugees out to block the roads. They crushed civilians with tanks, machine-gunned women and children, and "systematically" bombed hospitals and hospital ships. A large supply of "cold-blooded barbarians" revelled in doing these things "that no Briton could or would do."[4]

President Roosevelt himself did not publicly espouse such views at first. Instead he excoriated Hitler and his "political clique." It was "Hitler and his Nazis" who had the "gargantuan aspiration" of dominating the entire earth. It was "Hitler and his gang" whom the allied nations had to knock out. Privately, however, Roosevelt had approved of Vansittart's approach even before the declared war began. In November 1941, he had sent a collection of Vansittart's British radio hate speeches to William B. Donovan, coordinator of information and later chief of the Office of Strategic Services, to be used as American radio propaganda.[5]

Winston Churchill's prewar views on the reasons for the rise of Hitler had differed sharply from the Vansittart thesis. In 1935 he fully recognized Hitler's cruelty and ruthlessness, but, although Hitler had "loosed frightful evils," he had also performed "superb toils." Hitler had risen, said Churchill, because of the "lethargy and folly" of the French and British, who had not redressed the grievances of the treaties of Versailles and Trianon, had demanded "senseless" reparations, and had made no sincere attempt to come to terms with the various moderate German parliamentary governments.[6] Such prewar opinions had to become non-opinions for war purposes. The Vansittart argument that Hitler's climb to power simply reflected German iniquity and lust for conquest had to prevail.

The men around Roosevelt were active from the start in propagating the theme of total German iniquity and thirst for war. They included his closest official confidants, Henry Morgenthau, secretary of the treasury, proponent of the revengeful "Morgenthau Plan," and Sumner Welles, undersecretary of state. Harry Hopkins of course shared these views. They were expressed by Secretary of State Cordell Hull and other officials and were repeated and echoed and re-echoed by the press and radio and on innumerable platforms throughout the nation.

The campaign to build hatred of the whole German people assumed its full proportions in early 1943, with the adoption at Casablanca of unconditional surrender as the only acceptable basis of peace.

Millions of American soldiers would be invading a continent three thousand miles away in alliance with Communist Russia, with no prospect of return until the enemy was laid prostrate. Support for such a program required intense and widespread hatred of the entire German people, combined with fear of what would happen to the United States if the enemy were not rendered utterly powerless for the future.

Hatred was also needed for other reasons. Since December 1941, Stalin had firmly maintained his intention of taking all the territory he had seized in collaboration with Hitler in 1939. The West's vague deferment of these demands was to give way in March 1943, in a meeting of Eden and Roosevelt, to outright secret sanction, together with approval of Polish seizure of German territory and the expulsion of millions of Germans. The hollowness of the Atlantic Charter pledges would eventually become evident, and hatred and fear would be needed as a visceral substitute for belief in high moral purpose. Furthermore, the British air war against Germany had become chiefly an indiscriminate attack on masses of civilians, and, despite directives generally specifying military or industrial targets, American bombing in large part was to take on a similar character. Belief in the total depravity of the foe would help to obscure the moral implications of mass bombing. Last, but not least, hate was essential for the vindictive treatment of postwar Germany, plans for which were already sprouting in the Treasury Department.

The beginning of 1943 marked a notable increase in the outpouring of vengefulness against Germany and Germans. James W. Gerard, former ambassador to Germany, urged that when the Allies conquered Germany they hang 10,000 Prussians as a starter.[7] Joseph E. Davies, Roosevelt confidant and former ambassador to Russia, said the Germans should be treated like insane asylum inmates for two or three generations, and he predicted German use of poison gas and bacteriological warfare.[8] A New Jersey radio station even proposed to eliminate from use the word "kindergarten' because it was German, and in its contest to select a new term a newspaper publisher and a federal judge agreed to act as judges.[9]

The promotion of hatred of all Germans was guided and fueled by a quasi-governmental agency, the Writers War Board, set up early in the war by Secretary Morgenthau. He had picked Rex Stout, author of popular detective stories, to organize the board, and Stout and the dozen or so writers he chose as members naturally held the Morgenthau ideas. Members received no compensation, but the government paid office salaries and expenses. The board worked closely with the Office of War Information and had a quasi-official standing which, with the personal and professional connections of its members, insured effective entree to the radio, press and film industry and to opinion-forming channels generally. Its stated purpose was to mobilize writers behind the war effort, assisting with propaganda in connection with war loans, rationing and other essential home-front activities. Although indeed concerned with these throughout the war, by 1943 the board's chief effort had become promoting hatred of all Germans and the idea that they would start a new war unless prevented by a harsh peace following the Morgenthau ideas.

Two weeks after Roosevelt announced the slogan of unconditional surrender at Casablanca, the board opened an all-out hate campaign with an article by Stout in the *New York Times Sunday Magazine* entitled "We Shall Hate or We Shall Fail." Stout asserted that four generations of German leaders had been guided by the "adoration of force as the only arbiter and skullduggery as the supreme technique in human affairs." Hatred of the Germans was necessary "to establish the world on a basis of peace."

The country was not yet ready to espouse vengefulness against all Germans judging by the response to this call for unconditional hatred. According to the editor of the *Times*, the many letters received in reply were almost unanimously opposed to the views expressed. The National Education Association asserted that "these malignant indictments on entire nations and races are the characteristic weapons of dictators," and were "not suitable weapons for nations conducting a great crusade for the extension of liberty and justice to all peoples everywhere in the world." The Federal Council of the Churches of Christ in America said if hatred became the emotion that predominantly determined how the United Nations would act, the forces of evil would have won their greatest victory," and it will be impossible for mankind to achieve a just and durable peace." In a *Times* article answering the Writers War Board chairman, Dr. Walter Russell Boie, professor of practical theology at Union Theological Seminary, said such sentiments were "moral poison" which, if listened to, would bar all hope of a decent result of the war.

But the waves of hate propaganda were mounting to a tide which would sweep mass opinion before it. Before the days of television, the radio had enormous influence, and it was wide open to Stout's group, which not only arranged programs but assisted in the preparation of speeches. Quentin Reynolds—war correspondent, associate of *Collier's* magazine, and a wheelhorse for the Writers War Board—followed Stout's call to hatred on a leading nationwide program, "America's Town Meeting of the Air," urging hatred as a "healthy" emotion. The mental disease of Germany could not be cured—"you must kill." "We must go to the peace table with hatred in our hearts."[10]

The outpouring of hatred extended to German children. On another "America's Town Meeting of the Air" broadcast[11] a child actor taking the part of a German boy was introduced to represent German youth as saying: "America is a cesspool. . . . With the Führer to show us the way, it is our position to conquer the world." The author of a current play of which this passage formed a part assured the air audience that this was a true portrayal of German youth because it had been indoctrinated with lies and obscenities.

The subject of the "Town Meeting of the Air" September 30, 1943, was: "How must we deal with Germany after the war to win the peace?" The chief speakers were Vansittart, the British hate propagandist, and Richard M. Bruckner, author of a book, *Is Germany Incurable?* which the Writers War Board was promoting. Bruckner, introduced as a "noted psychiatrist," proposed the incarceration in institutions and labor battalions of large groups of "paranoid tending" Germans who had long dominated Germany. They included all persons with pre-1933 membership in the Nazi party; all pre-1933 officers in the armed forces, all junkers, and the police forces and various classes of civil servants. They would be treated as "typhoid carriers" and their children placed in foster homes.

Promoting fear of another war being started by a resurgent Germany became an increasing element in the propaganda. Germany had to be laid prostrate and kept down not only because all Germans were bad, but because they were a war-thirsty people, habitual starters of war, and unless harshly restrained they would start a new conflict as soon as they could. The people had to believe that Germany began not only World War II seeking world domination, but also World War I for the same purpose, and in fact had always been seeking to rule the world by force.

To establish this thesis in the popular mind, it was necessary to overturn the general historical verdict on World War I reached in calmer times. Most historians conducting research into the origins of that war had absolved Germany of exclusive, and some of even primary, blame for its outbreak. Their collective findings had been reflected in the 1930 edition of the *Encyclopaedia Britannica* which carried exhaustive analyses of the subject leading to a summation that there was no war "guilt" in the sense of a stain on any particular nation.

The war-guilt clause of the Versailles Treaty, in which Germany had been forced to admit responsibility for the war, was a dead letter, said the Britannica editor after summing up the research of a decade. The clause remained in force only because of domestic political necessities of the victorious nations. Most historians agreed with this view and, according to the editor of *Harper's*, writing in 1939, most ordinary Americans also. They had become convinced that "there had been guilt on both sides, not simply the German side."[12]

This belief, which had become generally accepted in peace, had to be buried for the purposes of war. The Writers War Board opened the campaign in an article by Stout in the *New York Times Book Review*.[13] Stout admitted that nearly all historical writing between the wars had controverted the idea that Germany had been solely or principally guilty of the First World War. But he assured *Times* readers that the authors of most of these books had "fatally deceived and misinformed their countrymen." He upbraided the publishers who had made such volumes available and recommended a spate of new books—not by historians—which argued the malignity of the entire German people. That the *Times* would give prominent space to the dismissal of the views of most serious historians by a writer of detective stories is an illuminating footnote to the emotion of the period, as well as to the influence of the Writers War Board with leading organs of public opinion.

History was now to be reversed. Germany had again become solely guilty of starting World War I. It had started five wars in 80 years. The theme was repeated by high government officials, newspaper editors and innumerable writers in the press and speakers on the radio. How successful this campaign was may be gauged by the somersault executed by the *Encyclopaedia Britannica*. Its several articles on "War Guilt" in the 1930 edition had run to more than 8,000 words, and the general finding was flatly contradictory to World War II propaganda. In its 1944 revision, the Britannica simply removed these articles—all of them. Under the same War Guilt heading, it substituted a brief note saying there was not sufficient space for treatment of the subject.*

*After Germany was conquered in World War II, reason again began slowly to regain the place that had been usurped by the emotional propaganda of war. By 1964 a leading London newspaper could say: "In retrospect, the 1914-18 war can be seen to have been a tragic misunderstanding, the war which nobody wanted and into which the European powers collided almost by accident."[14]

To the theme that Germany was a chronic starter of wars and was always thirsting for them, a fantastic proposition was now added: Germany was already making plans for a new war. *This Week*, the magazine section of the *New York Herald-Tribune* and many other leading newspapers, carried an article to the effect that a "Nazi underground" was being created in Germany to carry out these plans.[15] Many newspaper correspondents readily adopted the line. At first they cited captured German documents or obscure publications in places like Algeria as accepted fact. The *New York Times* carried a Washington dispatch of nearly a column, headed "Crafty Reich Plot Laid for Next War," attributing it simply to "French sources."[16]

The Associated Press quoted a London newspaper, which in turn gave as its authority a French underground publication, stating that the Germans, knowing the war lost, aimed at winning sympathy from their former enemies, establishing a "camouflaged dictatorship" in France, and attacking the Unitd States from French bases.[17]

Vansittart's views were widely publicized. The *St. Louis Post-Dispatch* ran two articles promoting Vansittartism on the same page, one explaining why Vansittart was an authority on Germans and the other setting forth his proposals for occupying Germany for a generation, putting Germans at forced labor, and executing tens of thousands of war criminals—all necessary to prevent another war.[18] The *Philadelphia Inquirer* editorialized that the Germans would try every "trick" and "whine" to win a soft peace so that—Hitler or no Hitler—they could try another "march of conquest."[19]

Publications of every ilk plugged the idea. Usually they preferred well-known names as authors, but they were not always particular. The *Reader's Digest* gave space to an anonymous writer to warn that no amount of education could change the forces of "centuries of predatory tradition inherent in the Prussian character," and that differentiating between regular German army officers and the Gestapo could result in a new war in 20 or 30 years.[20] Even *Barron's*, the business and financial weekly associated with the *Wall Street Journal*, published a long article which cited "reports from neutral capitals" as proving that Germany was feverishly at work in preparations for an economic and political offensive "to obtain the conditions essential to preparation for a third world war."[21]

Time magazine took full-page newspaper advertisements to tell the public "You and your family will never be safe. . . . as long as one of the most fierce and fertile tribes on this planet continues to believe that it should and eventually can, conquer and rule others."[22]

Even German prisoners in United States camps were part of the build-up for another war, according to the *Philadelphia Record*. "These men behind barbed wire in Jersey, Alabama and other states will be on hand for World War III, with their sons and daughters waiting for a third attempt to world domination."[23]

The idea was kept before the people on the most important nationwide radio programs by speakers who were frequently selections of the Writers War Board or its subsidiary, "The Society to Prevent World War III." On "America's Town Meeting of the Air," Louis Nizer—whose book, proposing harsh treatment of Germany, the board was assiduously promoting—asserted the Germans were trying to "save the necks" of the military for another war, and were storing money in neutral countries for the purpose. On the same program, Samuel Grafton, a syndicated columnist, urged the permanent exile or imprisonment, without trial, of at least 100,000 "members of the leading circles," to prevent another war. [24]

Prominent radio advertisers took it up as a patriotic message to use in the promoion of their products. On the Prudential "Family Hour," a nationwide weekly radio program of this old-line insurance company, listeners heard simulated "orders" from the German general staff to soldiers, given in heavy, gutteral German and translated: "World domination or world downfall is the German slogan. . . . We shall love peace as a means to new wars." The Prudential spokesmen told his hearers "They are planning to try it again in another twenty years."[25]

On this and other similar broadcasts there was no proof, no evidence; constant repetition had so conditioned the mass mind that the idea was just accepted. In June, a public opinion poll had indicated that 63 percent of the American people believed Germany, as soon as it was defeated, "would start making plans for a new war." Of those having any opinion 74 percent believed this.[26]

On June 22, Secretary Morgenthau, in a statement given first-page position throughout the country, even warned against the dangers of a German unconditional surrender, asserting it might be a "fake" arranged to facilitate the build-up for a new war.

On July 20, the long-planned plot of the underground opposition to Hitler culminated in an attempt to assassinate him with a bomb and to set up a new democratic German government. Hitler escaped by accident and the planned revolution collapsed. In retribution, approximately 5,000 persons were shot, hanged or tortured to death, the hangings continuing almost to April of the next year, almost to the time of surrender. News of the attempt, rather than being applauded in the United States and Britain, was greeted with venomous disparagement of the motives of the plotters. Typical was the front-page London dispatch in the *New York Times*, describing the attempt as a "game" of militarists whose aim was to seek an easier peace by supplanting Hitler and thus preserve the German army for a new war.[27]

As Hitler's fierce retaliation continued its sweep over Germany, the whole thing was derogated in the American press as a sideshow among murderers. Editorially the *New York Times* said the attempt suggested "the atmosphere of a gangster's lurid underworld" rather than what one "would normally expect within an officers' corps and a civilized state." The *Times* noted with apparent reproach that some of the highest officers of the German army had been concerned for a year with plans "to capture or kill the head of state and the commander-in-chief of the army." The plan was carried out "with a bomb, the typical weapon of the underworld."[28]

In the view of the *New York Herald-Tribune*, "American people as a whole will not feel sorry that the bomb spared Hitler for the liquidation of his generals. Americans hold no brief for aristocrats as such, and least of all for those given to the goosestep and, when it suits their purpose, to collaboration with low-born, rabble-rousing corporals. Let the generals kill the corporal or vice versa, preferably both."[29]

Prime Minister Churchill, in the House of Commons, August 9, described the plot as a case of highly-placed persons in the German Reich "murdering each other." Elmer Davis, director of the Office of War Information, told the American people that if a German revolution should take place with the overthrow of Hitler, it would just be a "phony" arrangement by German leaders to preserve the skeleton of their forces for another world war.[30] The public could not be allowed to believe that the attempt on Hitler's life was the work of brave and dedicated men risking everything to rescue their country from the Nazi grip. Such would have challenged the central thesis necessary to justify a war to unconditional surrender.

Sumner Welles, undersecretary of state until his resignation the preceding fall, spelled out that German plans for another war were well under way. He, rather than Secretary Hull, had been Roosevelt's close confidant in the Department of State, and his views were influential. In his book, *Time for Decision*, published in July 1944, Welles wrote that the German general staff, apprehensive of defeat, was already making plans for a new attempt to "dominate the world" when the time arrived. In preparation for this, its agents had been naturalized in neutral counries to begin the task. They would use funds already deposited in these countries to engage in business enterprises and seek through accomplices to control production and influence public opinion and election for the new war to dominate the world.[31]

The book received a wide and generally approving response in the press. The *New York Times* gave it a large and prominently displayed news story by James Reston.[32] A *Times* reviewer on the same day called the book "authoritative" and urged that Germany never again be permitted to have heavy industry, as "no one need fear an agricultural, small-crafts economy." The *Washington Post* editorially accepted Welles' assertion that agents of the German general staff were already planning for a new war, and said such machinations must be "nipped in the bud." Policy must be developed toward "all the disease spots on this planet," based on the Welles exposition.[33]

Welles repeated his thesis in newspaper and magazine articles, and, constantly promoted by the Writers War Board, it was accepted by the press generally. Any kind of a mere conjecture was used to support the idea of German plans for another war. An Associated Press Washington dispatch quoted unnamed "American officials planning administration of defeated Germany" as saying that the Nazis "may" be planting their own men in concentration camps so they could get into Allied confidence in preparation for World War III.[34]

It was a favorite subject for cartoonists. In the *New York Herald-Tribune*, German officers were depicted bending over "Plans for World War III" while one declined an invitation to a peace conference because they were too busy "planning the next world war." In the New York daily, *P.M.*, a German prisoner was pictured answering an American interrogation officer: "Of course I feel sorry. Now we poor Germans must start all over again to conquer the world." In the *Dallas Morning News*, a German militarist stood by a globe with his fist over the United States while generals in the background perused a document labeled "Plans for Next War." A *Sacramento Bee* cartoon warning against a soft peace pictured a hand held out to assist a fierce ape up a steep incline marked by a road sign, "To World Domination."

Hollywood was an effective proponent of hate propaganda. As early as September 1942, Walt Disney, the noted producer, had affirmed that "everybody" was in the mood to make hate pictures. "We have to get in that mood if we are going to win the war."[35] Hate films proliferated, with shining American or Allied heroes pitted against brutal Nazis. The crude malevolence of the Nazi characters in *The Death of a Nazi* was such that the *New York Times* reviewer compared them to villains of the old Mack Sennet comedies. When *The North Star* showed German army doctors bleeding children for their blood bank, killing one, *Time* hailed the picture partly because it was the "most successful attempt to show a sickening German atrocity in credible terms."

Hollywood did not forget the box office, and many of its hate pictures were heavily flavored with sex. *Hitler's Children*, a film of sheer brutality, depicted female "labor camps" where unmarried girls were forced to bear children for the Reich, the nub of the plot being that a girl would be sterilized if she refused. *Hitler's Madman* showed murder, pillage and enforced prostitution of Czech girls sent to the Russian front. Sex angles and the most brutal and shocking features of films were played up in advertising, and lurid posters showed fear-frozen women being menaced by inhuman Nazis.

Bosley Crowther, film critic of the *New York Times*, was moved to question the character of the appeal of some of the hate films. "It is part of the tragedy of total warfare that peoples should be encouraged to hate," he wrote. "But when a Hollywood-made motion picture pretends to suggest atrocities by dwelling in a strange erotic fashion on Nazi breeding 'farms,' when it shows a Nazi officer choosing from a group of captured girls, and all of them very pretty and seductive to the eye, the primary motive of the producer is open to serious doubt. And when a film shows tortures and brutalities in patently painful detail the appeal is more likely to morbidity than it is to any sense of outrage."[36]

Portrayal of Germans simply as evil and depraved gave way, as in other media, to the theme of Germans hatching a third world war. *The Master Race*, which appeared in the fall of 1944, was advertised as "revealing why we must beware the 'beaten' Germans." It pictured the ruins of the Third Reich giving rise to a fourth which would in time hurl itself upon the world. To the reviewer in the *Washington Star*, this warning seemed "entirely sound and rational." Readers were urged to see the film for a preview of what "unchastened German militarists have in mind for the future of decent, peace-loving peoples."[37] Numerous other movies carried the same message.

Educators joined in. Dr. Nicholas Murray Butler, president of the

Carnegie Endowment for International Peace and former president of Columbia University, said that when the war ended Germans could not be regarded as anything but convicted criminals. In a statement circulated to newspapers by the Writers War Board, he asserted that for a generation Germans could not be accepted as equal conferees in the postwar world. Hans Kohn, professor of history at Smith College , said in *Harper's* that Hitler was "less an individual than the German mass man in demoniac proportions."[38] The superintendent of schools of Philadelphia, also chairman of the educational policies commission of the National Education Association, proposed that all Axis school teachers who had stayed at their posts willingly during the war should be discharged and "forever barred from teaching again."[39]

The most preposterous suggestion came from—of all sources—an eminent anthropologist, Dr. Ernest A. Hooton of Harvard University. He proposed to dilute the German stock, adulterate the Nazi strain, and destroy the national framework by a process of "outbreeding." This would be accomplished by sending Czechs, Austrians and others into Germany, where they would settle and intermingle with the German people. Men of the German armies would be kept out of their native land while the "outbreeding" was in process by being put to forced labor in formerly occupied countries.[40]

11

The Writers War Board

Propaganda of the Writers War Board for a Carthaginian peace pervaded the entire field of communications. Its influence reached into editorial offices high and low, into the radio networks and into the movies. The board was a supplier and clearinghouse of hard-peace propaganda for editors, writers and broadcasters, arranging radio programs, providing speakers and ghost-writing magazine articles signed by prominent persons. It organized claques for hard-peace articles and books which it approved, while impugning the motives of writers who challenged its thesis and working assiduously to disparage their product. Organizations and individuals who proposed postwar reconstruction of Germany were attacked viciously. At the same time it sought constantly to promote trust in the aims of Soviet Russia. A large advisory council of well-known writers was set up as window dressing, but these knew little of what the actual operating group was doing.[1]

By January 1945, material was being sent to 3,500 writers, 1,150 army orientation officers and camp newspapers, 2,600 house organs of industrial plants, and 270 comic strip artists, cartoonists and editors of comic magazines. Canned editorials were being sent to 1,-600 daily newspapers, and editorials were supplied regularly to a syndicate with a clientele of 600 newspapers. Radio scripts went to 750 local stations, and dramatic material was distributed on request to 2,716 organizations. But the board's most effective work was conducted by personal contacts with editors, writers, and radio networks.

Much of its propaganda assisted war loans, rationing and other war-related activities, but the chief concern of the board was promoting hatred of the German people and a harsh peace. Hate pieces were arranged for all kinds of publications. An entire series of six such articles signed by well-known authors or persons of prominence was set up for the *American Legion Monthly*. In a board-arranged piece signed by Sumner Welles, readers were warned of German plans for a new war of revenge and domination. Another board-arranged article argued that all Germans were brutal. One proposed that every German home be searched for arms, with inspectors placed to see that no others were obtained, to prevent the Germans from starting a new war. Another directed hatred at the "entire generation" of German youth, asserting it was as poisonous and dangerous as a puff adder.

The board had entree nearly everywhere in the magazine world. Stout, as chairman, was invited to become a wartime adviser to the immensely influential Life-Time-Fortune group. Elsewhere the board was able to see articles before publication and influence the content. In the spring of 1944, the *Ladies Home Journal* commissioned a piece on reconstruction of German universities after the war. This was read in galley-proof by the board, where any idea of German resuscitation was anathema. Within a week Clifton Fadiman, writer and radio personality and Stout's right-hand man, was able to report that he had persuaded the *Journal* editor to abandon the story.

Mass magazines for the barely literate were a prime outlet for outright hate material. One such specified its needs as pieces to make the readers "hate Germany without exhorting them to do so." The requirements of a group of comic and confession magazines, according to the board minutes, were stories of German cruelty with "a shock and a sting" that would be "suitable for children."

The board went "all out"—its own favorite expression—to advance books arguing most vindictively its hate thesis, no matter how preposterous their content. Sometimes board members reviewed such books or were able to influence the selection of reviewers, and articles drawn from them were mailed to a wide newspaper and radio list. Arrangements were made for the authors to appear on leading radio programs, and for sympathetic radio commentators to mention the books and quote from them.

A big project was promoting the sale of the books, *What to Do With Germany*, by Louis Nizer, and *Germany Will Try It Again*, by Sigrid Schultz.

Nizer proposd that death penalties be demanded, not only of about 5,000 high Nazi officials and bureaucrats, but also of 150,000 leaders and subordinates in Nazi organizations. Every German officer above the rank of colonel, along with members of the Reichstag and many others, would be tried. Hundreds of thousands of Germans would be given jail terms ranging up to life, which they would serve in labor battallions.

But this would not cure the German "lust for war," which if not curbed might "blow out the light of civilization forever." All heavy industry must be removed from Germany or German control to thwart plans of German industrialists for a new war, for which strategic outposts were being set up. A "reform school" was necessary to cure the German mind. The educational system must be scrapped and education in democracy, conducted by the victors, must be made compulsory for all.

The Schultz book, a general diatribe against the war-thirsty German people, argued that Germany, in its effort at world domination, had planned great air raids against the United States, and it was to get Caucasus oil for these raids that Hitler had attacked Russia. How receptive the media were to absurd ideas if they promoted hatred toward Germans was illustrated by a review of this book in the *New York Times* by Orville Prescott. He said it was so lacking in documentation for its factual statements that it was "hardly to be taken as reporting." Nevertheless, it was valuable because of its "quality of repeated propaganda," and it should be "rammed down the throat of anyone who is still afraid to be beastly to the Germans."[2]

The board set up radio round-table discussions for these preposterous books, and supplied material to columnists. It arranged for speakers to use the title *Germany Will Try It Again* in war bond campaigns. Special window displays were obtained in 24 leading book stores throughout the nation. Articles drawn from the books and signed by their authors were sent throughout the country to radio commentators and to editors and writers.

The damaging of books which sought to offer objective assessment of Germany and the postwar problem was an urgent aim. One of these was *Germany, A Short History*, by George N. Shuster and Arnold Bergstrasser, both strongly anti-Nazi, appearing in the fall of 1944. Dr. Shuster, president of Hunter College, had warned of the menace of Hitler in 1937. Dr. Bergstrasser was a former German professor. To a reviewer in the *New York Times*, the book was "one of the best recent examples of learned condensation and popularization to appear in the field of modern history." But the authors related the steps by which the German nation had been led into war without realizing it, and cited facts showing that the people themselves had not desired or sought war. This of course contradicted the board's thesis that the entire German people had wanted the war to achieve domination of the world. The board arranged to have the book attacked on a nationwide broadcast of a popular radio commentator and conducted an incessant campaign to disparage the volume and its authors.

Other books also sought to deal with the postwar German situation dispassionately, and all were attacked wherever a spot could be found. In the spring of 1945, when the time was approaching for a harsh peace to be put into effect, the board arranged to do a job on the whole group. The *Saturday Review of Literature* agreed to run an extended piece with a reviewer of the board's own choosing. Written by Lewis Mumford, it appeared August 11, three months after Germany's surrender, as the principal article. The Shuster-Bergstrasser book was damned, and eight others which had met the board's antagonism were similarly treated while Vansittart was held up as a better guide to peace policy. To readers of the *Saturday Review*, the hand of the Writers War Board was not visible.

Hate was constantly promoted by radio. Among the best-known and most-widely broadcast commentators who preached hatred of all Germans were Quentin Reynolds and Walter Winchell. The views of Reynolds on "Town Meeting of the Air" have already been described. Winchell's views on the treatment to be accorded a conquered Germany were expressed to millions of mass listeners in terms of "a rattlesnake never deserves another chance." The Writers War Board supplied material to these and other commentators who espoused its line—the "all-outers," as it termed them.

The board and its offshoot, Stout's Society for the Prevention of World War III, which is discussed later, worked closely with "America's Town Meeting of the Air" and "America's Forum of the Air," two prestigious weekly programs which were broadcast nationwide. Stout not only selected many of the speakers on programs relating to Germany but was able to influence the choice of subjects and titles.

The board had a finger in the Saturday afternoon broadcasts between acts of the Metropolitan Opera. Stout spoke regularly on the Philco program. Fadiman was master of ceremonies for the Tuesday night program of the Council on Books in Wartime and was of course influential in the selection of books to be discussed. Innumerable radio forums were set up, and programs were constantly in preparation. Hate material was sent directly to commentators and disc jockeys on individual stations. One radio show preaching a harsh peace was recorded and distributed to more than 300 such broadcasters. Excerpts from broadcasts which followed the board's line were mailed to thousands of newspapers and other publications and to editors and writers.

Commentators who preached hatred of all Germans and a hard peace were commended by letters arranged to be sent to the broadcasting stations, signed by individuals. At the same time, the hatchet was kept sharp for those who differed. The board's minutes reveal that it audited the broadcasts of such speakers in an unsuccessful attempt to extract specific quotations with which it could damage them in the eyes of their commercial sponsors and the broadcasting stations. Commentators such as Fulton Lewis, Jr., who were attacked in material mailed out by the board, and who protested to the Office of War Information, were told that the board was not a government agency and hence not under its control.

Movies were promoted which embodied the thesis that all Germans were vicious, and effective work was done directly with the film industry. An instance of the board's influence was the change it was able to effect in the film, *Tomorrow the World*, even after its release. This film depicted the life of a German boy growing up under Hitler and accepting the Nazi ideology, but later repudiating it. The possibility of such reform was contrary to the board's propaganda and on its request the producer agreed to change the ending for future showings so that the boy's complete reform would not be implied.

The arm of the board reached into all sorts of places quite unrelated to communications media. In November 1944, it was learned that a resolution was being prepared for the annual convention of the CIO, condemning the Nazis but expressing sympathy for, and faith in, the German people. Stout made a special trip to Chicago where the meeting was being held, and succeeded in persuading union officials to offer a resolution condemning the German people as a whole and demanding a hard peace, which was duly approved by the assembled delegates.

How much heft the board wielded in the book world was shown by an incident unrelated to Germany, when more than 25 American publishers accepted an invitation to exhibit at a trade fair in Barcelona, in June 1944. The board dubbed the fair an "obvious fascist scheme" but could hardly take official action inasmuch as the Office of War Information had no objection to American participation. Members of the board, however, working through "individuals in publishing houses and elsewhere" (as the board minutes relate), were able to block participation by some of the most prominent houses, including Doubleday, Viking, Random House, Simon and Schuster and Reynal and Hitchcock.

In 1944, Stout organized a group with a distinct leftist slant calling itself the Society for the Prevention of World War III, which was devoted entirely to preaching hatred and fear of the German people and the thesis that only a harsh peace would prevent them from starting a new war. Initial financial support was obtained from Robert Woods Bliss, former ambassador to Argentina, privately channeled through the Brookings Institution of Washington. Friedrich W. Foerster, a 74-year-old German educator and writer who had spent most of his life in Switzerland since the early twenties, served as a figurehead for publicity purposes. Stout, as president, managed operations of the group, which included the most active members of the Writers War Board and a number of other writers, journalists and radio broadcasters who approved the Morgenthau-Vansittart ideas.

With no governmental liaison, the society was free to make open attacks on individuals and groups that opposed its policy. Its principal target was the Council for a Democratic Germany, a group of anti-Nazi Germans who had fled from the Hitler regime and who sought a democratic restoration of Germany after the war. This council was under the sponsorship of the American Association for a Democratic Germany, headed by Dean Christian Gauss of Princeton University and composed of prominent Americans. Aware of plans being made by the council for an initial public statement of purpose, the society issued a violent denunciation by Stout at the same time which, aided by press knowhow, successfully blanketed the council's announcement. Newspapers throughout the country carried Stout's assertion that "the 'salvage Germany' campaign is in full swing," and that "no one loyal to victory should help in the manufacture of a device for Germany's escape." The council's statement of purpose got little attention. Throughout the war, Stout and his group incessantly attacked this organization which, while strongly anti-Nazi, proposed a peace policy not governed by vindictiveness.

Through the numerous contacts of the Writers War Board, the "society" obtained much time on the air. Its speakers were on nine radio programs in less than two months in the fall of 1944. Most were on coast-to-coast networks. They appeared on the influential film news feature, *The March of Time*, produced by *Time* magazine.

137

All such presentations plugged the theme that only a harsh peace could prevent a war-thirsty Germany from starting a new war, for which it was already preparing.

12

Vindictiveness Becomes Policy

The propaganda for a hard peace was stepped up in the fall of 1944 as the Morgenthau ideas on the treatment of Germany became in effect national policy.* The "Morgenthau plan" proposed large-scale destruction of industry throughout Germany, with the complete dismantling and permanent removal of the principal industries of the Ruhr. Germany, the industrial heart of Europe, was to be reduced to a country "primarily pastoral" in nature. This plan, the philosophy of which was to be so disastrous to all Europe, was adopted by Roosevelt and Churchill at Quebec, September 15.

The plan saw its beginning as early as 1943, stemming from Harry Dexter White, Morgenthau's right-hand man in the Treasury, later to be identified by the chief of the Federal Bureau of Investigation as an active agent of Soviet espionage.[2]

These early proposals, which called for the destruction of German industry, had been tentatively approved by the President at the time.[3] The State Department's original prospective for postwar Germany was completed July 31, 1944. It envisaged no large-scale permanent impairment of all German industry, and on the contrary provided for rapid reconstruction and rehabilitation of war-torn areas, with eventual integration of Germany into the world economy to hasten European reconstruction. When Morgenthau got hold of this, he made a hurried trip to England with White to see American officials engaged in planning for postwar Germany and persuade them of the desirability of a harsh program. From General Eisenhower he got the emphatic declaration that Germany should "stew in its own juice" for several months after the Allied entry.[4]

A preliminary handbook to guide military government in Germany had been drawn up. It was moderate in tone and proposed a lenient occupation instead of continuing the war after the shooting

*Morgenthau himself had been voted, in a poll of 52 leading Washington correspondents, as the second "least useful" government official in the capital.[1]

stopped. It encouraged friendly soldier contacts with Germans and envisaged a gradual recovery of German industry. Morgenthau brought this back to Roosevelt, who, incensed by its moderate tone, ordered that it be recalled. In a sharp memorandum to Secretary of War Henry L. Stimson on August 26, Roosevelt said the German people must have it "driven home to them" that they had all been engaged in a "lawless conspiracy against the decencies of modern civilization." If they needed food "to keep body and soul together" they could be fed from army soup kitchens, "and they will remember that experience all their lives." It would make them "hesitate to start any new war." "Too many people" believed the whole German people were not responsible for what had happened.[5]

Roosevelt took Morgenthau to the Quebec conference to present his plan to Churchill. Violently opposed at first, the Prime Minister was apparently won over by a promise of six and a half billion dollars worth of credits at a time when England was hard-pressed financially. Although Morgenthau denied to Stimson that the loan had been agreed upon before the plan was approved, his diaries reveal that an oral promise had been previously made.[6]

Secretary of State Hull was not asked to Quebec. Although his own proposals for a postwar policy would have held Germany to a subsistence level, he read a copy of the Quebec agreement with "stupefaction." Secretary of War Stimson told the President the plan was "an open confession of the bankruptcy of hope for a reasonable economic and political settlement of the causes of the war." Its execution, he said, would be "a crime against civilization itself." Despite efforts to keep the agreement secret, its provisions leaked to the press where it was generally denounced with both Morgenthau and the President the objects of widespread attack.

The President then told Stimson he must have signed the document without much thought. Convinced, according to Stimson, that he had made a "false step,"[7] Roosevelt attempted to back away. At a press conference, he denied that any basic differences existed in the cabinet on treatment of Germany, and said that every story which had been published was essentially untrue in its basic facts. The press was given to understand that nothing had really been agreed upon, and the whole subject of permanent occupation policy was still under review by a cabinet committee of Hull, Stimson and Morgenthau.

That the President had signed the agreement without much thought is difficult to reconcile with the evidence of his extensive consideration and apparent approval of the plan before Quebec. Over the Labor Day weekend, Roosevelt had discussed an early version of the plan with Morgenthau at the latter's home and had added items of his own.[8] The plan, as approved at Quebec, had been gone over thoroughly with the President at two meetings of the cabinet committee on occupation policy, Secretaries Stimson, Hull and Morgenthau. Stimson expressed to the President his "unalterable opposition." Hull, whose ideas at first almost paralleled those of Morgenthau except for destruction of the Ruhr, modified his stand and eventually opposed the plan.

The President, Morgenthau related, had been "hungry" to obtain material which he could show Churchill at Quebec, and assured the Treasury secretary of full support for his program.[9] "As far as I'm concerned," he told Morgenthau, "I'd put Germany back as an agricultural country."[10] Secretary of the Navy James Forrestal wrote that the President himself proposed the plan at a cabinet meeting following one of his weekly luncheons with Morgenthau.[11]

Elmer Davis, director of the Office of War Information, called a press conference a week after the Morgenthau plan was approved to announce that Roosevelt had taken occupation policy into his own hands before Quebec, finding the early occupation manual too soft. Dismantling of industry had already been decided upon, and the policy would be a hard one as a precaution against Germany starting a new war.[12]

Indeed, the essentials of the Morgenthau plan, except for the permanent elimination of industry in the Ruhr (and the Saar), had already become official policy. White had obtained a preliminary Joint Chiefs of Staff occupation directive upon which the recalled moderate handbook was based, and had revised it so completely as to reverse the spirit of the original and incorporate most of the Morgenthau ideas. With the Morgenthau influence this was approved by the Joint Chiefs on September 22. Changes were later made at the instigation of the Treasury Department to render it more harsh.[13] Stimson wrote that continuous pressure in this direction was exerted throughout the winter. In the words of the Senate Internal Security Subcommittee, the Departments of State and War were made "virtually subservient to the Treasury" in planning for the occupation of Germany.[14] After Yalta, Morgenthau blocked an effort by the Department of State to reduce the harshness of the directive. Roosevelt, asked at this time by his son-in-law if he wanted the Germans to starve, was quoted by Morgenthau as replying, "Why not?"[15] Thus the propaganda for a harsh and punitive peace, which filled the press and radio to the end of the war and long afterward, was a reflection of the actual policy of the President.

Hull had warned Roosevelt before Quebec that any connection with the proposed Morgenthau plan would be bad political medicine in an election year. The press reaction after Quebec had confirmed this. The election was only a month away, and a new façade which did not involve the administration was needed. The Morgenthau-organized Writers War Board went into a huddle and set about attempts to remove administration identification from the plan while at the same time vigorously promoting the plan itself.

How readily the radio cooperated in this effort may be illustrated by a description of a nationwide broadcast on "America's Town Meeting of the Air."[16] A program had already been arranged as a discussion of the "Morgenthau Plan," the term universally used in the press, but the Blue Network obligingly eliminated the Morgenthau name and changed the title to "Should the Allies Change Germany from an Industrial to an Agricultural Nation?" The broadcast moderator obligingly assured the audience that the plan was now "without a father." Rex Stout, chairman of the Writers War Board and chief speaker, said that ascribing the plan to Morgenthau was "vicious nonsense" seeking to discredit Morgenthau and the administration, but at the same time declared it was necessary if another war was to be prevented. A Harvard Law professor similarly denied Morgenthau authorship, but urged the plan was needed "to give our grandchildren a chance."

The discussion was stacked by the selection of participants. Of two speakers presumably against the plan, Dr. Christian Gauss, dean of Princeton University, actually opposed it. The other was Sigrid Schultz, author of the fantastic book, *Germany Will Try It Again*, which the board was assiduously promoting. Her "opposition" consisted of proposing to destroy so much industry that 12 percent of the German population would be switched to farms. Rigorous export and import controls would be placed on the industry remaining, and all German mails would be censored for an indefinite period to find out where the Germans had hidden "loot" and were working for a "renewed attempt at world conquest."

The idea that the Germans would seek a new war after losing the current conflict was increasingly reiterated in the press. The Germans' hope, said the *Philadelphia Record*, July 6, "is to salvage enough out of this war to give Germany a base for preparing for World War III which they hope to win." By fall the idea had progressed to the notion that the Germans were already making such preparations. The leading article in the *New York Times Sunday Magazine*, August 8, 1944, headlined "The Nazis Dig in for World War III," asserted that planes probably were waiting to take Nazi leaders to other countries to work for the revival of Nazism, and it might "take generations" to cope with them. On the "American Forum of the Air," September 12, Dr. L. M. Birkhead, national director of the Friends of Democracy, said that "as a nation" Germany should be removed from the map.

The *New York Herald-Tribune*, on September 20, front-paged a story beginning, "The German high command, realizing that it has lost the second world war, . . . is already laying plans to fight a third world war with the hope of eventually attaining leadership of the world." The Writers War Board distributed this and similar journalistic products widely to press and radio. On *The March of Time*, film feature of *Time* magazine regularly shown from coast to coast, Sumner Welles, Lord Vansittart and the Writers War Board's right-hand columnist, Walter Winchell, warned that a stern policy was necessary to thwart German preparations for another world war.

From London, the correspondent of the *New York Times* wrote that Germany had started three wars in 83 years to dominate the world, and warned that the "virus of Prussianism" must be "bred out of her people." Large seizures of German territory would be made and 11,000,000 Germans would be expelled. Germany, existing "largely as an agricultural state," would be made to "pay dearly" for her crimes.[17]

James B. Conant, president of Harvard University, in effect espoused the Morgenthau philosophy in a New York speech October 7. "Drastic changes" had to be made in Germany's industry and much "redistribution of Germany" would be required, even though it meant "reorientation of the economic balance of the world."

The public was bombarded with arguments for a harsh peace to keep Germany from supposedly starting a new war. The extent of acceptance of this proposition in the press may be illustrated by the support given to it in a ten-day period by the widely respected *Christian Science Monitor*, a newspaper noted for its temperate and humane approach to the news. The *Monitor* published Conant's speech in full, November 1, and followed it a few days later by a special editorial page article by D. F. Fleming, professor of international relations at Vanderbilt University, asserting that Germany should be occupied for 30 or 40 years. This was accompanied by a cartoon showing Uncle Sam with a club, standing guard over "German Generals" inspecting "Plans for Third World War." The next day, the *Monitor* carried a front-page article by a former Greek government official, under a three-column headline, asserting that the current war was an integral part of Germany's "hundred-years war for the domination of the world."

On November 9, a *Monitor* front-page story proclaimed that the Germans were preparing to carry on the war from South America. A three-column headline said, "Nazis Speed Secret Weapons and War plans to Argentina." These weapons and plans, accompanied by technicians, were supposedly being transported by submarine. The authority for this bizarre tale was "responsible Argentines," which, it developed on further reading, were a single professor from a provincial Argentine University.

The story of the war from Argentina took hold and was repeated and expanded in the press generally. By December 14, the *Washington Star* was reporting that Spain was also being used in the new war plans. German money and materials were being shipped from Spain to Argentina as the "embryo of the new German war machine." Although the source of the *Star*'s story was a Soviet embassy bulletin, reprinting an article from the organ of Soviet trade unions, it was given a two-column headline on page one. An article on the *Washington Post* editorial page asserted that the German SS had incorporated units from other countries in plans to convert the organization into an international body and send it "underground" on a worldwide scale.[18] The public also read that underground warfare was to be conducted in Germany after the expected surrender. An Associated Press dispatch from an occupied German town reported that sabotage and guerrilla warfare was to be waged by partisan groups organized by districts, while a propaganda campaign was to be carried on by 200,000 Nazi followers in Europe and elsewhere. Picked troops already had been established in underground strongholds in the Austrian, Bavarian and Italian Alps. The story was "pieced together from information available from various sources."[19] Listeners to "America's Town Meeting of the Air" were told that three thousand German scientists had been placed abroad and were already at work devising new instruments of destruction for another war.[20]

The drums of hate beat incessantly. The United Nations Information Service issued a statement charging that the Germans were systematically starving children in occupied countries in a deliberate attempt to reduce their populations. It was asserted that a German field marshal had proposed this so that Germany would have twice the population of its neighbors. "Child Destruction, Axis Total War Sin," said the two-column headline in the *Washington Post*.[21]

But concern for children was limited if they were German children. On a nationwide radio forum the question was whether all Germans should be punished for Nazi atrocities, and the chief proponent urged the deportation of all German men between 20 and 40 years old. Admitting that this would punish millions of innocent children, he defended the proposal by asserting that these children were the "potential soldiers of World War III." Air listeners were asked to give their views by mail, and 53 percent of those holding an opinion voted for punishing all Germans. On the same program another speaker urged sentencing from two to three million Germans to hard labor. Dorothy Thompson, a widely syndicated columnist who did not subscribe to the idea of all Germans being bad, nevertheless would have executed 160,000 war criminals.[22]

While American soldiers fought to make Germans surrender, American propaganda was thus spelling out for them how disastrous that surrender would be. A Senate subcommittee on war mobilization got behind the principles of the Morgenthau plan, recommending that not only Germany's war industries but all its metallurgical and chemical industries be dismantled and removed to other countries. It proposed to punish 10,000 "imperialist-minded" German industrialists, along with the confiscation of all overseas assets.[23] "U.S. Seen for Ruthless Reich Control," said a *Washington Post* headline, December 13. The story, from London, reported plans for "complete and ruthless" abolition of German war industry, strict control of the economy, elimination of the aviation industry and the prospect of slave labor for the benefit of Russia.

This propaganda of vengeance helped open the American mind to harsh treatment of the German people, but it did not aid American soldiers in the battle line. From its announcement, the slogan of unconditional surrender—which army psychological experts considered a mistake—had given great support to Goebbels, the German propaganda chief, in strengthening the morale of the German army and people.[24] The Morgenthau plan provided him with more ammunition. General George C. Marshall pointed out to Morgenthau that his plan did not help in the American front lines, where loudspeakers were calling on German soldiers to surrender.[25] Every night in the fall of 1944 the German radio exhorted the people to fight and die rather than to permit the nation to be enslaved and turned into an agricultural state.[26]

But with Morgenthau in the saddle, and vengeance the cry, the cost in American lives was secondary. How many were lost thereby can only be guessed from the increasing desperation with which the Germans fought. German generals interviewed after the war were unanimous in testifying that the unconditional surrender policy enabled the Nazi government to keep the troops and people fighting long after they were ready to give up.[27] Interrogation of German prisoners in March 1945, revealed that their fierce last-ditch resistance had been motivated by fear of what would happen to them and their families in defeat.[28]

Yet their desperate stand appeared to be beyond American understanding. Ernie Pyle, Pulitzer Prize winner and correspondent for the *New York Telegram* and nearly 400 other daily newspapers, ascribed it to "inhuman bullheadedness." Such continued resistance would "so infuriate the world" that Germany was "apt to be committing national suicide."[29] Enemy resistance was presented in a manner to increase hatred, and as illustrating the unsavory qualities which Allied propaganda had attributed to Germans generally.

According to an Associated Press dispatch, some of the German prisoners taken were only 12 years old and had been "thrown into the front lines with guns and told to keep shooting."[30] But the battlefield desperation of German youth was ascribed by the *New York Times* to "unleashed savagery," resulting from its indoctrination with "treachery and murder."[31]

That the German people intended to start a new war when possible had become increasingly necessary propaganda throughout 1944 as the people had been progressively disillusioned about the Atlantic Charter while the war was intensifying. The original promises of a peace of freedom and justice to all, with no territorial seizures, were now washed up. No peace was to be considered, even though it included the complete overthrow of the Hitler regime, unless it was by unconditional surrender. When that was brought about, the victors proposed large seizures of territory and the ruthless driving of millions of people from their homelands, with punitive treatment of the conquered into an indefinite future. War for such an end had to be justified by fear of what would happen otherwise.

The undersecretary of war, Robert P. Patterson, now asserted there was "definite proof" that the Germans were planning a new war.[32] Patterson's statement provided official authority for the idea that Morgenthau-like treatment was essential. The managing editor of the *New York Times* wrote that such plans had to be stopped or all the effort against Hitler would be a useless sacrifice.[33] An "iron hand" had to be maintained on the Reich "to guarantee the inability of Germany to do her dirty work again."

On March 30, when German surrender was obviously only a matter of time, the Department of State put its imprimatur on the thesis that Germany was planning another war in a lengthy statement and nationwide broadcast, warning against alleged Nazi plans which would constitute a "constant menace to postwar peace and security" unless checked by the "peace-loving" nations. It was a curious product. No proof was offered. Stripped to their specific content, the alleged plans were innocuous, but the department's interpretation was interwoven so closely with its charges that, on cursory reading, it appeared to be an integral part. With the invidious interpretation removed, the "plans" were to:

—Renew commercial friendships in foreign countries to reinstate trade.
—Appeal to the courts in foreign countries to prevent unlawful property seiures by the victors; failing this, to repurchase the seized properties by means of local corporations of persons who met citizenship requirements.
—Offer technical and scientific help at low cost to industrial firms, and help in construction of technical schools and laboratories.
—Attempt to soften the expected harsh peace terms by pleas for fair treatment of Germans.

According to the Department of State, all this amounted to "well-arranged postwar plans for the perpetuation of Nazi doctrines and domination." If the Germans sought to renew commercial friendships, said the department, the object would be to restore cartels. Attempts in the courts to prevent unlawful seizure of German foreign properties were obviously iniquitous. Assistance to technical schools and laboratories in other countries would "afford the Germans an excellent opportunity to design and perfect new weapons." Efforts to soften harsh peace terms through what the department termed a "subtle" plea for fair treatment would have as their object "giving rebirth to all Nazi doctrines and furthering German ambitions for world domination."

Although the department cannily refrained from outright assertion that the Germans were compounding another war, the press filled in the gap. The *New York Times'* headline on the story was, "Nazis' Blueprint of New War Bared." *Time* reported on April 9 that allied officials had "solid evidence" of Nazi plans to carry on in Germany from secret arsenals. Thousands of specially trained Nazis would work illegally at home to sabotage the peace, while highly-trained agents would operate in other countries.

All this supported the claim that Germany had to be laid prostrate and kept so if the world was to be safe.

13

The War Ends, But Not the Frenzy

As the end of the war apparently neared in early 1945, ordinary pragmatism would have dictated abandoning efforts to promote hatred of the enemy if only to smooth the way for the victors to govern the conquered country. This was the course adopted by the Soviet. Even before Germany capitulated, Stalin on April 12 halted the ferocious anti-German output of Ilya Ehrenberg, the chief Soviet propagandist. With specific Soviet political objectives achieved, further hate propaganda was not merely useless but an impediment.

The American objective, however, other than creating an international organization of the victors, appeared to be insuring home support for a postwar policy of vengeance. The means to do so was certainly at hand: the American people were becoming aware of the horrors of Nazi concentration and extermination camps uncovered by the advancing troops. Press coverage of these horrors was extensive, with ghastly photographs, but the administration feared that this would not rouse vengeance fever to the desired pitch, and the War Department flew special delegations of members of Congress and leading newspaper editors to see the camps firsthand and provide greater publicity. Moving picture theaters treated their audiences to scenes of terribly emaciated prison inmates and piles of skeletons. Exhibits of photographs from the camps were held in various cities with large publicity. The resulting augmentation of hatred toward all Germans because of the Nazi atrocities tended to occupy the public mind, which was becoming progressively disillusioned with the dispositions of the Yalta conference.

Americans were told that such atrocities had been possible only with the approval of the entire German people. In the United States, where the press was not gagged and the freedom of individuals was relatively unfettered, this seemed to many a reasonable argument. Years later, a different picture could be presented. A correspondent for a leading London newspaper, covering a German trial of Germans charged in such crimes, could write:

> Yet, all in all, it was a ferociously guarded secret—in a gagged country in time of war—and I can believe that the mass of the Germans knew nothing of the extermination camps.[1]

But in the spring of 1945 any such suggestion was cried down. The mood of the mass was that of General Eisenhower in his VE Day broadcast, May 8, when he said the German nation had "eagerly absorbed" Hitler's "deliberate design of brutal, worldwide rape." Within six years, he was to assure the Germans themselves that he believed in their "freedom-loving quality," but that was after the cold war with the USSR had progressed to the Korean War and German help to contain the Soviet in Europe was wanted.

On the evening of VE Day, the nationwide radio program, "America's Forum of the Air," was given over largely to the espousal of vengeance. The moderator told his audience that the "vindictiveness, treachery and out-and-out enmity" of even German children posed a danger to occupation troops. The chief speaker was Louis Nizer, of Stout's Society for the Prevention of World War III. He was introduced as a man whose recent book had been made required reading for General Eisenhower's staff. He proposed that the Allies "re-educate" the Germans primarily by simply acting as conquerors, prohibiting all heavy industry and demanding forced labor as reparations. Mark Van Doren, professor of literature at Columbia University and also a member of the Society, proposed that re-education should consist of putting all German schools under the United Nations and just making Germans obey orders.

Prominent persons, otherwise presumably sane, demanded wholesale bloody vengeance. Joseph Pulitzer, publisher of the *St. Louis Post-Dispatch*, told a Carnegie Hall meeting arranged by Stout's society that punishing the guilty would require the execution of approximately a million and a half Germans. The guilty, "with no differentiation as to the degree of their guilt," should be shot. Germany should be occupied by the victors for at least one and possibly two generations, with the Germans put "on parole."[2]

Describing demands for a harsh peace (which it did not approve) the *United States News* on May 18 thus paraphrased the hard-line clamor:

> The Nazis must be murdered—every one of them. The Germans must be reeducated in the schools and colleges, in their books, films and radio. We must teach them a lesson and take away all their tools and machinery and keep them helpless for generations to come. If they starve for lack of food, it is

no more than they deserve. For didn't they tolerate Hitler and acquiesce in his cruelties?

Hatred was directed against German prisoners in the United States, even with the war over. Inasmuch as the Germans had permitted American prisoners to see American movies, the War Department had proposed that the film industry, having no German picture, make available American films with German dialogue dubbed in. The personal reaction of motion picture heads, as reported by the weekly organ of the entertainment industry, was "Let's give them rat poison instead."[3] In the early days of the American occupation, German prisoners in one camp were deliberately kept on a starvation diet by the commandant. At another camp Americans used Nazi torture devices to make prisoners confess misdeeds.[4]

A few voices attempted to counter the demand for vengeance. Robert M. Hutchins, president of the University of Chicago, in a speech to his students, deplored "the glee with which the most inhuman proposals are brought forward and the evident pleasure with which they are received by our fellow citizens."[5] Hutchins urged that Germany be treated "with justice and, if possible, with mercy. Otherwise we lay here and now the foundations of the next war. . . . Let us remember that vengeance is the Lord's."

"We must administer justice," urged David Lawrence in *United States News*. "We must repair, reconstruct, rehabilitate. . . . This is the real way to reeducate and reconvert human beings and to build firmly the foundation of human brotherhood which is so essential to lasting peace. . . . We shall hurt ourselves far more than we shall hurt the Germans if we give the brutish passions of vengeance within us full sway and become cynical of reason and justice."[6]

Frederick J. Libby, the Quaker who headed the National Council for the Prevention of War, pointed out that the victims of vengeance would not be the persons who had committed atrocities, but mostly men and boys whose only crime had been that they were born in Germany.

The nation, however, was hypnotized by hatred and the idea that Germany was making plans for another war. Senator Harley M. Kilgore, chairman of the war mobilization subcommittee of the Senate Military Affairs Committee, returned from Europe with the assertion that the Germans had "already conceived vicious plans for a third attempt at world conquest." These plans, according to "secret documents" which he did not identify, had supposedly been in the works since 1944.[7]

This propaganda was advanced by testimony before Senator Kilgore's subcommittee in hearings concerned with "the economic basis of German aggression." Bernard Baruch, former Roosevelt confidant and official adviser to James F. Byrnes, Director of War Mobilization, urged that Germany heavy industry be destroyed or removed to other countries. He proposed that, in addition to the Nazis and members of the Gestapo, the "war industrialists" and "war financiers" be sent to Russia for forced labor as reparations. If these things were not done, he said, "we face the certainty that Germany will make a third try to conquer the world. The *New York Times* placed Baruch's prescription for conquered Germany at the top of page one, and gave it two columns.[8]

This notion had become a fixation even in the American Intelligence division of supreme allied headquarters. At one time, the extermination of the entire general staff had been proposed as a preventive. In July, the idea was dropped by the United States group in the Allied Control Council for Germany, but a plan was substituted under which not only the general staff but about 10,000 field commanders and young staff officers who had gone into field service would be exiled to Russia, the United States and elsewhere. There they would be kept under constant surveillance to prevent them from scheming for a new war.[9] This plan in turn was abandoned, but it showed how widely the fantastic notion had taken root.

The press kept it alive. In August, *Atlantic's* leading article was "Germany's Third Try," a Vansittart piece solemnly asserting that the Nazis had plans for going "underground," especially in neutral countries, to prepare for the new war, which only harsh and prolonged occupation would prevent. The Associated Press reported that unnamed "Washington officials" who were charged with planning occupation administration believed that Nazi key men might have been planted in concentration camps to be in a strategic position to gain Allied confidence in preparation for the new war.[10] *The Stars and Stripes*, a newspaper published for the armed forces, sought to perpetuate the myth among the soldiers. On July 11, it carried a story that the Germans had already set in motion plans for a third world war.

How widely the ideas of Secretary Morgenthau had taken hold was illustrated by the reception given to his book, *Germany is Our Problem*, in October 1945, five months after the war against Germany had ended. This book—publication of which, Morgenthau said, had been approved by the President the night before he died, and for which Roosevelt had written an introduction—was an expansion of the Quebec plan, with modifications such as giving the Saar to France to accord with the Potsdam dispositions. Five million Germans to be expelled on destruction of the Ruhr industries would be replaced by French, British and Dutch, who would conduct a limited economic life under close supervision by the United Nations. Forced labor would be required under the command of the victors. Industrial plants throughout Germany would be seized as reparations, in addition to all foreign assets, as agreed at Potsdam. All this was to prevent Germany from starting a new war, for, said Morgenthau, the desire for war had been as firmly planted in the German as the desire for freedom in the American.

The War Department, while denying that this ferocious, ignorant and puerile book was actually to be used as a guide, sent several hundred copies to the staffs of all major commanders in Europe.[11] It was hailed in much of the press as enlightened and far-seeing. The reviewer in the Sunday *New York Times* said: "If we read and profit by Mr. Morgenthau's warning we should be able to prevent that third world war for which we know preparations have already been made." To another approving reviewer in the daily *Times*, Morgenthau demonstrated ". . . that Germany's will to war is unchanged." A reviewer for the *Washington Star*, said the book proved Morgenthau to be "not only an acute economist but also a statesman of broad vision."

In the *Washington Post*, a reviewer called the book a "powerful, prophetic study" which would make history. The reviewer for the *Survey Graphic* said: "It would be difficult to find any real flaw in Mr. Morgenthau's argument." In *Foreign Affairs*, a reviewer wrote that "advocates of a soft peace" must admit that the Morgenthau approach was "not motivated by revenge." Readers of the *American Political Science Review* were assured that there was nothing "vindictive" in the plan. The reviewer in the *Saturday Review of Literature* said the Morgenthau proposals "make good sense." To the reviewer in the *Christian Science Monitor*, Morgenthau's proposals were "humane, sensible and entirely free from vengeful sentiments."

14

Occupation as Revenge

While Morgenthau had not been able to gain approval for closing down the Ruhr and making Germany into a nation of farmers, he got his general ideas into the occupation directive, JCS 1067, which went to General Eisenhower in April 1945, just before the war ended. Germans, though conquered, were still to be treated as enemies. The occupation was directed to "take no steps looking toward the economic rehabilitation of Germany or designed to maintain or strengthen the German economy" except in general where necessary to prevent disease and insure order and to enforce a program of reparations. German consumption was to be held to a "minimum," so that "surpluses" could be used by the occupation, displaced persons, Allied prisoners of war or reparations.

Pending Allied agreement on details, the occupation was to embark on a general program of destroying, or removing for reparations, numerous categories of industrial plants and equipment, especially those producing merchant ships, synthetic rubber and oil, aluminum and magnesium. Where there was any doubt as to whether any industry was permitted, it was to be resolved in favor of destruction. All German courts were to be closed and reopened under occupation control after Nazi personnel were removed. All educational institutions were to be closed, with reopening of lower schools authorized after suitable denazification. Secondary schools and higher institutions were to be reopened under an interim program if they offered training immediately useful to the occupation.

Not only were Nazis and Nazi "believers" to be removed from government and any important private employment; numerous categories were to be arrested, including police officers above the rank of lieutenant and all mayors, even of villages, or persons of equivalent rank. Persons holding key positions in civic and economic organizations, industry, commerce, agriculture, finance, education, the judiciary and the press and publishing houses were likewise to be arrested, as it was "generally assumed in the absence of evidence to the contrary" that they were Nazis or sympathizers. The occupation was to be "aloof" and fraternization with German officials and people was barred.

The terms of the directive so shocked the advisers of General Lucius D. Clay, deputy commander in chief for military government, that one was dispatched to Washington in an attempt to obtain a modification. Unsuccessful, he finally resigned.[1]

The directive itself was kept highly secret for months. While the military government was not even permitted to acknowledge its existence, Washington vainly attempted to get the other victors to adopt it as policy. When in October the military government was permitted to make it known, General Clay, himself then a hard-liner, flew to Washington to urge modification of its unworkable terms. This attempt, however, like the previous staff protest, ended in failure. Although President Truman and other high officials conceded that drastic changes were needed, the tide of popular frenzy against the Germans barred alteration.

At the Potsdam conference in July, despite President Truman's statement that the Morgenthau plan was dead, the Morgenthau philosophy underlying the directive was further solidified as the basis of the treatment of Germany. Much of Germany's industrial plant was to be destroyed or carried off by the victors. Even factories making peacetime products were to be dismantled to hold general output down to a permitted low level. All industry, finance, and even scientific bodies and research and experimental institutions were to be controlled. The victors were to seize all external assets. In addition to industrial plants in the zone alloted to it, Russia was to get 15 percent of those removed from other zones in exchange for commodities from its zone, plus 10 percent more without balancing payments. Although actual boundaries were to be drawn at a "peace conference," the new Communist Poland was in effect permitted to keep seized German territory substantially in excess of that awarded at Yalta. A wave of German suicides followed the Potsdam agreements, more than 2,500 persons taking their lives within four days.[2]

Enforcement of this harsh program required that the occupation troops believe in it. Early in the war the army had begun building hatred of Germans along with a favorable view of Soviet Russia by means of specially prepared films. According to General George C. Marshall, such films had been made to show the causes of the war and the principles for which the nation was fighting, as knowledge of the facts was an indispensable part of military training. The facts, of course, were interpreted. In *The Nazis Strike*, the 1939 deal between Hitler and Stalin was portrayed as a Soviet move to gain time to prepare for defense against Germany, and tests showed it as effective in raising hatred.[3]

Another film, *Prelude to War*, brought 62 percent to the belief that in Germany "all children are taken away from parents shortly after they are born and raised by the government." The film assumed that Germany would, if possible, attempt to conquer the United States, and after seeing it, 83 percent believed that if the Nazis were successful in this they would close all the churches and make everyone worship Hitler. After seeing *Battle of Britain*, 76 percent agreed that British refusal to surrender had "probably kept American cities from being bombed by the Germans."

In late 1944, hatred was taught to the troops with prefabricated lectures. Discussion leaders were supplied with quotations from Vansittart and others of similar views to imbue the soldiers with a belief in the general malevolence and depravity of the people they were to conquer and police.

As the actual occupation approached, indoctrination films pictured Germany as a chronic starter of wars, and urged soldiers not to shake hands with Germans because their hands had been held up to Hitler. Specially prepared radio shows, with the use of hypothetical "typical" German individuals, endeavored to show that all Germans were malignant. "All Germans are guilty," said the announcer on one such show. "Show no friendliness to any of them. Give them no greeting, don't speak to them. They are your enemies."

Whatever temporary success all this effort had in building hatred among the occupation troops, it didn't last long for most of them. The occupation started right out arresting and reporting for court martial soldiers who violated the anti-fraternization order. In June, the military police arrested a thousand offenders and reported them for court martial, but the job was impossible. The GI attitude was reflected by a scrawl under a non-fraternization sign on the autobahn: "This don't mean me, buddy." In September, trials of offenders were abandoned.

The official ban on fraternization continued, although somewhat relaxed, and not until the end of the following year were Americans permitted to enter a German movie theater or vice versa. But most American soldiers soon came to regard the defeated Germans as simply human beings rather than scoundrels. Hard-liners at home deplored the tendency. Illustrative of this view was a *New York Times* correspondent's complaint of the "insidious effects" of associating with the defeated enemy, which was displayed under a two-column head at the top of page one. "Unfortunately." said the dispatch, too many American soldiers had become convinced that the Germans were "pretty decent guys after all."[4]

15

The Long Route to Sanity

The occupation was based on the premise that all Germans were collectively guilty of starting the war and of the Hitler regime's atrocities. Moreover, the nation loved war and was only waiting for a new chance to dominate the world by force. Germans had to be punished and politically re-educated, and while this was going on they had to be kept militarily powerless for an indefinite future. This meant they had to be rendered economically impotent. For occupation purposes Germany was divided among the victors and in cities and towns already partly or largely rubble, they proceeded with dismantling or destroying the means of production as agreed at Potsdam.

The American denazification policy—far more rigid than those of the other powers—hampered such production as was still being carried on in the American zone. Thirty-three categories of persons were subject to arrest, mostly because of membership in any of the numerous Nazi organizations, sometimes even including such persons as charwomen in Nazi offices.[1] Every German over 18 had to fill out a *fragebogen* with 131 questions. They dealt not only with actual Nazi affiliation, but also with whether he had belonged to a university fraternity, what his earnings had been, whether he or even his grandparents had held any title of nobility, whether he owned land, and numerous other matters related to the occupation's assumption that anyone of property or standing was a Nazi sympathizer unless proven otherwise.

The discharge of teachers in schools in the American zone ranged from 35 to 50 percent, resulting in classes ranging as high as 80 students. Trained railroad workers were discharged and replaced by unskilled personnel until the necessity of keeping the trains running compelled their reinstatement. Under the terms of the occupation directive, persons in important positions were generally assumed *ipso facto* to be Nazi sympathizers. As an instance of the controlling philosophy, the manager of the Opel automobile works near Berlin had refused to join the Nazi party, but his plant had produced military trucks and he was therefore discharged and blacklisted by the Americans. He worked at a service station until the British, less concerned with hypothetical assumptions about political sympathies, made him head of the Volkswagen plant in their zone. American authorities in Berlin barred Dr. William Furtwaengler from returning to his post as director of the Berlin Philharmonic orchestra because of alleged Nazi sympathies. Many persons discharged from substantial positions by the Americans were hired by their allies.

The tone of the American occupation was illustrated by General Eisenhower in Frankfort: "I say let Germany find out what it means to start a war."[2] American officers were not permitted to return the salutes of Germans in uniform, and the general policy of humiliating the conquered enemy found expression in innumerable actions and restrictions which relegated Germans to an inferior status.

When the occupation began, the food ration in the American zone was 900 to 1,000 calories. It was reported that more than half the babies born in Berlin in August died of starvation. In November, Washington decided that food would be sent to Germany to prevent starvation and disorder. The ration target was raised to 1,550 calories, but it fell to 1,275 a few months later, and even that was greater than the ration in the British zone. Coal miners' rations were raised of necessity because the men in their weakened condition could not produce enough fuel for the military, but little coal went to Germans. In the desperate winter of 1945-46, with their numbers swelled by millions of refugees expelled from their former homes, Germans crowded unheated railway stations, bunkers and bombed ruins for shelter.

Professor Karl Brandt, stationed with the food and agriculture branch of the office of military government, wrote that unless the situation was improved "the few buds of democracy will be burned out in the glory of death of the aged, the women and the children."[3] The Germans, a newspaper correspondent wrote, lived in a "remorseless enervating hell of leaking roofs, unheated houses and stomachs that are never satisfied. . . . a hell in which mothers starve to feed children."[4] Senator Homer Capehart of Indiana charged that a group of vengeful fanatics within the government was trying to destroy Germany through deliberate starvation.

An American officer interrogating half-starved Germans in American prison camps said many were in the same condition as prisoners Americans had released from German concentration camps.[5] But reports of these deplorable conditions brought no change in occupation policy, based on the JCS 1067 directive and the Potsdam agreements. The wartime propaganda had been only too successful. Only the recognition of political realities to which the United States had been war-blinded would eventually force a change. They were already beginning to emerge.

Germany had been divided into four zones, each occupied by one of the victorious nations, but all to be treated as a single economic unit. The Russians soon showed that they were not going to cooperate economically, as had been agreed at Potsdam, and relations with them deteriorated steadily. In February 1946, Stalin returned in a speech to the old Communist thesis of irreconcilable conflict with the capitalistic world. Russian newspapers charged the British and Americans with training anit-soviet troops among German prisoners of war. A vast North American Soviet spy apparatus was exposed in Canada. American officers were arrested as spies in the Soviet zone of Germany. Off-course American planes were shot down in Yugoslavia.

The wartime comradeship with Russia, pasted together with secret agreements, had collapsed, and the Soviet intent to control all eastern Europe had become apparent. In 1942, Prime Minister Churchill had been willing to grant all the Soviet demands in order to get an alliance with Russia. Now, on March 5, 1946, at Fulton, Missouri, he said an iron curtain had descended across Europe from the Baltic to the Adriatic and urged British-American cooperation to stem Soviet expansion. The United States government turned to erasing the favorable image of Russia it had sought so eagerly in wartime to create. American sources revealed in Frankfort that the Department of State had acquired captured German documents showing that Stalin had offered Hitler a full military alliance in 1941, which Hitler had refused because of the size of Russian territorial demands.[6]

With all Germany a morass and hope of Soviet cooperation abandoned, the United States arranged for economic unification of the American and British zones so that food and goods could move, setting the stage for later joining by the reluctant French. Announcing it at Stuttgart in September, Secretary of State Byrnes envisaged the day when the Germans would again have their own government. It was not a soft speech. Brynes upheld the French claim to the Saar and emphasized that Germany was to be kept militarily powerless. But it gave the Germans hope and was widely attacked by die-hard adherents of the Morgenthau philosophy.

Henry Wallace, former vice president and now secretary of commerce, in a speech which President Truman apparently had carelessly approved, praised the Soviet and warned against British imperialism. Florida's Senator Pepper suggested that some people wanted to fight Russia. Sumner Welles, in the *New York Herald-Tribune*, said that leaving the determination of Germany's future to the German people, "whose mass dementia was responsible for five wars of aggression within the past eighty years," would make possible the creation of a strong unified nation which "would endanger the security of Europe and jeopardize the safety of the United States." Newspapers gave prominent space to the assertion of a London group, including Lord Vansittart, that Germany was even then comparatively more powerul than in 1939. Walter Lippmann warned against a "revival of pan-Germanism," which would come from other powers bidding for the support of Germany under any future central government.

The Society for the Prevention of World War III asserted that unless the American people spoke up, "the forces that are working for Germany's regeneration will become irresistible." Influential in the large radio network offices, this group also worked beaver-like with independent stations, sending out hundreds of scripts to keep anti-Germanism alive. It also had important contacts in Washington and in the occupation machinery, established while Morgenthau was in office, which were used for hatchet jobs on persons who sought German economic restoration. One of its victims was Professor James K. Pollock of the University of Michigan, then serving as director of the regional government coordinating office under the occupation. Assailed by the society as an advocate of a soft peace because he had urged that revived German industry was indispensable for European reconstruction, he had been forced to resign.[7]

Diehard newspapers continued the hate campaign unabated, reiterating the thesis that a revived Germany would start a new war. A *Philadelphia Inquirer* cartoon showed a sleepy American sentry being watched by a fat German boy with a knife in his belt. The shade of Hitler above the boy said "Watch him. . . and when he falls asleep. . ." Correspondents of newspapers tended to feed the public anti-German appetite by seizing upon any material adverse to the former enemy.

But the general tone of the press was beginning to change. The grip of communism now extended through the Balkans. A Communist regime ruled Hungary, where the Communists in 1945 had gotten only 17 percent of a popular vote. Greece, where Britain was pulling out, was threatened by Moscow-managed guerrilla warfare, abetted by neighboring Soviet satellites. The USSR was putting the squeeze on Turkey for a land and naval base on the Dardanelles. Powerful Communist parties in France and Italy were attempting to block economic reconstruction while the Soviet sought to prevent economic improvement in the western zones of Germany. American publications were beginning to publish such articles as "Must We Fight Russia?" Senator Gurney, chairman of the Senate Armed Forces Committee, after a survey trip to Europe recommended an immediate miliary alliance with Spanish Generalissimo Franco, formerly held up as a tool of the Nazis.[8]

The occupation stopped its anti-German propaganda. Films seeking to build hatred with the argument that all Germans were responsible for Nazi atrocities were eliminated from troop indoctrination courses. Radio broadcasts telling the Germans they all were guilty were dropped. The troops were urged to do all they could to assist the Germans in reestablishing their country and their economy. [9] At home, official propaganda also changed. The public was now permitted to learn facts about the Soviet hitherto carefully suppressed. In February 1947,[10] it was revealed that American flyers forced to land near Vladivostok in 1944 had been imprisoned, some for more than a year. Planes making emergency landings, obviously friendly, had been attacked and seized. At one time there had been 131 Americans in closely guarded Soviet prison camps.

But the stripping of wartime varnish from Russia was slow in bringing fundamental change in the policy toward Germany. Dismantling of factories went on, and a network of controls minimized production in untouched plants. Germany always had to buy food and materials abroad, but imports, hampered by the lack of a sound currency, were also restricted by occupation edict. Vast numbers of people were still being subjected to minute denazification proceedings. In January 1947, with 450 tribunals working on denazification, 200,000 cases had been tried and 370,000 Nazis had been removed from their jobs, but there were still 1,300,000 to be heard.[11] As late as the fall of 1947, thousands of Germans who had never been tried or even indicted, and whose only proven crimes were the holding of good positions, were in prison camps. Even Germans with unquestioned anti-Nazi records found it almost impossible, two years after the war, to travel outside their own country.[12]

The 1946-47 winter was one of the coldest in history. Schools were closed and three-fourths of the industries in the American and British zones were closed down. No coal had been delivered to Germans for heating since October, and Germans followed carts delivering coal to the occupiers to pick up any pieces that fell off. In Berlin, two hundred people froze to death.

A newspaper dispatch thus described existing American policy:

> The Americans have approached Germany with enough confusion of purpose in themselves to perpetuate confusion in the German minds for considerably longer than the occupation lasts. We wanted to do the mutually exclusive things: to bring and hold the Germans down to an impossibly low level of economic life (which in this case meant also spiritual and moral life) and to rehabilitate them along democratic lines. And even in that sorry formula, the emphasis was where it should not have been, on the former instead of the latter part.[13]

With all Europe seemingly on the verge of economic collapse, to the benefit of communism, it had at last become necessary to accept that Germany was, in fact as well as phrase, the industrial heart of Europe, and that without its recovery there could be no real recovery elsewhere. President Truman saw that drastic changes in policy toward Germany were essential if Europe was to be rescued. But any effort to pull Germany from the depths had to deal with American public opinion, still gripped by wartime ideology. In February 1947, a public opinion poll had shown that 56 percent still believed Germany would "become an aggressor nation and want to start a new war." A massive assault on the thinking of the people had to be conducted to undo the results of previous propaganda.

Former President Herbert Hoover was drafted for the job. Officially, he headed a commission to ascertain conditions in Europe, primarily Germany. Actually, the conditions were known; the task was to mobilize public opinion in support of large economic assistance in which the former enemy would be included. During the war, Hoover had been consistently smeared because of his prewar stand against intervention and his warnings against the Soviet when Stalin was being officially portrayed as a noble partner in a war for democracy. Smeared no longer, he now was a man to whom the people would listen.

Hoover reported at the end of February that Germany had sunk to a level of existence not known in Europe in a hundred years. With the population in the western zone increased by 9,000,000 refugees, food production was only two-thirds the prewar figure and famine was widespread. He proposed large shipments of potatoes from the United States, where surpluses were being used for fertilizer, a feeding program for school children, the setting up of soup kitchens, and issuance of army rations. Above all, the dismantling of peacetime factories had to be halted so that exports could be produced with which to buy imports. The delusion that Germany could be reduced to a pastoral state had to be abandoned. Europe could not recover without Germany.

With President Truman's support, Hoover carried this message to the country. The Hoover report laid the basis for the Marshall Plan proposals, soon to be enunciated. In the meantime, the campaign to reverse public opinion and make aid to the former enemy possible was spurred by increasing recognition of the aims of the former ally. In March, Congress voted a large loan to shore up the Greek and Turkish governments against Communist pressure, and Truman announced the doctrine of supporting free peoples against subjugation by either armed minorities or outside pressure. State Department officials spelled out the charge of Russian pressure against Turkey. Secretary of State Marshall charged the USSR with seeking to keep Germany poor and under a form of government adapted to the seizure of absolute control.

The Marshall Plan for large-scale, long-term economic aid to cooperating countries over a four-year period was set forth June 5. From then until the European Recovery Act embodying its proposals was passed by Congress the following spring, an unremitting propaganda campaign sought to arouse popular support. While the Soviet Union, refusing participation by itself and its satellites, viciously attacked the plan and charged it was aimed at United States domination of Europe, official proponents asserted its necessity in order to contain communism.

The reversal in policy toward Germany had to be handled gingerly. A new and slightly softer occupation directive raised the level of permitted production somewhat. Experts were sent to Germany to help increase exports, and others to advise on rebuilding the cities, where devastation sometimes ranged as high as 85 percent. Military government officials were advised in the summer that Germany would be a participant in the Marshall Plan, but the fact was softpedalled for some months. Nevertheless, the change had come.

It had not come too soon. In Germany, everything was subordinated to getting food. People traveled from Frankfort to Bavaria to get potatoes.[14] In other countries, disorder was widespread. The Department of State asserted that Greek guerrillas were being directly aided by Communists from Yugoslavia, Albania and Bulgaria, Moscow satellites. France was beset by almost continuous riots. In Italy the Communist threat reached a point where newspaper dispatches predicted a takeover of the government unless immediate aid was forthcoming.[15]

The American occupation authorities joined to provide news derogatory of the Russians. General Lucius D. Clay, military governor, reported that German prisoners returned by the Soviet needed from three to six months to become fit for work. The public health branch of the military government pointed out that such prisoners averaged sixteen pounds below the minimum for health, and that half were suffering from disease.[16] Only a year before, special army lecturers were explaining to American occupation troops that Soviet ideals were not unlike those of a democracy, and that Stalin's prewar liquidation of his opponents in the Moscow trials of the thirties was "elimination of the fifth column."[17] Now the American occupation was warning Germans by radio against "following the phantom of communism" lest they "find themselves caught in the net of totalitarianism, with freedom gone, perhaps forever."[18] American radio programs told the Germans of forced labor, looting and concentration camps in the Russian zone.[19] Russian reparations claims were held up to the Germans as demands for a pound of flesh.

At home, the government again turned to its secret files to buttress the new direction and released the captured German documents of the 1939-41 period, revealing in detail the joint plans of Stalin and Hitler to divide the spoils of Europe. The Soviet Union said the United States wanted war. A Soviet spokesman in Berlin even asserted that the United States had plotted World War II to weaken both Germany and Russia. As Soviet vituperation increased, the possibility of war was widely discussed in the American press and was the subject of numerous conferences in the highest levels of government.

The administration now embarked on a campaign to arouse sympathy for Germany. Rather than being pictured as inherently malevolent and deserving of the worst they got, the Germans now were to be shown as human beings, cold, hungry and miserable. From President Truman went orders that occupation commanders were to start immediately a "continuous flow" of photographs documenting reports of famine conditions. The plight of children, women and the aged was especially emphasized. Pictures were to

165

show the emaciated condition of the people. Bread lines were to be photographed. Statistics were requested showing the increase in tuberculosis and the acceleration of the death rate.[20] A revived Germany now was essential to a Europe threatened by communism.

All the while, supporters of the Morgenthau ideas were fighting a stubborn rearguard battle. After the issuance of the Hoover report, Stout's Society for the Prevention of World War III had marshalled its forces against any effort to make Germany viable. Mrs. Franklin D. Roosevelt was the leading sponsor for a national conference on the German problem, arranged by this group. Morgenthau and Welles participated, as well as numerous other well-known persons devoted to a German hard-line, including Albert Einstein. They called for the halting of any subsidies to rehabilitate the German economy, prohibition of loans to Germany, transfer of ownership of all the heavy industries of the Ruhr and Rhineland to an international consortium, and rigid control of economic life. Speakers demanded that immigration of German scientists be stopped, and that German technicians and scientists, who the American armed forces had eagerly recruited as technical advisers, be sent home without United States citizenship.[21]

In a diatribe which received space in leading newspapers, the society charged that raising the level of permitted production in Germany had been put across by advocates of Germany First. Plans for raising production were "dangerous schemes of the cartelists" who had been the "accomplices" of Germany's "industrial warlords." Still influential on the air, this group was able to place one of its vice presidents, Edgar Ansel Mowrer, on a nationwide radio program where he charged that Germans remained "corrupt and potentially murderous."[22]

Hard-line news correspondents continued obliquely to insert anti-German material in their dispatches. Delbert Clark wrote in the *New York Times* [23] that "neo-Nazism" was rising and denazification was breaking down and that opportunists were seeking prestige as "former Nazis." Correspondents who sought to perpetuate feeling against Germans did not hesitate to base their stories on anonymous authority. Marquis Childs in the *Washington Post*[24] quoted an unnamed person holding a "responsible position" under the Soviet as saying that atrocities would begin if the occupation troops moved out. Raymond Daniell, *New York Times* correspondent, even while admitting the fact of great suffering "and perhaps even starvation," castigated the Germans for "morbid exaggeration of their plight."

Two generations of control over organs of public information would be required to make any "real change in the German attitude."[25]

The animus of former Undersecretary of State Welles seemed to grow rather than diminish as the trend toward aiding German recovery developed. While Congress debated the European Recovery Program, he approved an expressed view that "there is something in the German people that responds to barbarism, that likes kicking a man when he is down, that does not mind torture and brutality. . . . that thinks breaking your word is a sign of cleverness."[26]

But with the government itself now embarked on a reverse course, such outpourings were futile. The wartime pro-Soviet euphoria was fast diminishing and public opinion polls revealed that the Soviet danger was the strongest argument for the European Recovery Program. With Congress called into special session, Secretary of State Marshall urged emergency aid to Europe to save its free community. Germany was still to be kept impotent. In Chicago, November 10, Marshall proclaimed the "absolute necessity" of keeping Germany militarily powerless, disarmed for 40 years; nevertheless he said flatly that German industrial recovery was essential to the recovery of Europe. President Truman, in February, supporting ths aid plan, said the nation must act rather than hesitate in meeting the "growing menace" of the Soviet. The atmosphere was such that on March 5, 1948, General Clay sent a top-secret telegram to Army Intelligence in Washington, expressing the apprehension that war might come "with dramatic suddenness."[27]

Congressional approval of the aid program was followed in June by a Germany currency reform in the western zones, establishing a new and sound German mark which could be used to pay for imports. The Soviet had long been harassing the West's access to Berlin, in the Russian zone, for which in the wartime political euphoria no route or guarantee had been provided, although all powers shared occupation rights in the city. With the currency reform, the harassment became a total blockade, and the West responded by establishing a stupendous airlift which for more than ten months carried food, supplies and even coal to the Berlin western sector at the cost of 45 lives of American and British flyers.

The effort was now for the allegiance of the German people to the West. An army nutrition commission on August 6 urged the necessity of increasing food rations. The Germans were asked to submit estimates of their needs under the Marshall Plan. Some aluminum production was permitted, importation of fruit from Italy was allowed, and in general the rigid restrictions on imports were eased and German recovery began to get under way.

All the propaganda guns were now trained against the Soviet. The United States, which at Yalta had approved slave labor for German war prisoners, in February demanded a United Nations investigation of Russian slave labor camps, charging that from 8,000,000 to 14,000,000 persons were being held in them.[28] A great deal of rethinking had gone on, both in and out of government. The hardline press had swallowed some of its vindictiveness. The New York Times, referring wanly to the Atlantic Charter—"for which we fought"—postulated: "The bargains we made, far from promoting peace, merely compromised our own principles and exposed us to a new menace. The sooner we revise the rest of these bargains, the better it will be for the strength and conscience of the western world."[29]

Yet official policy toward Germany could hardly have been more contradictory. The United States went right along with its allies in tearing down factories, and not merely war plants. Even as the airlift in the Berlin blockade was flying bulldozers to Berlin, German plants which could have made them were being destroyed. Britain and France sometimes frankly aimed at eliminating competition. Soap factories were destroyed and Britain even blew up the Hamburg Harbor installations to block future German shipping rivalry. Protests against dismantling became louder in the United States and America's allies reluctantly agreed in 1949 to halt the process, but that was actually the year of greatest dismantling, and the destruction did not stop until 1950. Moreover, the American occupation still seemed more concerned with minute denazification that with promoting recovery. When a joint three-power agency approved a German industry show in New York, American occupation officials barred even non-active former members of the Nazi party from participation.[30]

Nevertheless, the German economy in the western zones was moving forward. A further increase in production was permitted, including many industries hitherto kept idle. Limited national government was established, with the military governors replaced by high commissioners. The myriad of economic controls were reduced. But dismantling continued and severe restrictions remained, still designated to circumscribe economic activities as well as to prevent the rise of military power.

In 1950 the prospect of an impotent Germany suddenly became

less attractive, as the Russian puppet government of North Korea attacked South Korea with a Soviet-trained army of 200,000, and intervening United States forces initially met disaster. With a hand-picked Communist government set up in the Russian zone of Germany, and with all eastern Europe under Communist control, new Russian moves were feared. If war came in Europe, Russia could not be contained without Germany on the side of the West and German troops in the field. The "absolute necessity" of keeping Germany disarmed and demilitarized for forty years, which Marshall had proclaimed in Chicago only three years before, vanished overnight. In September, the foreign ministers of the West recommended ending the state of war with Germany, announced that any attack on that country would be in effect an attack on the Western allies, and urgently proposed including German contingents in a European army.

All the influence of the West was now exerted to get a new German military force ranged at its side. General Eisenhower, as commander of the new North Atlantic Treaty Organization, formed to contain Russia, came to Germany to try to persuade the government to arm for defense. Six years before, he had said the German nation had "eagerly absorbed" Hitler's "design of brutal, worldwide rape." With the war in Korea against a Russian-equipped and supplied enemy requiring 15,000 replacements a month, Eisenhower told the Germans at Frankfort a quite different story. He believed in the "freedom-loving quality of the German people," and wanted to see them "lined up with others in the defense of the Western type of civilization."[31] In what a correspondent termed "a bold and clever" move, Eisenhower proclaimed that he wanted to see the German people and other free peoples building up their strength "as one gang" to defend freedom.[32]

But most Germans, contrary to Allied propaganda of a decade, wanted no part of any war. General reluctance to rearm was paralleled by intense resentment against Eisenhower personally. Much German sentiment was expressed by the Northwest German Radio when it asserted that Eisenhower bore a "not inconsiderable share of the loss of the peace." Furthermore, it charged that Eisenhower had enjoyed humiliating his defeated German enemies and had held up the Russians as friends of humanity.[33]

Allied propaganda which in the German view impugned the honor of the German soldier rankled especially. Eisenhower had so far subscribed to this propaganda that at the German surrender in Tunisia in 1943, he had refused to meet and shake hands with the defeated commander.[34] But necessity is a good brainwasher. Eisenhower now wanted Germans in uniform. Old views were no longer applicable. The somersault he executed paralleled that of his government. He publicly recanted, and told the Germans he had come to know that there was "a real difference between the regular German soldier and officer and Hitler and his criminal group."[35]

A public opinion poll in 1950 had shown that only 43 percent of the Germans favored rearming. Nevertheless the danger from Communist Russia appeared so great that the new government was finally won over. In 1952, the Bundestag rejected a policy of neutrality, and in 1955 the German government, now given full sovereignty and made a full member of the North Atlantic Treaty Organization, authorized raising an army of 500,000 to be placed under the Supreme Allied Commander in Europe. At Potsdam, the German military forces had been ordered "completely and finally abolished" to prevent Germany from starting a new war. Now it was different. The Germans were allies of the West and therefore, by definition, peace-loving.

Senator Hubert Humphrey, later Vice President, took his stand on November 23, 1958, at the Brandenburg Gate in Berlin to call that city the "citadel of democracy." In the same month, a Scots guard in London played "Deutschland über Alles"—which had been prohibited by the American occupation— when the West German president visited the queen at Buckingham Palace.[36]

An American army remains in Germany, not as an occupying force but for defense against Russia. German flyers train on United States airfields, and the two nations have jointly developed battle tanks and other weapons of war. The wheel has turned full cycle. But it was necessity that forced the United States to admit the old military truism that there is only one of two things to do to defeated enemies: exterminate them or make friends with them.

Part IV

Crusade by Bombing

16

Bombing Myths and Facts

In World War II, approximately 537,000 German civilians were killed by Allied bombing and 834,000 injured, not including police, civil defense workers, foreign-born workers and prisoners of war. Sixty-one German cities, with a total population of 25,000,000 were destroyed or greatly devastated. In Britain, an estimated 60,000 civilians were killed by German bombing and 86,000 injured. Many sections of London were devastated and various other British cities suffered heavy damage. The British military expert and historian, Capt. B. H. Liddell Hart, called it the "most uncivilized method of warfare the world has known since the Mongol invasions."

A myth which is still generally believed, despite the publication of British official histories and memoirs frankly stating the contrary, is that the bombing of civil populations began with the blitz of London in September 1940. Actually the bombing of German cities, as attested by official British histories, began nearly four months before any bombs fell on London, and the blitz itself was deliberately encouraged by Prime Minister Churchill. With British fighter airfields suffering acutely from Luftwaffe assaults, Churchill ordered a series of night raids on Berlin for the specific purpose of diverting German attacks from the airfields to London. After Berlin was attacked six times, the German air force was ordered to attack London, and, as Churchill anticipated, the pressure on the airfields was relieved. Thus began the blitz.

That Britain began the bombing was not revealed at the time. Not until 1944, when the tide of war had turned heavily against Germany, did the Air Ministry seeking credit for its achievements, admit it. The principal assistant secretary of the Air Ministry, J. M. Spaight, then wrote proudly: "We began to bomb objectives on the German mainland before the Germans began to bomb objectives on the British mainland." He said frankly that "because we were doubtful about the psychological effect of propagandist distortion of the truth that it was we who started the strategic offensive, we have shrunk from giving our great decision of May 1940 the publicity which it deserved."[1]

In 1935 and again in 1936, Hitler had made proposals for the prohibition of bombing outside battle zones [2] but met no response in Britain, where longrange bombers were being designed and plans being drawn up to make the bombing of Germany the nation's chief weapon in the event of war. The "whole *raison d'être*" of the Bomber Command, organized in 1936, "was to bomb Germany should she be our enemy."[3] The German Air Force, on the other hand, was designed primarily for close support of the army. Sir Arthur Harris, chief marshal of the British Bomber Command, states that the Germans had no strategic bombers at all, and even in daytime the Luftwaffe "was fitted only to carry out the work of a tactical air force, not strategic attack."[4]

At the outbreak of the war in Europe, President Roosevelt asked the belligerents to refrain from bombing undefended towns or civilian populations. Both Britain and Germany agreed to such a restriction, which was in accordance with the generally accepted rules of warfare barring bombardment except in support of armies in the zone of battle. Prime Minister Chamberlain in June 1938 had strongly condemned any suggestion that victory in war should be sought "by the demoralization of the civilian population through the process of bombing from the air," asserting it was "absolutely contrary to international law." When the war began, he said the British government "would never resort to the deliberate attack on women and children and other civilians for purposes of mere terrorism." The stricture now was only against bombing civilians for "mere terrorism," which did not preclude bombing them for other purposes. Nevertheless, for eight months both Britain and Germany narrowly restricted bombing to what was conceded by both sides to be legitimate military and naval targets.

Bombing of the German homeland without delay was urged strongly at the outbreak of war by many prominent figures. The Labor party leader in the House of Commons, supported by a former Conservative minister, proposed that the entire Black Forest region be set fire with incendiary bombs.[5] Others proposed immediate air attacks on German cities. Such counsel was temporarily rejected, and the British restricted bombing to military objectives "in the narrowest sense of the term." The Germans proceeded likewise, being, according to the Royal Air Force official historians, "under orders as stringent as our own." Under these circumstances, the

British air force could not carry out its "most far-reaching plans, including those for attack on German industrial resources." This did not "unduly disturb" the air staff, however, which assumed that Germany would eventually begin bombing British cities, thus liquidating all restrictions on its own operations. In the meantime, the RAF was greatly strengthened, radar techniques were brought to much higher efficiency, and the bombing force expanded, while the Bomber Command awaited the time when it could "take the gloves off."[6] The more time that elapsed, the closer the British would be to having in operation the longrange bombers which had been planned in 1936 specifically for attacks on German industrial cities in the event of war. Fear that American public opinion might be alienated if Britain took the initiative in bombing civilian areas also counseled restraint.[7]

The bombing of Germany was begun May 15, 1940, when a force of 99 planes was dispatched against "oil and railway targets" of the Ruhr by night. "Thus began the Bomber Command strategic air offensive against Germany," say the British official historians of the air offensive.[8]

The British, whose own prewar planning had been based on the assumption that their bombers would probably operate against Germany from bases in the Low Countries,[9] took the position that the bombing of German cities outside battle zones was justified by German bombing when Rotterdam was attacked. Actually, no matter what the Germans did, British plans from the start of the war had been to restrain themselves from bombing German cities only so long as they were not losing. In October 1939, the war cabinet had approved launching a full-scale assault on cities in the Ruhr district, to be made "if enemy action against France or ourselves looks like being decisive."[10] Such assault obviously did not depend on a German attack on Rotterdam.

At any rate the argument that the German attack on Rotterdam justified the beginning of the British bombing offensive against German cities was rejected by the principal British military expert and historian. Though the bombing of Rotterdam and Warsaw horrified the world, he points out that "it did not take place until the German troops were fighting their way into these cities. It thus conformed to the 1935 definition [Hitler's proposal for a universal agreement to confine bombing to the fighting zone] as well as the old rules of siege bombardment."[11]

Spaight likewise writes: "When Warsaw and Rotterdam were bombed, German armies were at their gates. The air bombardment was an operation of the tactical offensive."[12] According to Major General J. F. C. Fuller, there was "little doubt" that British strategic bombing pushed Hitler into his assault on Britain.[13] The Royal Air Force official history says: "The attack on the Ruhr. . . . was an informal invitation to the Luftwaffe to bomb London."[14]

The bombing of London did not follow the bombing of the Ruhr. After the Birtish army was evacuated from Dunkirk in late May, Hitler, mistaking the temper of the British people, made peace overtures and expected Britain to abandon the war. Leave was granted to many in the German army, and part of the Luftwaffe was shifted elsewhere. But Britain would not quit. The night bombing of Germany continued. If war plants could not be found, the aim was general dislocation of war industry, especially around Hamburg, Bremen, the Ruhr and Frankfort. On June 23, Bomber Command was directed to prepare for setting German crops and forests afire with a special incendiary pellet expected to be ready in early July.[15]

Throughout June, Hitler continued to expect a peace settlement. When he realized it was not forthcoming, he ordered the Luftwaffe to prepare the way for an invasion, which had not been contemplated and for which no plans had been made.[16]

In the air battles that followed, the Luftwaffe aimed at military objectives, and the RAF official historians write that, as late as the latter part of August, "the governing object of the enemy was still the destruction of the RAF and especially of Fighter Command."[17] So effective were the German attacks on airfields that toward the last of the month it appeared that British reserves of fighter aircraft would be exhausted within three weeks. In this situation (after bombs had been falling on German cities for months), the German bombers seeking to attack air installations near London lost their way and dropped their bombs on London. That these bombs were dropped by error, and that the Luftwaffe was still operating "under orders to conform to the old and longstanding rules of bombardment," is attested by Liddell Hart.[18]

But with British fighter reserves in a crisis, Churchill, in the words of Air Marshal Sir Robert Saundby, "decided to play a bold card." He would take the heat off the airfields by attacking Berlin and thus divert German attacks to London itself, rather than military objectives.[19] On August 25, 81 bombers were dispatched in the first of a series of night raids on the German capital. Not until September 7, after the sixth bombing attack on Berlin, did the Luftwaffe begin the blitz in retaliation. Saundby says the attack on Berlin "caused the

German air force to switch from its damaging concentration on the British fighter airfields to the less dangerous bombing of London and other cities. . . . Although this meant that the civilian population had to suffer, it was a turning point in the battle, and greatly improved the British chances of victory."[20]

Spaight wrote: "Retaliation was certain if we carried the war into Germany. . . . There was a reasonable probability that our capital and our industrial centers would not have been attacked if we had continued to refrain from attacking those of Germany."[21]

Liddell Hart wrote that the Germans were justified in describing the attack on London as a reprisal, following six successive RAF attacks on Berlin. "Moreover, they took the initiative a few weeks later in proposing a mutual agreement to restrict such city bombing—although they still had the immense advantage in bombing strength."[22]

But the British, who had repelled the Luftwaffe by the end of September, wanted no bombing truce. Improved heavy bombers were being increasingly produced, and the much heavier longrange planes projected in 1936 were on their way. Attacks were pressed against Berlin and cities of the Ruhr, while the Germans bombed London and British industrial cities. The German raids dwindled in the spring of 1941 and all but ceased as the Luftwaffe was shifted toward Soviet Russia, although a few moderately heavy raids were later mounted. Reprisal raids were conducted on English historic towns after the big incendiary attacks on Luebeck, Rostock and Cologne in the spring of 1942. After these raids there was little strategic bombing of England, except for an occasional attack, until the arrival of the first robot bombs in June 1944, followed by the rocket bombs in September.

The original British bombing plans had envisaged destroying the enemy's industrial and military power through attacks on specific targets, but it was soon found that these targets were difficult or impossible to hit by night bombing. It was an easy progression to outright aiming at civilian populations. As early as September 1943 bomber captains were told to attack any target in an industrial area when they could not find the target specified. When Mannheim was attacked in December, the orders were to concentrate "on the center of the town." Prime Minister Churchill was a strong proponent of bombing people as people. In July 1941, the RAF historians wrote, he was an "enthusiast. . . . for the mass bombardment of German towns," and in August, "repeatedly" urged it.[23] In January 1941, when oil installations were named as the principal target, he "regretted that oil plants were for the most part far removed from centers of population." The "increasing insistence" of the Prime Minister and of members of his government on a "more ruthless" bombing policy is noted by the official historians.[24]

By the summer of 1941, British bombing was, in effect, indiscriminate. Only one-third of all aircraft recorded as having attacked their stated targets were found to have gotten within five miles of them, and in the Ruhr only one-tenth. These were averages. On moonless nights, only one-fifteenth of the attacking planes got within five miles. The "appalling inaccuracy" of the bombing was illustrated on October 1, when, with the specified objectives of Karlsruhe and Stuttgart, planes of the Bomber Command were reported over 27 other German cities.[25] In July, bombers were ordered on cloudy nights—which were three out of four—to make "heavy, concentrated and continuous area attacks on large working-class and industrial areas."[26] In February 1942, a directive named "the morale of the enemy civil population and in particular, of the industrial workers" as a primary objective. The chief of air staff spelled it out: "I suppose it is clear that the aiming points are to be the built-up areas, *not*, for instance, the dockyards or aircraft factories where these are mentioned. . . . This must be made quite clear if it is not already understood."[27]

Leading members of the British government apparently had no qualms about aiming at residential sections. Sir Archibald Sinclair, Minister for Air, expressed himself privately as being in "complete agreement" on general policy with a member of Parliament who urged "the bombing of working-class areas. . . . slaying in the name of the Lord." Foreign Secretary Anthony Eden suggested attacking primarily lightly defended towns under 150,000 population in order to produce greater psychological effects, even though these towns contained "only targets of secondary importance."[28] But to mount a massive offensive aiming at the widespread destruction of cities throughout Germany required a much larger allocation of resources than hitherto had been granted. Some members of the War Cabinet questioned the military effectiveness of such allocation. The Bomber Command therefore planned a series of giant attacks, testing new incendiary techniques, to show the doubters how much destruction mass bombing could cause.

The old city of Luebeck was chosen for the first attack, March 28. The commander in chief of the Bomber Command says: "It was not a vital target, but it seemed to me better to destroy an industrial town of moderate importance than to fail to destroy a large industrial city."[29] The official historians state frankly that the city, "a relatively unimportant place," was chosen "because it was one of the most inflammable parts of Germany."[30] The medieval part of the city, which would burn most easily because of its closely packed houses, was selected as the target. A large area, including the cathedral and numerous other ancient historical buildings, was destroyed by incendiary bombs. There was so little defense that bombers flew as low as 2,000 feet.

Whether the bombing had a military objective or was purposely directed at civilians depended on who did it. When Luebeck was attacked, a five-line British communique said that a heavy assault had been made on the city, "an important port." The fact that the prime reason for choosing Luebeck for the attack was to test new incendiary techniques on a city that would burn easily was not revealed. Newspapers did not mention the human tragedy or the fact that the 12th century cathedral and many other architectural monuments had been destroyed. However, when the Germans in reprisal bombed a town on the south coast of England, in a far lighter raid a few days later, civilian suffering was feelingly described in the *New York Times* and other newspapers. "Rescue workers spent most of the Good Friday holiday searching for the bodies of victims. One tavern filled with people enjoying their quiet half pints of beer suffered a dead hit by a high-explosive bomb, and nearly everyone in the pub was killed." Damage was done to "hospitals, churches and pubs."

The ancient city of Rostock was chosen a few weeks later as a further test of the new incendiary techniques used on Luebeck. Like Luebeck, according to the official historians, Rostock "was inflammable because it contained many medieval buildings, and, again, like Luebeck, it was only lightly defended." In a series of four night attacks, 60 percent of the city was destroyed by fire.

It is illuminating to compare a RAF official historian's account of the attacks on Rostock with the accounts which Americans read in their newspapers at the time. In the press, the attacks were portrayed as directed at the Heinkel aircraft works (which were situated on the outskirts of a suburb). Actually, the great mass of the attacking bombers had the built-up center of the ancient city, not the aircraft plant, as their designated target. On the first night, only 18 of the 161 attacking bombers aimed at the Heinkel plant. The remainder were ordered "to concentrate on the town as a whole."[31] The British Air

Ministry reported that the Heinkel plant apparently had been "gutted," although it was not even hit. Throughout the four attacks, American news reports emphasized the aircraft factory as the chief target. By the end of the raids, the plant had indeed suffered substantial damage, but more than 75 percent of the bombs had been aimed, by directive, at the center of the town itself.[32]

But the destruction of Luebeck and Rostock had not been sufficient to achieve the Bomber Command's purpose. Devastation was needed on a scale which, in the words of Air Marshal Saundby, would "capture the imagination of the British public and impress the government." To achieve this, a force of 1,000 bombers was sent against Cologne, May 30, destroying a square mile of the built-up area and raising a sea of fire that could be seen for 150 miles. Churchill was "greatly impressed" and critics were silenced. According to Saundby, the imagination of both the American and British publics was "captured." After this assault, Bomber Command got the priorities it was seeking.

Newspaper reports of the bombing warfare were generally quite different from the facts as later revealed. When Coventry was bombed it was presented to the American public as wanton frightfulness visited upon a city chiefly notable for its historic interest. The American press graphically reported the destruction of the ancient cathedral, and the *New York Times* account said "it was not Coventry's factories that took the worst punishment from the raiders, but human life, little homes, churches, hospitals." The city was described as "specializing in the manufacture of cars and cycles."

A different picture is offered by the Royal Air Force official historians, who frankly discredit "the popular conception of this raid as a virtually indiscriminate assault on a city center." Rather than being primarily devoted to making cars and cycles, it was a vital center of war equipment manufacturing. The historians agree that at least "many" of the German planes had specific targets, and most of them were hit, including twelve important aircraft plants and nine other industrial works. [33] The light engineering industries of the city, according to the chief of the British Bomber Command, "were almost indispensable to the production of a great range of weapons and war equipment."[34]

How far the wartime selection of facts is perpetuated into the future by indifference if for no other reason may be illustrated by the article in the current *Encyclopaedia Britannica* on Coventry, compared with that on Luebeck. Of Coventry, one can read that the center of the town was laid waste and more than 50,000 houses destroyed during the German air raids of 1940 and 1941, with a description of the ancient buildings destroyed or damaged. But the editors did not bother to revise their standing article on Luebeck, of approximately the same length, which describes the various medieval architectural treasures of that town as though there had been no war. If the medieval section of the city containing these historical buildings was destroyed by British incendiary bombs, readers will not learn it from the edition published eighteen years after the war ended.

As in all wars, the enormity of the crime depended on which side committed it. When several English schoolchildren were killed in a German bombing raid, it was in the headlines of American newspapers. When the Associated Press reported from Stockholm (April 5, 1945) that 33 German schoolboys had been killed by the bombing of Spandau, it was only as a casual mention in the last line of a dispatch.

As 1942 ended, the vast destruction of German cities was yet to come. At Casablanca, in January 1943, a joint directive for "morale" bombing was issued for the British and American air forces which, as Air Marshal Harris said, "allowed me to attack pretty well any German industrial city of 100,000 inhabitants and above." In March, Harris began "the task of destroying the Ruhr." For five months, cities of this area, including Dusseldorf, Essen, Duisburg and also Cologne were bombed. With the exception of the Krupp works in Essen, these attacks were aimed directly at the center of the town because it would burn more easily. The destruction of factories, in the word of Air Marshal Harris, "could be regarded as a bonus."[35]

On January 6, President Roosevelt had told the Congress and the people, "day in and day out we shall heap tons upon tons of high explosives on their war factories and utilities and seaports." Residential areas were not mentioned, but in July the United States Air Force, now coming more effectively into operation, joined the RAF in destroying half the dwellings of Hamburg and heavily damaging many more. The Americans bombed three days and the British four nights. Techniques had so progressed that 400 planes in 15 minutes could drop as many bombs as 1,000 planes had dropped on Cologne in an hour. Hamburg was in the grip of an extraordinary heat wave which raised even night temperatures above 90 degrees, and the incendiary bombs raised a giant fire typhoon which, in the words of one observer, went "beyond all human imagination." Nearly ten square miles of the most densely built-up section of the city were destroyed.

In these assaults and others in August, more than 48,000 inhabitants three-fifths being female, perished in flames.

The principal British official historians of the air offensive write frankly that the night operations against German cities could be "perhaps not inaccurately described as 'terror bombing,' "[36] but no such admission, of course, was made in wartime. After the Rostock attacks, neutral sources had reported that workers' dwelling areas were the principal target, but this was denied in Parliament by Sir Archibald Sinclair, secretary of state for Air. Similar denials were made throughout the war. As the official historians wrote, Sinclair's public statements "invariably suggested that Bomber Command was aiming at military or industrial installations, as of course it sometimes was. . . . Only in this way, he explained, ...could he satisfy the enquiries of the Archbishop of Canterbury, the moderator of the church of Scotland and other significant religious leaders whose moral condemnation of the bombing offensive might be disturbing."[37]

Operating by daylight, American planes were directed to aim at specific industrial and railway targets, and air force officials resisted British pressure to adopt general area bombardment as a stated policy. American operations were termed "precision" bombing, and when the skies were clear the term was relatively applicable insofar as any bombing, especially from great heights, could be precise. As a practical matter, the weather made visibility impossible much of the time and attacks were made blind, by radar. This entailed, according to the official American history, "some compromise" with the aim of precision bombing. A large industrial area could generally be located, but specific factories could not be identified unless they were isolated and unusually extensive. Furthermore, in the late 1943 campaign most objectives were chosen "frankly for their suitability as targets for a force still inexperienced in the techniques of radar bombing." However, "it seemed better to bomb low-priority targets frequently, even with less than precision accuracy, than not to bomb at all."[38] From mid-October 1943 to mid-February 1944, most American bombing was by radar, which in bad weather allowed bombers to do "a type of area bombing which presumably kept pressure on the enemy."

The American official historians' frank description of a large proportion of such American attacks clearly indicates that they were in effect little or no different from British night area bombing. Between October 15 and December 15, 1943, out of 151 "combat boxes" operating by radar, only six dropped their bombs within a mile of the aiming point; seventeen within two miles; 30 within five miles; and the remainder far away. At Bremen, which was heavily attacked, no high explosives fell within two miles of the aiming point and only five "combat boxes" placed their bombs within five miles.[39] The effectively indiscriminate nature of this bombing is indicated by the historians' statement that "as area bombings went, these missions seem to have been effective."[40]

The British began colossal night bombing of Berlin in November 1943, continuing through March 1944, during which month the United States Air Force joined with heavy daylight assaults. The combined offensive resulted in the destruction of approximately three and a half square miles of the built-up section of the city. On March 8, Berlin was attacked by 2,000 U.S. planes, including more than 850 bombers which dropped 350,000 incendiary bombs and 10,000 explosives. During most of this period weather was such, according to Air Marshal Harris, that "scarcely a single British crew caught a single glimpse" of its objective. "Thousands upon thousands of tons of bombs fell through unbroken cloud which concealed everything below it except the confused glare of fires. We knew, of course, from what the Germans said, that we were hitting Berlin."[41]

The frequent contrast between American press reports of USAF bombing and the facts as later revealed is well illustrated by the heavy daylight assault made on Berlin on March 6, 1944. The official communique described the attack as made on "factories, airfields and other military installations in the metropolitan district of Berlin with good results." An Associated Press dispatch said "numerous fires and devastation were left among high-priority war plants and other targets." The American official historians, on the contrary, later admitted that "bombs were scattered here and there, mostly within the greater Berlin area, but few near any of the high-priority industrial targets."[42]

The instructions generally were to bomb the stated targets if possible, and if not, to bomb whatever was available. On January 11, 1944, USAF planes were to bomb aircraft plants in and around Brunswick. But "in case the weather should close in and prevent visual bombing, it was planned to bomb the city of Brunswick and surrounding area by radar." In a February 21 raid on Brunswick, the bombardiers "succeeded in dropping a heavy tonnage of bombs on the city, but without damaging the aircraft factories directly."[43]

Even when targets were hit, a far greater amount of bombs was frequently dropped on other parts of the city in which the target was situated. When the I. G. Farben plant was attacked by the USAF on January 7, 1944, only 39 tons of bombs, out of a total of 277, actually fell on the factory, the remainder being dropped "over Ludwigshafen." Of an entire series of attacks made about this time, the official historians say the missions constituted "essentially an attack against industrial areas." As late as January 1945, the Eighth Air Force, with blind daylight bombing, had "an average circular probable error of about two miles . . . . which meant that many of its attacks depended for effectiveness upon drenching an area with bombs." At one point, even the official historians felt constrained to describe these operations as "so-called" precision bombing.[44] The official account is replete with such instances of blind bombing in which the results were effectively the same as those of British attacks aimed outright at built-up residential areas.

But in the newspapers it was "precision" bombing. The air columnist for the *New York Herald-Tribune*, in an article syndicated to the *St. Louis Post-Dispatch* and other papers, waxed almost lyrical over American bombing accuracy. He referred to "our trained bombs which hunt their way through solid overcast and smack into the middle of fog-shrouded war plants." "Our ice, smog and cloud-eating navigators who seem to need but an address to score on a fuel dump," and "our saturation bomb patterns, as accurately laid as though plotted by a civil engineer. . . ."

It would be reassuring to think that the American people were told their bombs were hitting only specific military and industrial targets because they would have recoiled from bombardment of civilians. Such was not the case. They wanted mass bombing of German cities, military targets or no. Soon after the Casablanca directive was published, a public opinion poll indicated that 81 percent approved of intensified air attacks on the German civilian population to undermine morale and "to destroy their capacity for further resistance." The natural hatred of the enemy which war itself generates had been stimulated and encouraged by propaganda, which pictured the German people as already preparing for a war in the future. Furthermore, Americans had been told, and believed, that the Germans had started the blitz of London without provocation, and therefore deserved anything they got. But the most effective justification of mass bombing of German cities was that it would shorten the war. The slogan of "unconditional surrender," coined by Roosevelt at Casablanca, coupled with the promises of a harsh peace, meant that the enemy would fight to the last ditch. Bombing German civilians was all right because it would presumably save the lives of American soldiers who had to fight not merely for victory but to render the enemy prostrate.

Such voices as were able to make themselves heard against obliteration bombing received short shrift. To the protest in February of Lord Lang, Archbishop of Canterbury, against mass air attacks on civilian populations, the *Washington Star* piously replied that "the good forces of mankind must strike their sword remorselessly against evil (as Michael did against the prideful Lucifer). . . ." Furthermore, if it shortened the war, such "concentrated violence" was "in a sense, even merciful."

A picture of the state of press and public opinion was presented in March 1944 by the general reaction to an appeal by 28 eminent clergymen and other leaders against obliteration bombing. Their appeal was a foreword to an article in *Fellowship*, a pacifist publication, which described the horrors of Allied bombing as seen by correspondents of Swedish and Swiss newspapers, comparing them with the worst tortures of the Middle Ages. It called upon Christians "to examine themselves concerning their participation in the carnival of death" and to acquaint themselves with "the realities of what is being done in our name in Europe."

The appeal was virtually ignored in the news columns of the American press, with a few exceptions. The *New York Times* displayed the story prominently on the first page.[45] The *New York World-Telegram* carried an informative story, and the *Philadelphia Inquirer* printed an Associated Press dispatch. Doubtless there were others, but of twenty other major newspapers surveyed, not one carried a line of news about it.

The *Times* answered the protest editorially by asserting that "the Germans started this practice by indiscriminate attacks on British cities," and defended mass bombing as the most merciful manner of fighting inasmuch as it was calculated to end the war more quickly. The editorial answer of the *World-Telegram* and other Scripps-Howard newspapers similarly argued that bombing was saving lives, as it would shorten the war. The *Philadelphia Inquirer* argued that obliteration bombing violated no rule of civilzed warfare, inasmuch as the bombed places defended themselves with fighter planes and hence were not "open cities."

Some newspapers which had refused to print a news account were impelled, probably because of the prominence given to the appeal by the *Times*, to mention it in editorial attacks. The *New York Herald Tribune* belatedly referred to the protest, asserting that most people would not want to halt the bombing of cities "short of absolute certainty that it will not save a single allied life or lessen the war's length by a single day." Three days later, this newspaper, which still had not told its readers what it was all about, gave nearly a column to a statement by a group attacking the appeal, which it had not seen fit to print when issued.

In the national capital, the *Washington Post*, which had also ignored the appeal as news, was moved to a curious editorial dichotomy. It would be illogical not to bomb German cities, for bombing was "the one weapon for which the enemy has no defense", inasmuch as enemy air opposition appeared to be weakening rapidly. At the same time, the *Post* warned that if the bombing of German cities were halted, the Germans might even bomb American cities. A *Post* editorial columnist then attacked the protest as designed to benefit Nazi propaganda, asserting that the Allies had resorted to bombing "belatedly only with reluctance" because it would shorten the war.

The *Washington Star* also found justification in the belief that bombing German cities would "shorten the duration and insure victory." The *Chicago Sun*, referring vaguely to "protests which have come from some distinguished American and British clergymen," also said the prospect of shortening the war was "ample justification" for mass bombing.

The hitherto surly Soviet press lent its voice to the effort to silence critics of saturation bombing. Numerous American newspapers that had ignored the clergymen's protest straightfacedly carried a pious appeal from the Red Army's official newspaper for more bombing devastation as an "honorable task" in the battle of "leading humanitarians."

The syndicated columnists, appearing in newspapers throughout the land which had printed no news of the protest, joined in rebuttal or disparagement. But they did not describe the protest except in the vaguest terms, and their readers had little notion of precisely what was being discussed. Walter Lippmann whose column was published in newspapers with a combined circulation of ten million, obliquely defended mass bombing by assuring "conscientious clergy and laymen" who had protested against bombing policy that the devastation of Germany was only a consequence of battle, not a purpose. The objective was "to make the enemy lay down their arms, not to kill them." Dorothy Thompson, with a syndicated circulation of seven million, denounced "pacifists" generally, asserting that they were perhaps more responsible for the war than anyone else. William L. Shirer saw the only alternative to such bombing as "slavery to the Nazis."

The *New York Times*, news story drew a heavy response of letters to the editor, which, by editorial count, favored continuance of area bombing in the proportion of 50 to 1. Many of the communications were violent. A leading novelist called the appeal a "coordinated effort at sabotage," and asked how the appeal signers could achieve justice, tolerance and humanity "without socking the rapacious German nation with every pound of explosive available." In the view of one writer, the destruction of German cities was an obligation "to all our fellow Christians." To another, the appeal was a "maudlin chant" which swept him with "undiluted fury." Another, urging continued mass bombing, said "the German army from private to general was equally guilty of murder, rape and massacre."

Freedom House, a group which included prominent Protestant and Catholic churchmen, as well as educators, publishers, writers, and Wendell L. Willkie, the 1940 Republican presidential candidate, called the appeal a "distinct shock." This group asserted that "peace-loving people" faced the issue of "destroying the enemy or disappearing from the stage of history."

Churchmen were prominent among those defending mass bombing. Episcopal Bishop William T. Manning of New York wrote that the protest was "gravely harmful," both spiritually and morally. The president of the National Association of Evangelicals for United Action asserted that "we protestants repudiate the un-American pacifism of the appeal." The chaplain of the New York County American Legion said the appeal was an incentive to the enemy to continue the fight.

The Rev. Daniel A. Poling, president of the International Christian Endeavor Society, pastor of the Philadelphia Baptist Temple, and editor of the *Christian Herald*, asked whether the signers of the appeal wanted to lose "the chance to build a better world." Poling's statement was carried on the wires of the United Press and was published widely in newspapers where the protest itself had been ignored. Bishop G. Bromley Oxnam, president of the executive committee of the Federal Council of Churches of Christ and secretary of the Council of Bishops of the Methodist Church, assured his hearers on the influential "March of Time" broadcast that the obliteration

187

bombing of German cities was a "necessity" however revolting the idea.

Anything that would further condition the public mind to acceptance of saturation bombing of Germany received immediate currency. The *London Chronicle*, on the basis of a vague report from Algiers, informed its readers that the German general staff, seeing defeat, was already planning a new war against the United States in 25 years. It was relayed to American papers by the Associated Press and widely used. Within four days a letter citing these alleged plans as a reason for continued saturation bombing was given space in the *New York Times*. A respected weekly journal used for high school current events study throughout the country did its bit by reporting that Marshal Kesselring had advised German flyers to bomb women and children.

On March 15, the air columnist of the *New York Herald-Tribune* laid allied bombing on the line: "The destruction of Germany—all of Germany—has begun. . . . It is a total war against the German people. It is war on plants, houses, churches, public buildings, parks, hospitals, orphanages . . . . civilian and soldiers alike. When we finish with Berlin, we must move to the next city."

Most newspapers continued to ignore, excuse, or deny the facts of Allied saturation bombing. When eminent members of the French clergy in May appealed against such attacks, the *New York Times* asserted that only the Axis powers had pursued a policy of terrorization of civilian population; Allied air assaults were quite different, being calculated to save the lives of soldiers by making it easier to win the war. The German robot bomb attacks on London in June were "indiscriminate murder of civilian population," while assaults on German cities had a "definite military purpose." German air warfare was such that the nation "had forfeited the right to complain about anything the world inflicts on her in retribution and atonement."

Whenever German air or artillery action resulted in the death of civilians it was described in news dispatches in such a way as to imply that the Germans had been aiming at civilians. As one example, during the Normandy invasion a United Press dispatch told of shells from the retreating German army falling in the streets of Carentan, killing or wounding more than 20 women and children. "The story from Berlin," said the correspondent sarcastically, "probably would be that they were after the bridges across the Douve. But the shells I saw fall today exploded nowhere near the bridges." This dispatch was carried throughout the country, and a typical headline was "Nazi Troops Continue to Kill Civilians by Shelling Carentan."[46]

It was quite a different thing when, in the invasion, Allied bombers reduced the center of Caen of rubble, with heavy civilian casualties, leaving the few German soldiers in the citadel unharmed. Likewise when the RAF, with similar loss of civilian life, demolished great areas of LeHavre from which the enemy had long since withdrawn. A British war correspondent, writing about it years later, told of such bombing inaccuracy, in broad daylight without opposition, that a divisional commander refused to attack if he had to be,"looking over his shoulder" for Allied bombs. After the RAF announced the bombing of a gasoline[47] tank surrounded by German soldiers in a Dutch village, this correspondent found that the gasoline tank had been a water tower and the German soldiers, Dutch orphans. But such tragic misadventures on the Allied side received no headlines in wartime because they could not be reported at all.

Bombing of German cities, largely reduced during the early months of the invasion, was resumed on a much heavier scale in the fall of 1944, and in the last quarter the weight of bombs dropped on Germany exceeded that of the entire previous period of the war. American flyers were still briefed to aim primarily at specific industrial or military targets, particularly oil installations or transportation. But most of the American attacks were made blind through clouds, and three-fourths of the bombs dropped by the Eighth Air Force fell more than 1,000 feet from the targets. The Fifteenth Air Force did only slightly better. Of this, the American official historians remark, "radar bombing was better than no bombing." The Luftwaffe had been so greatly weakened that the Royal Air Force now sometimes attacked in daylight, like the USAF. Its main target was Berlin, and so great had RAF strength become that on October 6 it was able to send 1,250 bombers over the city.

In British war circles, the idea of gigantic air strikes against one or more large German cities that hitherto had been spared had taken hold, and this developed into plans for destroying the chief cities of east Germany as the Russians moved toward them. By January, in addition to Berlin, such eastern cities as Dresden and Leipzig appeared, in the view of Prime Minister Churchill, to be "especially attractive targets" for devastation. With the London newspapers filled with harrowing accounts of the scenes in these cities, flooded with civilian refugees from the Russian advance, the Air Ministry seemed to hesitate. But Churchill would brook no delay. His "insistent intervention"[48] brought the ministry into line and on January 27 the word was given to go ahead.

Three days later, General George C. Marshall, U.S. chief of staff, gave his "strong approval" of the proposal. American air leaders at Malta joined with their British counterparts to spell out Churchill's aims in a directive for the air forces which contrasts markedly with the American claims of bombing only specific industrial and military targets. Heavy attacks were to be made to "cause great confusion in civilian evacuation from the east" and thus hamper possible reinforcements for the Russian front.[49] In the words of the American official historians, it was hoped that these raids "would increase the panic and confusion already prevalent in those cities, which were thoroughly frightened by the sudden Russian advance and full of refugees."

With the Luftwaffe practically finished as a fighting force, the destruction of Berlin continued with a heavy assault on February 3, when 1,000 bombers attacked while escort fighter planes strafed anything in sight. Approximately 25,000 persons were killed in the German capital, much of which had been long since reduced to rubble. The American official historians say it was felt that "a good attack on the eve of the Yalta conference might help convince the Soviet Union of American willingness to assist it."[50] Many years later, General Carl Spaatz, commander of the United States Strategic Air Forces, was to state frankly that the USAF had bombed Berlin "indiscriminately, making no effort to confine ourselves to military targets," [51] but this was not admitted at the time. On the contrary, in response to a query about terror bombing, General Spaatz assured Washington positively that the Americans were not making indiscriminate attacks on cities, but, in the words of the official historians, were "attacking transportation facilities inside cities in missions which the Russians had requested and seemed to appreciate."[52]

The destruction of Dresden has never been satisfactorily explained. The armies of General Eisenhower were advancing on a wide front toward the Rhine, and dwindling German opposition was but a last desperate resistance to unconditional surrender. Roosevelt, Stalin and Churchill were already in Yalta. The normal population of around 600,000 was swollen by hundreds of thousands of homeless refugees of the estimated five millions fleeing from the Russians. The city, which vied with Vienna as the most beautiful baroque city of

Europe, was undefended. Even the anti-aircraft guns had been taken elsewhere.

Sir Robert Saundby, deputy commander of the British Bomber Command, did not believe bombing Dresden was a military necessity, and so expressed himself, years after the war.[53] At the time, when the order came, he was so disturbed by it that he queried the Air Ministry. Ordinarily such a matter would be handled by the Air Ministry immediately, but this message was forwarded to Churchill at Yalta, and the reply was instructions to bomb Dresden at the first suitable opportunity.

The British struck the night of February 13, with a carefully prepared plan which envisaged the deliberate raising of a gigantic fire storm such as had occurred in Hamburg by chance. Two separate heavy assaults were arranged. The target area, which was the center of the city, was first marked out by target-indicator bombs. The first indicator, as revealed by RAF photos taken concurrently with its discharge, was dropped on the largest hospital complex in Germany from a height of less than 800 feet. This was followed by a bombing attack which carpeted the area and left the city in flames.

The second bombing attack, chiefly with thermite incendiary bombs, was set for three hours later, so that fire-fighting brigades and relief suppliers which might arrive from other cities would themselves become victims. The target again was the center of the city. A Luftwaffe airfield five miles from the city was brilliantly illuminated by the attackers' "Christmas tree" bombs, but the British flyers did not attack it, saving their bombs for Dresden itself. There was no air opposition and no flak from the ground because Dresden had no anti-aircraft guns. The city was methodically carpeted by incendiary bombs, and a master bomber directed the attacking planes to peripheral areas that were not yet in flames. The resulting fire storm was of indescribable immensity. Returning bombers could see the glare for 150 miles.

The next day, 1,350 American Flying Fortresses attacked the city, a scene of unrelieved horror, with flames and smoke rising three miles. Accompanying fighter planes, with instructions to drop to roof-top level and strafe "targets of opportunity," opened fire on masses of people leaving the city and almost anything else in sight. One flew so low it collided with a wagon. The river bank, already piled with corpses, to which survivors had fled from the flames, was a special target. Even the huddled remnants of a children's choir were machine-gunned on a street bordering a park.[54]

The following day, United States bombers again attacked, 210 planes dropping 461 tons of bombs, all blind through clouds and smoke. The Associated Press, referring to this attack, said "great air battles" were raging throughout Germany, with the implication that there was such at Dresden. There was no mention of the fact that the city was undefended.

The fire storm had been of such dimensions that it picked up crowds of people and hurled them along the streets. Because of the presence of vast hordes of refugees, no one knows how many were killed. Some estimates placed the number at 200,000, others as low as 35,000. The estimate of the wartime German civil defense head was 60,000, taking no account of the injured.

Hospitals, churches, dwellings, all met the same fate. In one hospital, 200 persons died, including 45 expectant mothers. Some sections of the city could not be entered for days and even weeks so fierce was the fire. Corpses and remnants of bodies were everywhere. At first efforts were made to bury the dead, but there were not enough able-bodied persons to do it, even though the charred and shriveled remains of bodies were dumped into mass graves. Air raid cellars with a 12-inch liquefied mass of human remains on the floor were covered with quicklime. Finally, as the danger of disease became widespread, the remaining bodies were burned on great funeral pyres.

But the United States Air Force was not through. On March 2, American bombers attacked "marshalling yards" in Dresden. There, the American official story ends. The British official historians record that a large American attack on Dresden was actually carried out April 17, but the American official historians do not mention it.

Why was Dresden bombed? British statements issued immediately after the attacks described Dresden as "a great industrial city," describing its great importance in war manufacturing, with "large munitions workshops" and various other war plants. This line was faithfully followed in American newspapers, the Associated Press reporting that Dresden had "great engineering industries." In truth, radar and other electrical components actually were manufactured in outlying suburbs, five to nine miles from the center, and a few small firms in the city itself made aircraft parts and other products of some importance. But no such plant was within the congested area marked out for the RAF attacks,[55] which was the general area of American attack also.

Dresden was also described as a transportation center of great importance in connection with the possible movement of German reinforcements to the eastern front. The officially stated target of American bombers was railway installations. In support of this, a communique after the second U.S. attack said that photographs taken "through breaks in the clouds" showed explosives and incendiaries "headed towards" the principal railway station and falling on a main rail line. But three days after the first attack trains were running regularly through the "New Town" section of Dresden. The railway line over which such reinforcements should have moved lies between a mountain range and the Elbe River. Presumably it could easily have been destroyed without destroying Dresden. No railroad ran through the central target area.

A deception that perhaps should have another name was the claim that the attacks had been made in response to Russian requests. In the first British statement, the attacks were described as having been promised by the Allied leaders at Yalta. Significantly, this claim was omitted in a bulletin three hours later, which merely termed the attacks an example of "close cooperation between the Allies." Both the Associated Press and the United Press reported that it was "suggested unofficially in London" that the blows at Dresden and other cities had been made because Air Chief Marshal Sir Charles Portal had returned from Yalta with "instructions from the Big Three" to assist the Red Army. Subsequent dispatches implied, without specifically stating, that the Russians desired the destruction of Dresden, and emphasized the assistance which the assaults on Dresden and other east German cities were presumably giving to the Russians. The Associated Press on February 14 quoted the British Air Ministry as stressing the great value of Dresden for conducting any defense against the Russian armies, and the next day its dispatch referred to the city being "in the path" of the Soviet forces.

The communiques, of course, made no mention of a specific objective later recorded bt the official historians, "to increase the panic and confusion already prevalent" in cities filled with refugees. The omitted objective was supplied on February 18 by and Associated Press correspondent after a briefing at Supreme Allied Headquarters. "Allied Air Chiefs," he cabled, "have made the long-awaited decision to adopt deliberate terror-bombings of German population centers . . . . as a ruthless expedient of hastening Hitler's doom. . . . The all-out air war on Germany became obvious with the unprecedented daylight attack on the refugee-crowded capital, with civilians fleeing from the Red tide in the East."

193

The story was suppressed in Britain after a brief appearance, but was widely published on the front pages of American newspapers. Supreme headquarters immediately denied the contents of the dispatch, and asserted that American bombing was solely aimed at destroying towns as transportation or oil centers. It was a pure accident that Dresden was crowded with refugees. Secretary of War Stimson called a press conference to back up the headquarters statement, denying it was American policy to attack cities as refugee centers. But Stimson himself had some doubts. He sought and received on March 6, assurance from General George C. Marshall, chief of staff, that Dresden actually was an important transportation center and that the attacks had been requested by the Russians.[56]

Newspapers rushed to the defense of the supreme headquarters denial. The *Washington Star*, while admitting the distinction was a fine one, argued that hampering transport to divert scarce supplies to civilian relief was a legitimate objective of war, quite different from bombing just "to kill or terrorize people." The *Washington Post* averred that the American aim was "to do the least, not the most possible, harm to civilians" although the enemy had "not scrupled to employ terroristic bombing."

Official history, however, confirms the accuracy of the Associated Press report of the SHAEF briefing. "Terror bombing" was doubtless the correspondent's own phrase, but it succinctly expressed the Western Allies' intention as given. The briefing officer had "described how the air forces were to bomb large population centers and then attempt to prevent relief supplies from reaching and refugees from leaving them. . . ."[57]

Moreover, briefings to RAF flyers before an attack on Chemnitz, about 30 miles away, the day after the Dresden attack, spelled out that the bombing was aimed at refugees. There were many legitimate targets in Chemnitz, but the RAF men were told "your reasons for going there tonight are to finish off any refugees who may have escaped from Dresden."[58]

The claim that the Russians had asked for the destruction of Dresden did not stand the test of time. The American official historians made the best of it by saying that "perhaps" the decision approved at Malta to attack the eastern cities "grew out of foreknowledge of a formal Russian request for such assistance which was put forward a few days later at Yalta." They avoid claiming that the Russians asked for an attack on Dresden itself, but imply the same by saying that this assistance "was to take the form of blocking the major transportation centers . . . . such as Berlin, Leipzig, Dresden, Cottbus, Chemnitz and others."[59]

The American Department of State stuck to the story as late as 1953. In that year, Russia organized a propaganda memorial demonstration in Dresden for the victims of "Anglo-American terror bombing." The department authorized a statement in Bonn that the attacks had been approved by the Soviets. When the papers of the Yalta conference were published, it was revealed that the Russians had asked specifically only that Allied air forces "paralyze the junctions of Berlin and Leipzig."[60] Dresden was not included. The Russians themselves had declined to bomb Dresden in late 1944, when pressed by the British air staff with Churchill's approval.[61] The British official historians write that, after requesting the bombing of Berlin and Leipzig, the Russians showed little further interest in the strategic air offensive. "As far as its application to targets in eastern Germany was concerned, they seemed to have been anxious to restrict rather than to encourage its development."[62]

At the end of March, giant raids were conducted in which all available American and British bombers and fighter planes ranged throughout the Reich simultaneously. The stated American targets were "grade crossings, stations, barges, docks, signals, tracks, bridges and marshalling yards." It was hoped "to produce a stupefying effect on morale"[63] to assist the land offensive. With virtually no opposition from the Luftwaffe, bombers attacked from low altitudes and fighter planes conducted independent strafing and bombing operations. In two days it was estimated that 950 such targets had been struck. The Fifteenth Air Force alone, with 700 heavy bombers and 350 fighters, bombed 30 different towns in a single day.

Most of the objectives were small places that had not been bombed before and were able to offer little or no defense. The American official history records show that the German people had received "an unforgettable demonstration of Allied air power." The Swiss received a demonstration, also. The town of Schaffhausen was bombed for a second time. On March 4, nine B-24's bombed Basle and six others attacked Zurich. They dropped 34 tons of bombs on these cities, mistaking them for Freiburg, which was 25 miles from Basle and 45 from Zurich.

Toward the end even small villages were bombed and strafed by Allied planes. German fighter defense in effect no longer existed, and strafing planes attacked not merely trains but the smallest of targets. Anything that moved along the highways was attacked. City dwellers bicycling into the country seeking food were objectives of low-flying fighters. It sometimes appeared to be a grim game. A child, pulling a little wagon laden with potatoes, was gunned. When two farm women, plowing with their only horse, sought refuge in a ditch, an attacking plane nevertheless killed the horse. These and many other such incidents related first-hand to the author are illustrative of the manner in which, long after the war was effectively won, allied planes operated. Of course, no description of such operations appeared in the American press.

The fact of terror bombing by the British was admitted frankly, though privately, by Prime Minister Churchill on March 28, in a minute which did not see the light until long after the war. Concerned that the victorious allies might come into possession of an utterly ruined Germany in which the occupiers might not be able to find housing, he wrote to his chief of air staff: "It seems to be that the moment has come when the question of bombing of German cities simply for the sake of increasing the terror, though under other pretexts, should be reviewed. . . . The destruction of Dresden remains a serious query against the conduct of Allied bombing." He suggested more precise concentration upon military objectives, "rather than on mere acts of terror and wanton destruction, however impressive." The British official historians note that this, coming from the man who had urged area attacks on German towns for four years and had suggested the bombing of the great eastern cities, including Dresden, did not sit well with the air staff. The Prime Minister was persuaded to withdraw this minute and substitute for it a "more discreetly and fairly worded document," which made no mention of terror bombing or wanton destruction.[64]

It cannot be said that the American people believed their bombs were striking only military and industrial targets, even though the news dispatches almost invariably emphasized these. A moral numbness had gripped the nation. The fixed demand for unconditional surrender meant that the war would be fought to the bitter end, and any method of warfare was accepted which promised that fewer Americans would be killed. Hatred, naturally engendered by the war itself and actively promoted by the government and numerous private groups, was augmented by the psychological necessity of the people to blind themselves to the moral issue of attacking civilian populations.

The general American view of the bombings was precisely the view expressed by the Russians when they sought to have Herman

Goering, as commander-in-chief of the German Air Force, charged with killing civilians and wanton destruction by aerial bombardment of cities. As described by General Telford Taylor, associate American counsel, the Soviet representatives argued: "The German attacks had been the work of Nazi war criminals, who had rained death on innocent workers and their wives and children. The Allied attacks, on the other hand, had been carried out by the avenging forces of democracy in order to seek out the Fascist beasts in their lairs and stamp out imperialism and nazism." But the ground was too slippery. Recognizing the nature of their own attacks on cities, the Western Allies refused."[65]

Full cycle was turned when the danger of Russian dominance of Europe became acute. General Spaatz, who had mass-bombed Berlin, Dresden and other east German cities for the stated purpose of aiding the Russian advance, now wrote: "The people of the United States, no less than their government, are determined that Berlin shall not be surrendered to the Communists." He proposed to make the former German capital, still struggling to emerge from the devastation of Allied bombing, the permanent headquarters of the United Nations.[66]

By 1964, the Starfighter jet pilots of the German Air Force were doing 90 percent of their flying practice over the deserts of Arizona.[67]

In the United States mass hatred of Germany diminished, while the Germans, with some United States aid and prodigious effort of their own, rebuilt their ruined cities. American cities were intact, but whether the people themselves escaped psychologically unscathed is a disturbing question. Wrapped in the belief of its own righteousness and the myth that Germany started the bombing offensive, America has appeared to have few qualms about the wholesale air war conducted against German civilian populations.

In England, the same belief and the same myth still hold the popular mind, but there are more critical voices. In the view of Noble Franklund, official historian of the British air offensive, many have come to believe that World War II strategic bombing "marked the beginning of the descent of war morality down a slippery slope."[68]

A strange official reticence began to envelop the part played by the British air offensive against German cities as soon as the war was over. Churchill, in his victory broadcast, made only a cryptic reference to it. According to the British official historians, "The Prime Minister and others in authority seemed to turn away from the subject as though it were distasteful to them and as though they had forgotten their own recent efforts to initiate and maintain the offensive." They note that there is "surprisingly little" about the bombing offensive in Churchill's memoirs.[69]

A British view of the mass bombing of Germany, which makes the reader pause, was provided by a *London Times* reviewer. Ending an exhaustive critique of the British official history of the strategic air offensive, he said: "One closes these volumes feeling, uneasily, that the true heroes of the story they tell are neither the contending air marshals, nor even the 55,888 officers and men of Bomber Command who were killed in action. They were the inhabitants of the German cities under attack; the men, women and children who stoically endured and worked on among the flaming ruins of their homes and factories, up till the moment when the Allied armies overran them. . . ."[70]

Conclusion
The Imaginary Peril

President Roosevelt brought the nation into declared war against Germany by successive hostile steps, each of which led to another and in itself constituted an act of war, although presented as an effort to keep peace. The transfer of fifty destroyers, the Lend-Lease Act, the convoying of British ships, and the 1941 amendment of the Neutrality Act to permit armed American ships to carry any cargoes desired into any war zones—all were acts of war. By the time the Neutrality Act was amended in November 1941, American naval vessels were already attacking German ships far from American shores, and Hitler's declaration of war was merely a formal recognition of the situation that existed.

These steps were made possible by the presidential propaganda that Hitler planned to attack the United States after conquering Britain. It was a gigantic fraud. The pictures Roosevelt drew of Nazi planes over American cities; South America divided into vassal states; conquest of the United States facilitated by Nazi agents in key places; overthrow of democracies all over the world and the "strangling" of the United States and Canada—all these and other horrific visions of peril presented in innumerable speeches were outright fabrications.

In none of the many German documents seized after the war was any support whatever found for the notion that Hitler had any idea of attacking the United States then or in the future. There is no indication that it ever entered his mind. Nor had he planned to conquer England. Twice he sought peace with England; once after conquering Poland and again after the British debacle in France. His ruthless ambitions were unrestrained by principle, but they did not include any conquest across the English channel, much less across the Atlantic.

What B. H. Liddell Hart, the noted British military expert (he was knighted for his services to the military), called "one of the most extraordinary features of history" was that when Hitler invaded

Poland he had made no plans at all for dealing with British opposition. Nor had any such plans been made by the time France crumbled. "It thus becomes very clear," he wrote, "that Hitler was counting on the British government's agreement of a compromise peace on the favorable terms he was disposed to grant, and that for all his high ambitions he had no wish to press the conflict with Britain to a decisive conclusion."[1]

After the conquest of Poland and the division of spoils with the Soviet, Hitler unsuccessfully sought peace with Britain and France. Apprehensive of danger from Russia, he resolved on an offensive against France to force peace in the west so that he would be free to move eastward. He believed that if the French were defeated, Britain would withdraw from the war. The German generals were so strongly opposed to moving against France that they even considered a plan to turn the western armies toward Berlin and overthrow the Nazi regime, but Hitler prevailed and the offensive was carried out.[2]

That Hitler was not seeking conquest of Britain was clearly shown by his attitude at Dunkirk in late May 1940. After the German tank divisions had overrun northern France and cut off the British army from its base, Dunkirk was the only remaining escape port. With the British army many miles away and the German tanks within sight of Dunkirk, Hitler personally ordered the tanks to halt for three days until the fleeing British could reach the port and organize themselves for evacuation. This, said Liddell Hart, "preserved the British forces when nothing else could have saved them."[3] Diverse military reasons were advanced for the halt, but General G. Blumentritt, chief of staff to Field Marshal R. G. von Rundstedt, German commander in the west, believed that an important factor in Hitler's decision was the desire to conciliate Britain.

Hitler's views of Britain, as expressed in a meeting with General von Rundstedt and staff, when the German tanks were halted, were related by General Blumentritt as follows:

> He then astonished us by speaking with admiration of the British Empire, of the necessity for its existence, and of the civilization that Britain had brought into the world. . . . He compared the British Empire with the Catholic Church— saying they were both essential elements of stability in the world. He said that all he wanted from Britain was that she should acknowledge Germany's position on the Continent. The return of Germany's lost colonies would be desirable but not essential . . . . and he would even offer to support Britain with troops if she should be involved in any difficulties anywhere. . . . He concluded by saying that his aim was to make peace with Britain on a basis that she would regard as compatible with her honor to accept.[4]

After the collapse of France in June, Hitler considered the war practically over, and gave his generals so to understand. Leave was granted, and part of the Luftwaffe was shifted to other fronts. On June 22, Hitler ordered the demobilization of thirty-five divisions.[5] At this time, with survivors of the Dunkirk debacle being reorganized, there was only one satisfactorily armed and ready division in England. If the Germans had landed in England within a month after the fall of France, says Liddell Hart, there would have been little chance of resisting them.[6] But Hitler had had no desire to invade England and had made no plans for it. On the contrary, he believed that Britain would agree to a settlement.

But the British were not interested. Rebuffed, Hitler halfheartedly ordered plans to be drawn up for an invasion to force a settlement so that he could safely turn toward Russia. No invasion preparations of any kind had been made. The German troops had been given no training for seaborne and landing operations. No landing barges had been built. The invasion was first set for August and then delayed to September, while an assortment of river boats and barges was collected. The German generals and admirals alike were averse to the idea; nevertheless, the Luftwaffe was assigned to destroy the British air defenses, and thus began the air Battle of Britain.

From the start, no one in von Rundstedt's headquarters believed the invasion would actually be attempted. Hitler, his mind turned eastward, paid little attention to the invasion plans, and von Rundstedt did not take them seriously. The slightness and amateurishness of the preparations were such that by September the Luftwaffe flyers wondered whether they were being sacrificed to maintain a façade for an operation that was being abandoned. In September, the generals and admirals renewed their objections, and Hitler readily acquiesced in a "postponement" of the project which became effectively an abandonment.[7]

Even after passing up the opportunity to capture the British army at Dunkirk, in Liddell Hart's view, Hitler would have almost certainly defeated Britain if he had concentrated on it. "For although he had missed the best chance of conquering her by invasion, he could have developed such a stranglehold by combined air and submarine pressure as to ensure her gradual starvation and ultimate collapse."[8]

Whatever Hitler's ambitions, conquering Britain was not one of them, much less attacking the United States. That the nation could be brought to war by belief in such an imaginary peril is testimony of the war-making powers of the President, who can not only create propaganda for war but, more important, create the situations which make war inevitable.

Just as the propaganda that Nazi Germany planned to attack the United States was used to bring the United States into war, the equally absurd idea that Germany would start another war for world domination unless utterly prostrated prolonged the war unnecessarily at the cost of millions of lives. As has been seen, this idea by the end of the war had metamorphosed into the claim that Germany was *already* making plans for a new war.

Such propaganda was essential to give any semblance of reason to the decision not to end the war short of unconditional surrender; the Germans had to be fixed so they could not start the new war. Regardless of whether the Nazi regime was abolished and a democratic regime set up, the world would not be safe because the whole German people was only awaiting the chance of a new war for "world domination."

Leaders of the widespread anti-Nazi movement in Germany were rebuffed in their efforts to obtain from the West some indication of the kind of peace to expect if they brought about a successful revolution. Instead of encouraging opposition to Hitler, the attitude of the West insured that a successful revolution could not be carried out. When the West should have been engaged in a mighty propaganda effort to undermine Hitler's hold on the German people, it was concerned only with promising vengeance to them. So the Germans fought on until the West and Russia conquered unconditionally and a large part of Europe was turned over to communism.

Notes

CHAPTER 1 *Prelude to War*

1. 1945 revision.
2. Arthur Krock, *The New York Times*, June 20, 1947.
3. Arthur Krock, *Memoirs* (New York: Funk and Wagnalls, 1968), p. 146.
4. *Ibid.*, pp. 183, 184.
5. *Time*, September 18, 1939, p. 9.
6. Samuel Eliot Morison, *History of United States Naval Operations in World War II*, v. 1, *The Battle of the Atlantic* (Boston: Little Brown and Company, 1948), p. 34.
7. Winston Churchill, *The Second World War*, v. 3, *The Grand Alliance* (Boston: Houghton Mifflin Co., 1950), p. 23.
8. *Memoirs of General the Lord Ismay* (New York: Viking Press, 1960), p. 216.
9. Robert E. Sherwood, *Roosevelt and Hopkins* (New York: Harper and Brothers, 1948), p. 124.
10. Thomas A. Bailey, *The Man in the Sreet* (New York: Macmillan Co., 1948), pp. 11-13.
11. Senate Committee on Foreign Relations, *Lend-Lease Bill* (Washington: U.S. Government Printing Office, 1941), Part 1, p. 211.
12. *Ibid.*, pp. 159, 115, 89ff.

CHAPTER 2 *The Secret War on the Atlantic*

1. Robert E. Sherwood, *Roosevelt and Hopkins* (New York: Harper and Brothers, 1948), p. 272.
2. *Ibid.*, p. 274.
3. Samuel Eliot Morison, *History of United States Naval Operations in World War II*, v. 1, *The Battle of the Atlantic* (Boston: Little, Brown and Company, 1948), p. 50. The foreword of this work by Secretary of the Navy James Forrestal states that it "is in no sense an official history." Nevertheless, Dr. Morison was commissioned a captain in the Navy for the sole purpose of preparing the history, and "all naval activities, afloat and ashore, were directed to make available to Captain Morison such records as he might desire to consult." The Navy Department did "everything possible to enable him to make his research exhaustive and to afford him firsthand impressions." For all practical purposes, therefore, the history is entitled to be termed official.
4. *Ibid.*, p. 54.
5. *Ibid.*, p. 54.
6. *Ibid.*, pp. 74, 78.
7. *Ibid.*, p. 78.
8. *The New York Times*, December 4, 1941.

9. Morison, *op. cit.*, p. 110.

10. *Ibid.*, p. 98.

CHAPTER 3   *The Atlantic Charter versus Russia*

1. Speech to the American Youth Congress, February 10, 1940.

2. *The New York Times*, June 30, 1941.

3. *Ibid.*, June 24, 1941.

4. Ambassador Laurence A. Steinhardt to the Secretary of State, in *Foreign Relations of the United States, 1941* (Washington, D.C.: Government Printing Office) v. 1, p. 764.

5. *Ibid.*, p. 766.

6. *Ibid.*, pp. 767, 768.

7. Winston Churchill speech to Parliament, January 28, 1942.

8. Anthony Eden, *The Reckoning* (Boston: Houghton Mifflin Co., 1965), p. 316.

9. Robert E. Sherwood, *Roosevelt and Hopkins* (New York: Harper and Brothers, 1948), p. 4. January 2, 1972.

10. *The New York Times*, January 2, 1972.

11. Winston Churchill, *The Second World War*, v. 3, *The Grand Alliance* (Boston: Houghton Mifflin Co., 1949), p. 444.

12. *Ibid.*, p. 441.

13. Sumner Welles, *Where Are We Heading?* (New York: Harper and Brothers, 1946), p. 17.

14. Sherwood, *op. cit.*, p. 362

15. *Foreign Relations, 1941*, *op. cit.*, pp. 376, 377.

16. *Ibid.*, p. 784.

17. *The New York Times*, August 24, 1941.

18. Sherwood, *op. cit.*, p. 372.

19. Winston Churchill, *The Second World War*, v. 4, *The Hinge of Fate* (Boston: Houghton Mifflin Co., 1950), p. 327. Also *Foreign Relations of the United States, 1942* (Washington: Government Printing Office), v. 3, p. 537.

20. *Washington Post*, December 20, 1944.

21. *Washington Star*, December 20, 1944.

22. *Foreign Relations, 1941*, *op. cit.*, p. 996.

23. *Ibid.*, p. 999.

24. *Ibid.*, p. 832.

25. *Ibid.*, p. 1,000.

26. *Philadelphia Bulletin*, October 2, 1941.

27. *Foreign Relations of the United States, 1941* (Washington: Government Printing Office), v. 1, p. 1,001.

28. Sherwood, *op. cit.*, pp. 391, 392.

29. *The New York Times*, October 6, 1941.

30. *Foreign Relations, 1941*, *op. cit.*, p. 1,002.

31. Sherwood, *op. cit.*, pp. 392, 393.

32. *Ibid.*, p. 380.

33. *Ibid.*, pp. 448, 449.

34. Winston Churchill, *The Second World War*, v. 3, *The Grand Alliance* (Boston: Houghton Mifflin Co., 1950), p. 682.

CHAPTER 4 *A Tight Lid on Soviet Aims*

1. The reference is to an anti-Soviet British group alleged to be sympathetic to Nazism.

2. *Foreign Relations of the United States, 1942,* (Washington: Government Printing Office), v. 3, pp. 506, 507.

3. *Foreign Relations of the United States, 1941,* (Washington: Government Printing Office), v. 1, p. 194.

4. *Foreign Relations, 1942, op. cit.,* pp. 511, 512.

5. Cordell Hull, *The Memoirs of Cordell Hull,* (New York: Macmillan Co., 1948), 1,166-69.

6. Robert E. Sherwood, *Roosevelt and Hopkins* (New York: Harper and Brothers, 1948), p. 362.

7. Winston Churchill, *The Second World War*, v. 3, *The Grand Alliance* (Boston: Houghton Mifflin Co.,1950), p. 441.

8. Winston Churchill, *The Second World War*, v. 4, *The Hinge of Fate* (Boston: Houghton Mifflin Co., 1950), p. 327.

9. *Foreign Relations, 1942, op. cit.,* p. 537.

10. Sherwood, *op. cit.,* p. 526.

11. *Foreign Relations, 1942, op. cit.,* p. 538.

12. *Ibid.,* pp. 538-40.

13. *Foreign Relations of the United States, 1942,* (Washington: Government Printing Office), v. 3, p. 569.

14. Hull, *op. cit.,* v. 2, p. 1,169.

15. *Foreign Relations, 1942, op. cit.,* pp. 435-37.

16. Letter from Rep. Martin Dies, in column of David Lawrence, *Washington Evening Star*, April 11, 1955.

17. *The New York Times*, March 30, 1942.

18. Staton testimony before the Senate Internal Security Subcommittee. See the *Washington Star*, March 2, 1954.

19. October 1, 1942, press conference.

20. *The New York Times,* November 9, 1942.

21. Two of the "four freedoms" enunciated during the period of the Russo-German alliance had not been mentioned in the charter, promulgated shortly after the beginning of a de facto Russo-American alliance. Religious freedom had been accepted by the Russians in the Declaration of the United Nations only after Roosevelt had urged upon them a specious interpretation of the phrase. Freedom of speech did not get in at all.

CHAPTER 5 *The Charter Secretly Abandoned*

1. *Foreign Relations of the United States, 1942,* v. 3, pp. 199, 200, and *Foreign Relations of the United States, 1943,* v. 3, pp. 319, 320.

2. Elliott Roosevelt, *As He Saw It* (New York: Harper and Brothers, 1948), p. 117.

3. Robert E. Sherwood, *Roosevelt and Hopkins* (New York: Harper and Brothers, 1948), p. 696.

4. Winston Churchill, *The Second World War*, v. 4, *The Hinge of Fate* (Boston: Houghton Mifflin Co., 1950), p. 686.

5. Hans Rothfels, *The German Opposition to Hitler* (Chicago: Henry Regnery, Company, 1962), pp. 133, 134.

6. Ronald C. D. Jasper, *George Bell, Bishop of Chichester*, (London: Oxford University Press, 1967), pp. 266-71.

7. J. F. C. Fuller, *The Second World War* (London: Eyre and Spottiswoods, 1948), pp. 355, 269.

8. *Washington Post*, January 28, 1943.

9. *The New York Times*, February 21, 1943.

10. *Foreign Relations of the United States, 1943*, (Washington: Government Printing Office), v. 3, pp. 13-15. Notes of Harry Hopkins, present at the conference.

11. *Washington Post*, March 19, 1943.

12. Published in June. Forty-eight percent of those responding, and 55 percent of those described as "well-informed," said yes. Those who believed Russia would try to bring about Communist governments in other European countries were 40 percent and 46 percent, respectively.

13. *Foreign Relations, 1943, op. cit.*, pp. 373-74.

14. *Foreign Relations, 1943, op. cit.*, pp. 431, 442.

15. *New York Herald-Tribune* and *The New York Times*, January 30, 1943.

16. *Foreign Relations of the United States, 1943*, (Washington: Government Printing Office), v. 3, pp. 501, 504.

17. *Ibid.*, v. 3, p. 510.

18. William H. Standley and Arthur A. Ageton, *Admiral Ambassador to Russia* (Chicago: Henry Regnery Co., 1955), p. 333.

19. "The Battle of Survival," *London Times Literary Supplement*, February 23, 1962.

20. United Press dispatch from Delaware, Ohio, March 8, 1943.

21. *Foreign Relations of the United States, 1943*, (Washington: Government Printing Office), v. 3, p. 364.

CHAPTER 6 *Covering Up Soviet Atrocities*

1. *Time*, July 17, 1972.

2. *Interim Report* of the House of Representatives Select Committee to Conduct an Investigation and Study of the Facts, Evidence and Circumstances of the Katyn Forest Massacre, July 2, 1952. Hereafter referred to as the House Katyn Committee.

3. *Foreign Relations of the United States, 1942*, (Washington: Government Printing Office), v. 3, p. 1,104.

4. House Katyn Committee, *op. cit.*, p. 15.

5. *Foreign Relations, 1942, op. cit.*, p. 185.

6. *Final Report* of the House Katyn Committee, December 22, 1952.

7. Hearings before the House Katyn Committee, November 13, 1952, pp. 2,246-2,251.

8. Winston Churchill, *The Second World War*, v. 4, *The Hinge of Fate* (Boston: Houghton Mifflin Co., 1950), p. 760.

9. *Foreign Relations of the United States, 1943*, (Washington: Government Printing Office), v. 3, p. 396.

10. Hearings before the House Katyn Committee, November 12, 1952, p. 2,072.

11. *Stalin's Correspondence with Churchill, Atlee, Roosevelt and Truman* (New York: E. P. Dutton and Co., 1958), p. 121. This is an English translation of an official publication of the Ministry of Foreign Affairs of the U.S.S.R.

12. *Foreign Relations, 1943, op.cit.*, p. 396.

13. *Time*, April 26, 1943.

14. *Newsweek*, April 26, 1943.

15. *Washington Post*, April 28, 1943.

16. A breakdown of their political affiliations and backgrounds was given by Stanislaw Mikolajczyk, prime minister of the Polish government, in *Collier's*, August 12, 1944.

17. *Atlanta Constitution*, April 30, 1943.

18. *Atlanta Journal*, April 28, 1943.

19, *The New York Times*, April 27, 1943.

20. *Ibid.*, May 1, 1943.

21. *Chicago Sun*, April 30, 1943.

22. *Washington Star*, April 30, 1943.

23. *Washington Post*, April 30, 1943.

24. *Ibid.*, April 25, 1943.

25. *Chicago Sun*, April 30, 1943.

26. *Final Report* of the House Katyn Committee, *op. cit.*, p. 9.

27. Hearings before the House Katyn Committee, November 12, 1952, p. 2,124.

28. *Final Report* of the House Katyn Committe, *op. cit.*, p. 5.

29. Hearings before the House Katyn Committee, November 13, 1952, p. 2,203.

30. *Washington Post*, July 6, 1952.

31. *Ibid.*, December 26, 1952.

CHAPTER 7 *On to Teheran*

1. *Washington Post*, April 29, 1943.

2. *The New York Times*, May 14, 1947.

3. House Committee on Un-American Activities, *Hearings Regarding Communist Infiltration of the Motion Picture Industry* (Washington: Government Printing Office), October 20, 1947.

4. *Foreign Relations of the United States, Conferences at Cairo and Teheran, 1943*, (Washington: Government Printing Office), pp. 3-5.

5. *Harper's Magazine*, October 1943.

6. Winston Churchill, *The Second World War*, v. 5, *Closing the Ring* (Boston: Houghton Mifflin Co., 1951), p. 288.

7. *Morgenthau Diary*, Report of the Internal Security Subcommittee of the Senate Committee on the Judiciary (Washington U.S. Government Printing Office, 1967), p. 16.

8. Jan Ciechanowski, *Defeat In Victory* (New York: Doubleday and Co., 1947), pp. 229, 232.

9. *Ibid.*, pp. 235-37. Nowhere is there any indication in Hull's memoirs that he knew of the Roosevelt-Eden accord of the preceding March on this subject.

10. *Ibid.*, pp. 235, 236.

11. *The New York Times*, November 13, 1943.

CHAPTER 8   *Teheran—Secrecy Until the Election*

1. *Foreign Relations of the United States, Conferences at Cairo and Teheran, 1943*, (Washington: Government Printing Office), pp. 594, 595. Charles E. Bohlen minutes.

2. *Ibid.*, p. 594.

3. *Ibid.*, pp. 599, 604.

4. "How We Won the War and Lost the Peace," by William C. Bullitt, *Life*, August 30, 1948.

5. Frances Perkins, *The Roosevelt I Knew* (New York: Viking Press, 1946), p. 142.

6. *Ibid.*, p. 83.

7. *Ibid.*, p. 84.

8. Elliott Roosevelt, *As He Saw It* (New York: Duell, Sloan and Pearce, 1945), pp. 183, 207.

9. *The New York Times Magazine*, January 2, 1944.

10. Edwin E. James, in *The New York Times*, February 27, 1944.

11. Rep. Fred Bradley, Michigan.

12. *The New York Times*, March 9, 1944.

13. Cordell Hull, *The Memoirs of Cordell Hull* (New York: Macmillan Co., 1948), v 2, p. 1,110.

14. *The New York Times*, March 23, 1944.

15. *Ibid.*, March 25, 1944.

16. *Ibid.*, April 5, 1944.

17. *The New York Times*, March 28, 1944.

18. *Saturday Evening Post*, May 13 and May 20, 1944.

19. *The New York Times*, January 14, 1944.

20. Winston Churchill, *The Second World War*, v. 6, *Triumph and Tragedy* (Boston: Houghton Mifflin Co., 1953), pp. 73, 227.

21. *Life*, August 7, 1944

22. *Newsweek*, October 16, 1944.

23. Walter Millis, ed., with the collaboration of E.S. Duffield, *The Forrestal Diaries* (New York: Viking Press, 1951), p. 14.

24. Arthur Bliss Lane, *I Saw Poland Betrayed* (New York: Bobbs Merrill, 1948), p. 61.

25. *The New York Times*, October 29, 1944.

26. Churchill, *op. cit.*, pp. 241, 242.

27. Sumner Welles, *Where Are We Heading?* (New York: Harper and Brothers, 1946), pp. 9, 16.

28. Winston Churchill, *The Second World War*, v. 4, *The Hinge of Fate* (Boston: Houghton Mifflin Co., 1950), p. 890.

29. *The New York Times*, December 31, 1944, p. 18.

CHAPTER 9 *The Deceptions of Yalta*

1. Winston Churchill, *The Second World War*, v. 6, *Triumph and Tragedy* (Boston: Houghton Mifflin Co., 1953), p. 341.

2. James F. Byrnes, *Speaking Frankly* (New York: Harper and Brothers, 1947), p. 24.

3. *Time*, January 8, 1945.

4. Edgar Ansel Mowrer, in *Time*, January 8, 1945.

5. Edwin L. James, in *The New York Times*, February 3, 1945.

6. *Foreign Relations of the United States, Conferences at Malta and Yalta* (Washington: Government Printing Office), pp. 177, 193, 196, 622, 632, 983.

7. Roosevelt's solution had been a "compromise" which followed the Soviet formula so closely that Stalin approved it virtually without change.

8. Byrnes, *op. cit.*, p. 43.

9. These "peace-loving" nations were defined at Yalta as those which entered the war on the side of the Allies by March 15. Among the nations excluded thereby were Switzerland and Sweden.

10. *Foreign Relations, op. cit.*, p. 677.

11. *The New York Times*, March 3, 1945.

12. Samuel I. Rosenmann, editor, *The Public Papers and Addresses of Franklin D. Roosevelt* (New York: Random House, 1938-50)

13. *Time*, March 3, 1945.

14. Anthony Eden, *The Reckoning* (Boston: Houghton Mifflin Co., 1965), p. 604.

15. Churchill, *op. cit.*, p. 424.

16. The White House statement, according to the minutes of the conference, was not factually correct; when the conferees in formal session had agreed on three votes for Russia, there was no bargain, and nothing was said about three votes for the United States. Later urged by Byrnes, Roosevelt had asked for and obtained Stalin's acquiescence to additional votes for the United States. The concession to Russia had been made originally without any quid pro quo. The United States later dropped its claim.

17. Eden, *op. cit.*, p. 609.

18. Arthur Bliss Lane, *I Saw Poland Betrayed* (New York: Bobbs Merrill, 1948), p. 117.

19. Stanislaw Mikolajczyk, *The Rape of Poland* (New York: McGraw-Hill, 1948), pp. 161-242.

CHAPTER 10 *The Build-up*

1. *Saturday Review of Literature*, May 24, 1941.

2. *The New York Times*, January 3, 1943.

3. *Saturday Review of Literature*, September 23, 1944.

4. Sir Robert Vansittart, *Black Record, Germans Past and Present* (Toronto: Musson Book Co., 1941). Vansittart's description of German air practices approximated the actual instructions to British and American air forces in the destruction of Dresden and nearby cities—instructions that were carried out. See chapter 15.

5. Elliott Roosevelt, *Franklin D. Roosevelt, His Personal Letters,*, v. 3 (New York: Duell, Sloan and Pearce, 1950), p. 1, 234.

6. Winston S.Churchill, *Great Contemporaries* (New York: G. P. Putnam's Sons, 1937), pp. 226, 227, 231.

7. *Washington Star*, January 11, 1943.

8. *The New York Times*, January 30, 1943. (In April 1942, a *Des Moines Register* poll had indicated that 57 percent of Iowans were willing to use gas on military objectives, and 36 percent would use it without such qualification if it would save American lives.)

9. *The New York Times*, January 3, 1943.

10. "America's Town Meeting of the Air" (Blue Network), January 31, 1943.

11. *Ibid.*, May 13, 1943.

12. Frederick Lewis Allen, *Only Yesterday* (New York: Harper and Brothers, 1939), p. 321.

13. *The New York Times Book Review*, March 21, 1943.

14. *Observer,* London, August 23, 1964.

15. *This Week*, in the *New York Herald-Tribune*, February 6, 1944.

16. *The New York Times*, March 12, 1944.

17. *Washington Post*, March 6, 1944.

18. *St. Louis Post-Dispatch*, March 10, 1944.

19. *Philadelphia Inquirer*, May 9, 1944.

20. *Reader's Digest*, February 1944.

21. Max Immanuel, in *Barron's*, April 10, 1944.

22. *Washington Star* and other newspapers, June 6, 1944.

23. *Philadelphia Record*, May 7, 1944.

24. "America's Town Meeting of the Air" (Blue Network), February 10, 1944.

25. "Family Hour" (Columbia Broadcasting Corp.), June 11, 1944.

26. *The New York Times*, June 10, 1944.

27. *Ibid.*, July 20, 1944.

28. *Ibid.*, August 9, 1944.

29. *New York Herald-Tribune*, August 9, 1944.

30. *Washington Post*, September 15, 1944.

31. Sumner Welles, *The Time for Decision* (New York: Harper and Brothers, 1944), pp. 336, 342, 343, 345, 346.

32. *The New York Times*, July 19, 1944.

33. *Washington Post*, July 20, 1944.

34. *Ibid.*, September 5, 1944.

35. "American Forum of the Air" (Red Network), September 9, 1942.

36. *The New York Times*, November 24, 1943.

37. *Washington Star*, November 10, 1944.

38. *Harper's Magazine*, April 1944.

39. *Education and the People's Peace* (Washington: National Education Association and American Association of School Administrators, April 1944).

40. United Press dispatch, in *The New York Times*, October 11, 1944.

CHAPTER 11   *The Writers War Board*

1. The material here presented about the Writers War Board is taken chiefly from the board minutes and publications. The board minutes, now in the Library of Congress, were kept secret for some years after the war because of an expressed fear of "witch hunters."

2. *The New York Times*, January 24, 1943.

CHAPTER 12   *Vindictiveness Becomes Policy*

1. *Washington Times Herald*, May 1, 1944.

2. *Interlocking Subversion in Government Departments, Part 16*, Report of the Internal Security Subcommittee of the Senate Committee on the Judiciary (Washington: U. S. Government Printing Office, November 27, 1953). The concentration of Communist agents and sympathizers in the Treasury Department is told in detail in *Morgenthau Diary*, a Report of the Judiciary (Washington: Government Printing Office, 1967). White, although apparently not an actual party member, was the center of a conspiratorial Communist group, according to the report. In 1948 he was found dead from a dose of sleeping pills a few days after denying participation in Communist activities before the House Committee on Un-American Activities. Five members of the Treasury group took the Fifth Amendment when questioned on Communist activities by congressional investigators. Col. Bernard Bernstein, Morgenthau's personal representative on the U. S. Control Council in London, was identified by the subcommittee as a strong supporter of pro-Communist causes. Lauchlin Currie, White House assistant and formerly on the Treasury staff, who cooperated with the group, fled the country after testifying before the House Committee on Un-American Activities.

3. *Morgenthau Diary, ibid.*, p. 12.

4. *Ibid.*, p. 15.

5. Cordell Hull, *The Memoirs of Cordell Hull* (New York: Macmillan Co., 1948), v. 2, p. 1,603.

6. *Morgenthau Diary, op. cit.*, p. 35.

7. Henry L. Stimson and McGeorge Bundy, *On Active Service in Peace and War* (New York: Harper and Brothers, 1947), pp. 580, 581.

8. Henry Morgenthau, Jr., in the *New York Post*, November 28, 1947.

9. *Morgenthau Diary, op. cit.*, p. 26.

10. *Ibid.*, p. 34.

11. Walter Millis, ed., with the collaboration of E. S. Duffield, *The Forrestal Diaries*, (New York: Viking Press, 1951), p. 11.

12. *The New York Times*, September 23, 1944.

13. *Morgenthau Diary, op. cit.*, p. 78.

14. *Ibid.*, p. 78.

15. *Ibid.*, p. 59.

16. "America's Town Meeting of the Air" (Blue Network), October 5, 1944.

17. Raymond Daniel, in *The New York Times*, September 24, 1944.

18. Paul Winkler, in the *Washington Post*, December 2, 1944.

19. *Washington Post*, December 14, 1944.

20. "America's Town Meeting of the Air" (Blue Network), December 28, 1944.

21. *Washington Post*, November 12, 1944.

22. "America's Town Meeting of the Air" (Blue Network), December 28, 1944.

23. *The New York Times*, November 13, 1944.

24. Capt. Harry C. Butcher, *My Three Years With Eisenhower*, (New York: Simon and Schuster, 1946), p. 518.

25. *Morgenthau Diary, op. cit.*, p. 656.

26. James F. Byrnes, *Speaking Frankly* (New York: Harper and Brothers, 1947), p. 181.

27. Capt. B. H. Liddell Hart, *The Other Side of the Hill* (London: Cassell and Co., 1948), p. 304.

28. *Newsweek* March 26, 1945.

29. *New York World-Telegram*, September 6, 1944.

31. *The New York Times*, January 2, 1945.

30. *Washington Post*, November 27, 1944.

32. *Christian Science Monitor*, December 12, 1944.

33. Edwin L. James, in *The New York Times*, February 11, 1945.

CHAPTER 13   *The War Ends, But Not the Frenzy*

1. *The Observer*, London, January 26, 1964.

2. *The New York Times*, May 23, 1945.

3. *Variety*, May 26, 1945.

4. Robert Murphy, *Diplomat Among Warriors* (New York: Doubleday and Co., 1964), p. 294.

5. *Time*, May 21, 1945.

6. *United States News*, May 18 and June 22, 1945.

7. *The New York Times*, June 22, 1945.

8. *Ibid.*, June 23, 1945.

9. *Ibid.*, July 22, 1945.

10. *Washington Post*, September 5, 1945.

11. *The New York Times*, December 30, 1945.

CHAPTER 14   *Occupation as Revenge*

1. Robert Murphy, *Diplomat Among Warriors*, (New York: Doubleday and Co., 1964), p. 251.

2. *Time*, August 26, 1945.

3. C. I. Hovland, A. A. Lumsdaine, and F. D. Sheffield, *Experiments on Mass Communications* (Princeton, N. J.: Princeton University Press, 1949), pp. 23-59.

4. *The New York Times*, September 28, 1945.

CHAPTER 15   *The Long Route to Sanity*

1. Robert Murphy, *Diplomat Among Warriors*, (New York: Doubleday and Co., 1964), p. 294.

2. *Time*, October 22, 1945.

3. Letter to the *Washington Post*, March 29, 1946.

4. *Washington Daily News*, March 27, 1946.

5. John Dos Passos, in *Life*, March 11, 1946.

6. *The New York Times*, March 19, 1946. With the exception of a demand for control of the Dardanelles and a free hand in adjacent lands, what Stalin actually got in cooperation with the West was approximately what Hitler had refused him.

7. *Ibid.*, August 7, 1946.

8. *Ibid.*, October 6, 1946.

9. *Ibid.*, December 4, 1946.

10. *Ibid.*, February 13, 1947.

11. Eugene Davidson, *The Death and Life of Germany* (New York: Knopf, 1959), p. 158.

12. *The New York Times*, April 15, 1947.

13. *Wall Street Journal*, March 11, 1947.

14. Alfred Friendly, in the *Washington Post*, September 12, 1947.

15. *Washington Post*, September 14, 1947.

16. *The New York Times*, October 1, 1947.

17. Melvin J. Lasky, *The New Leader*, September 21, 1946.

18. Associated Press dispatch from Frankfort, Germany, December 14, 1947.

19. The New York Times, December 15, 1947.

20. *Ibid.*, October 14, 1947.

21. *Ibid.*, March 7, 1947.

22. "America's Town Meeting of the Air" (Blue Network), March 6, 1947.

23. *The New York Times*, September 7, 1947.

24. *Washington Post*, September 10, 1947.

25. *The New York Times Magazine*, December 14, 1947.

26. *New York Herald-Tribune*, February 24, 1948.

27. Walter Millis, ed., with the collaboration of E. S. Duffield, *The Forrestal Diaries*, (New York: Viking Press, 1951), p. 387.

28. *The New York Times*, February 14, 1949.

29. *Ibid.*, March 24, 1949.

30. *Ibid.*, March 10, 1949.

31. *Newsweek*, January 29, 1951.

32. *The New York Times*, January 21, 1951.

33. *Newsweek*, January 29, 1951.

34. Murphy, *op. cit.*, p. 255.

35. *The New York Times*, January 24, 1951.

36. *Newsweek*, November 3, 1958.

CHAPTER 16   *Bombing Myths and Facts*

1. J. M. Spaight, *Bombing Vindicated* (London: Bles, 1944), pp. 74, 68.

2. *Ibid.*, p. 39.

3. *Ibid.*, p. 60.

4. Sir Arthur Harris, *Bomber Offensive* (London: Collins, 1947), p. 86.

5. Martin Gilbert, in the *Sunday Times Magazine*, London, September 6, 1964.

6. Denis Richards and Hilary St. G. Saunders, *The Royal Air Force, 1939-1945* v. 1, (London: Her Majesty's Stationery Office, 1953), pp. 36, 37, 42, 67.

7. Martin Gilbert, in the *Sunday Times Magazine*, London, September 6, 1964.

8. Sir Charles Webster and Noble Frankland, *The Strategic Air Offensive Against Germany, 1939-1945*, v. 1 (London: Her Majesty's Stationery Office, 1961), p. 144. When the phrase "British official historians" is used, it refers to this work. The Royal Air Force history, previously quoted, also official, is more limited in scope.

9. Air Marshal Sir Robert Saundby, *Air Bombardment* (London: Chatto and Windus, 1961), p. 111.

10. Webster and Frankland, *op. cit.*, v. 1, p. 136.

11. Capt. Sir B. H. Liddell Hart, *Defence of the West* (New York: William Morrow & Co., 1950), p. 318. Capt. Liddell Hart, held by many to be the world's leading military expert, was knighted for his services to England during the war and before. He served as historical adviser to the British Broadcasting Corporation for its serially televised portrayal of World War II.

12. Spaight, *op. cit.*, p. 43.

13. J. F. C. Fuller, *The Second World War* (New York: Duell, Sloan and Pearce, 1954), p. 222.

14. Richards and Saunders, *op. cit.*, v. 1, p. 122.

15. Webster and Frankland, *op. cit.*, v. 1, p. 148.

16. B. H. Liddell Hart, *Encyclopaedia Britannica*, 1963 edition, v. 23, p. 791-K.

17. Richards and Saunders, *op. cit.*, v. 1, p. 178.

18. B. H. Liddell Hart, *History of the Second World War* (New York: G. P. Putnam's Sons, 1971), pp. 192, 594.

19. Saundby, *op. cit.*, pp. 104, 105.

20. *Ibid.*, p. 104.

21. Spaight, *op. cit.*, pp. 73, 74.

22. Liddell Hart, *Defence of the West, op. cit.*, p. 318.

23. Richards and Saunders, *op. cit.*, v. 1, p. 378.

24. Webster and Frankland, *op. cit.*, v. 1, pp. 161, 162.

25. *Ibid.*, v. 1, pp. 178, 185.

26. Richards and Saunders, *op. cit.*, v. 1, p. 377.

27. Webster and Frankland, *op. cit.*, v. 1, pp. 323, 324. The British official historians report that in the 1943 attacks on Berlin, "the difficulty was to find the industrial areas or workers quarters in so large an area."

28. *Ibid.*, v. 3, p. 115.

29. Harris, *op. cit.*, p. 105.

30. Webster and Frankland, *op. cit.*, v. 2, p. 121 and v. 1, pp. 324, 391.

31. Richards and Saunders, *op. cit.*, v. 1, p. 128.

32. Webster and Frankland, *op. cit.*, v. 1, pp. 393, 394.

33. Richards and Saunders, *op. cit.*, v. 1, p. 211.

34. Harris, *op. cit.*, p. 87.

35. *Ibid.*, p. 147.

36. Webster and Frankland, *op. cit.*, v. 3, p. 116.

37. *Ibid.*, v. 3, p. 116.

38. Wesley Frank Craven and James Lea Cate, editors, *The Army Air Forces in World War II*, United States Air Force Historical Division (Chicago: University of Chicago Press, 1951), v. 3, p. 13.

39. *Ibid.*, v. 3, p. 20.

40. *Ibid.*, v. 2, p. 727.

41. Harris, *op. cit.*, p. 187.

42. Craven and Cate, *op. cit.*, v. 3, p. 51.

43. *Ibid.*, v. 3, p. 36.

44. *Ibid.*, v. 3, p. 58.

45. *The New York Times*, March 6, 1944.

46. *Chattanooga News-Free Press*, July 13, 1944.

47. H. D. Ziman, "Bombed by the RAF," in the *Daily Telegraph and Morning Post*, London, October 27, 1961.

48. Webster and Frankland, *op. cit.*, v. 3, p. 103.

49. Craven and Cate, *op. cit.*, v. 3, p. 725. General Marshall, from the start, apparently had no qualms about air warfare directed at civilian populations. As early as November 1941, at an off-the-record press conference, he said that if war with Japan came, bombers would be dispatched immediately to set the cities of Japan on fire. "There won't be any hesitation about bombing civilians." As quoted by Robert Sherrod, *I Can Tell It Now* (New York: E. P. Dutton and Co., 1964), p. 42.

50. *Ibid.*, p. 725.

51. *Newsweek*, January 5, 1959.

52. Craven and Cate, *op. cit.*, v. 3, p. 726.

53. Foreword by Sir Robert Saundby to David Irving, *The Destruction of Dresden* (London: William Kimber, 1963).

54. Irving, *op. cit.*, pp. 152, 180, 181. The author of this comprehensive and painstaking work has drawn on official records, numerous personal accounts by residents of Dresden, members of the air forces who took part in the attack, and others. Its authoritativeness is vouched for in a foreword by British Air Marshal Sir Robert Saundby.

55. *Ibid.*, p. 71.

56. Craven and Cate, *op. cit.*, v. 3, p. 731. and footnote 84.

57. *Ibid.*, v. 3, p. 727.

58. Irving, *op. cit.*, p. 155.

59. Craven and Cate, *op. cit.*, v. 3, pp. 724, 725.

60. *Foreign Relations of the United States, Conferences at Malta and Yalta* (Washington: Government Printing Office, 1955), p. 583.

61. Webster and Frankland, *op. cit.*, v. 3, p. 108.

62. *Ibid.*, v. 3, p. 106. Today, with Dresden under Communist control, there hangs in the Zwinger, the city's famous art gallery and museum, a greatly enlarged photograph of the city after the bombing, a scene of ruin stretching as far as the eye can see. A placard describes the "terror bombing" of the British and Americans, and concludes: "A terrible accusation against those guilty of this mass murder."

63. Craven and Cate, *op. cit.*, v. 3, pp. 732-35.

64. Webster and Frankland, *op. cit.*, v. 3, pp. 112, 113, 117.

65. *The New York Times Magazine*, August 27, 1950.

66. *Newsweek*, January 5, 1969.

67. Bonn dispatch to *The Times*, London, August 20, 1964.

68. Noble Frankland, *The Bombing Offensive Against Germany* (London: Faber and Faber, 1965), p. 110.

69. Webster and Frankland, *op. cit.*, v. 3, p. 284.

70. *The Times Literary Supplement*, London, October 20, 1961.

CONCLUSION   *The Imaginary Peril*

1. B. H. Liddell Hart, *History of the Second World War* (New York: G. P. Putnam's Sons, 1971), p. 87.

2. B. H. Liddell Hart, *The Other Side of the Hill* (London: Cassell and Co., 1948), pp. 112-16. In an official capacity, Liddell Hart interviewed many German military leaders after the war.

3. Liddell Hart, *History of the Second World War, op. cit.*, p. 74.

4. *Ibid.*, p. 83.

5. *Ibid.*, p. 87.

6. *Ibid.*, p. 709.

7. Hart, *The Other Side of the Hill, op. cit.*, pp. 152-61.

8. Liddell Hart, *History of the Second World War, op. cit.*, p. 709.

Index

218